ST BASIL THE GREAT

On Christian Doctrine and Practice

ST VLADIMIR'S SEMINARY PRESS
Popular Patristics Series
Number 47

The Popular Patristics Series published by St Vladimir's Seminary Press provides readable and accurate translations of a wide range of early Christian literature to a wide audience—students of Christian history to lay Christians reading for spiritual benefit. Recognized scholars in their fields provide short but comprehensive and clear introductions to the material. The texts include classics of Christian literature, thematic volumes, collections of homilies, letters on spiritual counsel, and poetical works from a variety of geographical contexts and historical backgrounds. The mission of the series is to mine the riches of the early Church and to make these treasures available to all.

Series Editor
BOGDAN BUCUR

Associate Editor
IGNATIUS GREEN

* * *

Series Editor
1999–2020
JOHN BEHR

ST BASIL THE GREAT

On Christian Doctrine and Practice

Translated, with Introduction and Annotations, by

MARK DELCOGLIANO

ST VLADIMIR'S SEMINARY PRESS
YONKERS, NEW YORK
2012

Library of Congress Cataloging-in-Publication Data

Basil, Saint, Bishop of Caesarea, ca. 329–379.
  [Sermons. English Selections]
  On Christian doctrine and practice / St. Basil the Great ; translated, with
introductions and annotations, by Mark DelCogliano.
        p. cm. — (St. Vladimirs Seminary Press popular patristics series ; no. 47)
        Includes bibliographical references and index.
        ISBN 978–0–88141–458–5
        1. Sermons, Greek—Translations into English. 2. Sermons, Early Christian.
  I. DelCogliano, Mark. II. Title.

  BR65.B33E6 2012
  230—dc23

                                                                    2012034668

COPYRIGHT © 2012 BY

ST VLADIMIR'S SEMINARY PRESS
575 Scarsdale Road, Yonkers, NY 10707
1-800-204-2665
www.svspress.com

ISBN 978–088141–458–5
ISSN 1555–5755

PRINTED IN THE UNITED STATES OF AMERICA

To
Lewis

Contents

Preface

My work on translating these Moral Homilies began in earnest as a result of a happy confluence of events. In the years 2005–2007 I collaborated with Andrew Radde-Gallwitz on a translation of Basil's *Against Eunomius*, which had never before appeared in English. While the revising of that translation continued until early 2009, I missed the challenge of rendering Basil's Greek afresh into English and so sought another translation project. Basil's untranslated Moral Homilies seemed like a good option. So in the course of writing my dissertation in the years 2007–2009 I drafted translations of portions of the Moral Homilies relevant to that project and started translating other Moral Homilies for the sheer fun of it to avoid working on the dissertation. After I completed my dissertation, I realized that I had what could be the nucleus for a volume of translations of selected Moral Homilies. Soon, however, I learned that Susan R. Holman was also planning a volume of English translations of selected Moral Homilies and that some of the homilies I intended to translate (or had already translated) were to be included in her volume. In order to resolve this dilemma, she graciously suggested that I contribute four translations to her volume, which would then become a joint work, and allowed me to include a few homilies in my volume which she had planned to include in hers. I am very grateful for Susan's generosity and willingness to negotiate. The translations and introductions that appear in this volume were the focus of my work in the years 2010–2011.

This volume would not have seen the light of day if it were not for the help and support of others. I thank Fr. John Behr for his enthusiasm for the project from the moment I proposed it to him and for accepting it for publication in the Popular Patristics series. I thank Fr. Benedict Churchill of SVS Press for his guidance throughout the project. I thank Susan Holman not only for the reasons mentioned above, but also for sharing with me her draft translation of *Sab* and for her willingness to participate in an exchange of ideas via e-mail regarding the historical context of *Mund* and *Lak.* Because of her critiques I was able to articulate my own position on these matters more clearly. I thank Timothy McConnell for sharing with me his draft translation of *Verb.* I thank Andrew Radde-Gallwitz for our ongoing discussions of Basil and other fourth-century concerns. His insightfulness and clarity of thought never fail to stimulate my own thinking and help me clarify my own ideas. I thank Amy Levad, whom I am just darn lucky to have as a wife, not least of all because, being also in academia, she understands a scholar's need to spend long hours of concentration immersed in texts. Her generosity enabled me to submit the final manuscript in the nick of time, as a few days after submitting it our daughter, Iris Abigail, came in to our life, a bit earlier than expected. Immediately I was privileged to witness the mother's tenderness and self-sacrifice that Basil praised in *Lak* 8. This volume is dedicated to Lewis Ayres, my teacher, doktorvater, collaborator, colleague, and friend, in gratitude for all that he has done and continues to do for me.

Abbreviations

General

Gk.   Greek
LXX   Septuagint (Greek Bible)
ms(s)   manuscript(s)
MT   Masoretic Text (Hebrew Bible)

Series

CSEL   Corpus Scriptorum Ecclesiasticorum Latinorum
CCSL   Corpus Christianorum Series Latina
FOTC   The Fathers of the Church
GCS   Die griechischen christlichen Schriftsteller der ersten [drei]
           Jahrhunderte
NPNF   Nicene and Post-Nicene Fathers
PG   Patrologia Cursus Completus: Series Graeca
PPS   Popular Patristics Series
SChr   Sources Chrétiennes
VCS   Vigiliae Christianae Supplements

Dictionaries, Encyclopedias, and Reference Works

ABD   *Anchor Bible Dictionary*. Ed. David Noel Freedman. 5 vols.
           New York: Doubleday, 1992.
BBV   *Bibliotheca Basiliana Vniversalis*. Paul Jonathan Fedwick. 5
           vols. Turnhout: Brepols, 1993–2005.
CPG   *Clavis Patrum Graecorum*. Maurice Geerard. 5 vols.
           Turnhout: Brepols, 1974–1983. Cited by source number.

DCB   *Dictionary of Christian Biography, Literature, Sects and*
           Doctrines. Ed. William Smith and Henry Wace. 4 vols.
           London: John Murray, 1877–1887.
DSpir   *Dictionnaire de spiritualité ascétique et mystique, doctrine*
           et histoire. Ed. Joseph de Guibert, Marcel Viller, and
           Ferdinand Cavallera. 45 vols. Paris: Beauchesne, 1932–1995.
DThC   *Dictionnaire de théologie catholique.* Ed. Alfred Vacant,
           Eugène Mangenot, and Emile Amann. 15 vols. Paris:
           Letouzey et Ane, 1902–1950.
LS   *The Hellenistic Philosophers.* Ed. A.A. Long and D.N.
           Sedley. 2 vols. Cambridge: Cambridge University Press,
           1987. Cited by source number.
NCE   *New Catholic Encyclopedia.* 2nd ed. Detroit: Gale, 2003.
RAC   *Reallexikon für Antike und Christentum.* Ed. T. Klause et al.
           Stuttgart: Hiersemann, 1950-.
SVF   *Stoicorum veterum fragmenta.* Ed. Hans Friedrich August
           von Arnim. 4 vols. Leipzig: Teubner, 1903–1905. Cited by
           source number.
TRE   *Theologische Realenzyklopädie.* Ed. Gerhard Müller, Horst
           Balz, Gerhard Krause. 36 vols. Berlin: De Gruyter, 1976–
           2004.

Edition

De Sinner Gabriel Rudolf Ludwig De Sinner, *Sancti Patris nostri*
           Basilii, Caesareae Cappadociae archiepiscopi, opera omnia
           quae exstant, vel quae sub eius nomine circumferuntur, ad
           manuscriptos Codices Gallicanos, Vaticanos, Florentinos
           et Anglicos, necnon ad antiquiores editiones castigata,
           multis aucta: Nova Interpretatione, criticis Praefationibus,
           Notis, variis Lectionibus illustrata, nova sancti Doctoris
           Vita et copioissimis Indicibus locupletata. Tomus Primus et
           Secundus: Opera et studio Domni Iuliani Garnier, Presbyteri
           et Monachi Benedictini, e Congregatione Sancti Mauri.

Tomus Tertius: Opera et studio Monachorum Ordinis Sancti Benedicti, et Congregatione Sancti Mauri. Editio Parisina altera, emendata et aucta. Paris: Gaume Fratres, 1839.

Basil's Moral Homilies

Att	*In illud, Attende tibi ipsi* (*On "Be Attentive to Yourself"*)
Bapt	*In baptisma* (*On Baptism*)
Chr	*In sanctam Christi generationem* (*On the Holy Birth of Christ*)
Dest	*In illud, Destruam horrea mea* (*On Luke 12.16–21*)
Div	*In divites* (*Against the Rich*)
Ebr	*In ebriosos* (*Against Drunkards*)
Fam	*Dicta tempore famis et siccitatis* (*Delivered in Time of Famine and Drought*)
Fide	*De fide* (*On Faith*)
Gord	*In Gordium martyrem* (*On Gordius the Martyr*)
Grat	*De gratiarum actione* (*On Giving Thanks*)
Hum	*De humilitate* (*On Humility*)
Iei1	*De ieiunio I* (*On Fasting I*)
Iei2	*De ieiunio II* (*On Fasting II*)
Inv	*De invidia* (*On Envy*)
Ira	*Adversus iratos* (*Against those Prone to Anger*)
Iul	*In martyrem Iulittam* (*On Julitta the Martyr*)
Lak	*Dicta in Lakizis* (*Delivered in Lakizois*)
Malo	*Quod Deus non est auctor malorum* (*That God is Not the Cause of Evil*)
Mam	*In Mamantem martyrem* (*On Mamas the Martyr*)
Mart	*In quadraginta martyres* (*On the Forty Martyrs*)
Mund	*Quod rebus mundanis adhaerendum non sit* (*On Detachment from Worldly Things, and on the Fire that Occurred Outside the Church*)
Prov	*In principium Proverbiorum* (*On the Beginning of Proverbs*)
Ps1	*In Psalmum i* (*On Psalm 1*)

Ps7	*In Psalmum vii* (*On Psalm 7*)
Ps14a	*In Psalmum xiv A* (*On Psalm 14 I*)
Ps14b	*In Psalmum xiv B* (*On Psalm 14 II*)
Ps28	*In Psalmum xxviii* (*On Psalm 28*)
Ps29	*In Psalmum xxix* (*On Psalm 29*)
Ps32	*In Psalmum xxxii* (*On Psalm 32*)
Ps33	*In Psalmum xxxiii* (*On Psalm 33*)
Ps44	*In Psalmum xliv* (*On Psalm 44*)
Ps45	*In Psalmum xlv* (*On Psalm 45*)
Ps48	*In Psalmum xlviii* (*On Psalm 48*)
Ps59	*In Psalmum lixi* (*On Psalm 59*)
Ps61	*In Psalmum lxi* (*On Psalm 61*)
Ps114	*In Psalmum cxiv* (*On Psalm 114*)
Ps115	*In Psalmum cxv* (*On Psalm 115*)
Sab	*Contra Sabellianos, et Arium, et Anomoeos* (*Against the Sabellians, Anomoians, and Pneumatomachians*)
Trin	*Adversus eos qui per calumniam dicunt dici a nobis deos tres* (*On Not Three Gods, against those who calumniate us, claiming that we say that there are three gods*)
Verb	*In illud, In principio erat Verbum* (*On the Beginning of the Gospel of John*)

Other Works of Basil

Ep.	*Epistulae* (*Letters*)
Eun.	*Contra Eunomium* (*Against Eunomius*)
Hex.	*Homiliae in hexaemeron* (*Homilies on the Six Days of Creation*)
Litt.	*Ad adolescentes, quomodo possint ex gentilium libris fructum capere* (*To Young Men on How They Might Derive Benefit from Greek Literature*)
Reg. brev.	*Regulae Brevius Tractatae* (*Short Rules*)
Reg. fus.	*Regulae Fusius Tractatae* (*Long Rules*)
Spir.	*Liber de Spiritu sancto* (*On the Holy Spirit*)

General Introduction

In the summer of 362 the church of Caesarea in Cappadocia was at a crossroads. Its longtime metropolitan bishop, Dianius, had just died. The election of his successor was hotly contested, with several rival factions each proposing their own candidate. Even when a number of bishops from nearby cities gathered in Caesarea to participate in the consecration of the new bishop, agreement proved elusive. At long last a band of soldiers stationed in Caesarea took matters into their own hands. They seized one of the leading citizens of the city, a man named Eusebius, and dragged him before the visiting bishops to have him consecrated. Though Eusebius was not even a baptized Christian, he was a man of excellent character and less objectionable than the candidates endorsed by the rival parties. Immediately the visiting bishops baptized and ordained him. And thus Caesarea had a new bishop.[1]

In order be an effective bishop Eusebius would have been faced with two challenges. First, he needed to surround himself with a competent clergy to compensate for his own lack of ecclesiastical experience and theological knowledge. Second, he needed to gain credibility with and win the favor of the rival factions to unite the Caesarean church. As it turned out, there happened to be a promising young reader in his church whose promotion to the presbyterate, Eusebius thought, could help him on both counts.[2] His name was Basil.

[1]Gregory of Nazianzus recounts of the election of Eusebius in *Oration* 18.33. Eusebius was the bishop of Caesarea in Cappadocia from mid-362 until 370; he is not to be confused with Eusebius, the bishop of Caesarea in Palestine, the famous church historian, exegete, and theologian, who died in 339.

[2]The office of reader (or lector) was one of the minor clerical orders whose appointees, as the name implies, were entrusted with public reading at the liturgy. The office of presbyter is roughly equivalent to today's priest. The order of reader continues in the Orthodox church today, and Orthodox Christian priests are often still referred to as presbyters.

Born in 329 or 330, this scion of a Christian family from the
nearby province of Helenopontus had received the best education
that money could buy in the ancient world.[3] After studying grammar
and rhetoric in Neocaesarea and Caesarea as a teenager, in 348 or
349 he went to Constantinople for a year, and then to Athens for five
years, for advanced studies in rhetoric and philosophy. Upon returning to Caesarea in 355 or 356, he taught rhetoric and established a
reputation in the region as one of the foremost orators of his generation. But soon Basil abandoned a teaching career and decided to
adopt the ascetic life, as so many other Christians in Cappadocia and
elsewhere in the Roman Empire were doing at this time.[4] After being
baptized by Dianius, he established a small community of ascetics
on his family estates in Annisa. Here they immersed themselves in
prayer and in the study of Scripture and Christian theology.

After two or three years of ascetic retreat, Basil had become
increasingly recognized not only for his rhetorical prowess but now
also for his ascetical, biblical, and theological expertise. Dianius
ordained Basil a reader in the Caesarean church, and in January 360
brought his newly-ordained cleric with him to a church council in

[3]This sketch of Basil's life is drawn from Mark DelCogliano and Andrew Radde-
Gallwitz, St. Basil of Caesarea: Against Eunomius, FOTC 122 (Washington, DC:
Catholic University of America Press, 2011), 6–18. The best modern biography of
Basil remains Philip Rousseau, Basil of Caesarea (Berkeley / Los Angeles / London:
University of California Press, 1994). Good, shorter accounts of Basil's life and work
can be found in Blomfield Jackson, "Prolegomena. Sketch of the Life and Works of
Saint Basil," NPNF 2.8, xiii–lxxvii; Jean Gribomont, "Basil, St." in NCE 2: 135–139; and
Stephen Hildebrand, St Basil the Great: On the Holy Spirit, PPS 42 (Crestwood, NY:
St Vladimir's Seminary Press, 2011), 11–21. A trilogy of books by Raymond Van Dam
depicts Basil, as well as Gregory of Nazianzus and Gregory of Nyssa, in their Cap-
padocian and Roman context: Kingdom of Snow: Roman Rule and Greek Culture in
Cappadocia (Philadelphia: University of Pennsylvania Press, 2002); Becoming Chris-
tian: The Conversion of Roman Cappadocia (Philadelphia: University of Pennsylvania
Press, 2003); and Families and Friends in Late Roman Cappadocia (Philadelphia:
University of Pennsylvania Press, 2003).

[4]On the ascetic movement in Asia Minor at this time, see Susanna Elm, Virgins
of God: The Making of Asceticism in Late Antiquity (Oxford: Clarendon Press, 1994),
25–223, and Anna M. Silvas, The Asketikon of St Basil the Great (Oxford: Oxford
University Press, 2005).

Constantinople to avail himself of both Basil's theological advice and rhetorical power. The creed adopted by the council endorsed a Trinitarian theology that was broadly Homoian, a position with which Basil could not agree.[5] When Dianius was compelled by imperial agents to subscribe to this creed in the summer of 360, Basil became disillusioned with his bishop's orthodoxy and returned to his ascetic retreat. But in the summer of 362, when he heard that his bishop was on his deathbed, Basil returned to Caesarea and was reconciled with Dianius before he died.[6]

So when Eusebius succeeded Dianius, he realized that Basil could be a great service to the Caesarean church. No longer seen simply as orator of profound skill, he was also recognized as a leading authority on the theological debates over the Trinity that were currently rocking the church and viewed as an expert by the various groups of ascetics that were popping up all over Cappadocia. Hence by elevating Basil to the rank of presbyter Eusebius hoped to acquire a superb preacher, a theological advisor, and favor with the ascetics. Basil received ordination at the hands of Eusebius in late 362 or early 363.[7]

One of Basil's primary tasks a presbyter was to preach. In fact, we possess one of the first homilies he delivered after he was ordained (*Prov*). It may even be his very first homily, though we cannot be certain. In the opening lines of the homily Basil reports that Eusebius asked him to preach on the opening verses of the Book of Proverbs,

[5]On the theological debates raging at the beginning of Basil's ecclesiastical career, see DelCogliano and Radde-Gallwitz, *St. Basil of Caesarea*, 18–35, as well as the more extensive discussions in Lewis Ayres, *Nicaea and its Legacy: An Approach to Fourth-Century Trinitarian Theology* (Oxford: Oxford University Press, 2004); and John Behr, *The Nicene Faith* (Crestwood, NY: St Vladimir's Seminary Press, 2004).

[6]Basil, *Ep.* 51.

[7]Paul Jonathan Fedwick, "A Chronology of the Life and Works of Basil of Caesarea," in idem, ed., *Basil of Caesarea: Christian, Humanist, Ascetic. A Sixteen-Hundredth Anniversary Symposium* (Toronto: The Pontifical Institute of Mediaeval Studies, 1981), 3–19. In all matters of dating I have followed Fedwick. It should noted that Basil had a falling out with Eusebius by late 363 for some unspecific reason and retreated again to his family estates. He did not resume his presbyterial duties in Caesarea until late 365. On this dispute, see p. 52 below.

which in the early church was considered notoriously difficult to understand. Basil also hints that Eusebius was testing him, wanting to see if he could live up the rhetorical and theological reputation he had already established for himself. The homily he preached is replete with insight, erudition, and dazzling rhetoric. It must have taken over an hour to deliver, perhaps as long as an hour and a half. In the absence of the many forms of entertainment and media that we enjoy today, ancient audiences were willing and even eager to hear a long speech and were as captivated by good oratory as we are by a blockbuster movie. When Basil concluded his homily, no one was in doubt. He had passed the bishop's test.

For the remainder of his career Basil preached on a regular basis. Besides the various Sundays, feasts, and celebrations of the church's liturgical calendar, he preached at synods and other ecclesiastical gatherings. As his episcopacy progressed Eusebius came to rely more and more upon Basil for the pastoral care of his flock, particularly when it came to preaching. For example, during the Cappadocian famine of 369 Basil preached a series of homilies on social justice, whose overall theme was an impassioned plea for the rich to help the starving poor and needy.[8] As a presbyter, Basil must have delivered hundreds of homilies and then hundreds more when he succeeded Eusebius as bishop of Caesarea in 370. Only about fifty of his homilies are extant. While this is undoubtedly a small fraction of his total output, it is not inconsiderable and affords us the opportunity to get a sense of Basil as a preacher.

His goal in preaching first and foremost seems to have been to benefit his audience. Though Basil was a skilled rhetorician and one of the best theologians the church has ever produced, his homilies were not intended to be oratorical showpieces or theological treatises, however much they turned out to be so. Just as Scripture was written for our benefit, so too must the preacher strive to benefit his

[8]Rousseau, *Basil of Caesarea*, 136–44. The homilies Basil preached during this period are *Div*, *Dest*, *Fam*, and *Ps14b*. These homilies are translated by C. Paul Schroeder, *St Basil the Great: On Social Justice*, PPS 38 (Crestwood, NY: St Vladimir's Seminary Press, 2009).

audience with his words.[9] Basil's hope was that each member of his audience would hear something in his homily that he or she could use to make further progress in the Christian life: insight into overcoming a particular vice or acquiring a particular virtue, a greater desire to help the poor and needy, a deeper understanding of the Trinity, and so forth. Basil was also aware that his audience could only digest so much at once. A couple of his homilies conclude with a comment to this effect.[10] This concern not to overwhelm his audience also demonstrates Basil's goal of benefitting his listeners. His homilies typically conclude with an exhortation to put into practice or adopt what he has discussed in the homily. Finally, like Origen, Basil usually ends his homilies with a prayer to Jesus Christ and a doxology based on 1 Peter 4.11: *to whom be glory and might for ever and ever. Amen.*[11]

In his homilies Basil uses a variety of rhetorical techniques and tactics to achieve the goal of benefitting his audience, to help them be attentive to his words and remember his lessons.[12] While some of the rhetoric of Basil's homilies may seem "flowery" to us today, in a predominantly oral culture such as Basil's it was deemed essential, desirable, and delightful. It is true that there was a long tradition in the Greco-Roman world of orators placing more emphasis on rhetorical pyrotechnics than on substantive content, but good orators such as Basil were adept at making the rhetorical form of their speeches serve their content, not vice versa.[13] One of the most effective rhetorical techniques he uses (and which comes across in

[9]See *Prov* 1; *Lak* 5; *Inv* 5; *Sab* 4; and *Verb* 4.

[10]See *Mund* 8; and *Verb* 4.

[11]On Origen's custom, see Joseph T. Lienhard, *Origen. Homilies on Luke, Fragments on Luke*, FOTC 94 (Washington, DC: The Catholic University of America Press, 1996), xxiv.

[12]See James Marshall Campbell, *The Influence of the Second Sophistic on the Style of the Sermons of St. Basil the Great* (Washington, DC: Catholic University of America Press, 1922).

[13]Most of the homilies translated in this volume are stylistically sophisticated, yet there are a few that fall below the standard which Basil set for himself. See the introductions to the individual homilies for more details.

translation)[14] is extended metaphors and analogies. For example, in one homily he compares the devil to robbers who ambush unsuspecting travelers as they make their way along the road (*Mund* 1). In another, a person struggling with various vices and passions is compared to the steersman trying to keep his ship from sinking during a squall (*Prov* 15). Another technique used by Basil with some regularity is *ecphrasis*, the detailed and picturesque depiction of some object. Basil employs *ecphrasis* with great effect when describing those who have succumbed to some vice to underscore their irrationality and ridiculousness, for example, the man filled with envy (*Inv* 2), the rich man who makes countless excuses for not helping the poor and needy (*Mund* 8), the man seething with anger (*Lak* 3), and the greedy person (*Lak* 5). Such depictions were surely intended to be as amusing as they were educational.

Basil's homilies cover a range of topics. There are sermons, for example, on the virtues and the vices, on Christian practices such as fasting, on the care of the poor and needy, in praise of the martyrs, on theological topics such as the Trinity, on interpreting various psalms and other passages of Scripture, and so forth. His nine homilies on the six days of creation, known collectively as the *Hexaemeron*, is considered his masterpiece by ancient and modern commentators alike.[15] All of his homilies on other topics, that is, all of his homilies outside of the *Hexaemeron*, are also grouped together as collection and known as the Moral Homilies.[16]

[14]Some of the rhetorical techniques used by Basil depend upon the sound of Greek words themselves and other kinds of Greek wordplay that are lost in translation.

[15]The most recent edition is Emmanuel Amand de Mendieta and Stig Y. Rudberg, *Basilius von Caesarea: Homilien zum Hexaemeron*, GCS n.f. 2 (Berlin: Akademie-Verlag, 1997). An English translation based on an older edition can be found in Agnes Clare Way, *Saint Basil: Exegetic Homilies*, FOTC 46 (Washington, DC: The Catholic University of America Press, 1963).

[16]The exception is two homilies on the origin of humanity, which are appended to the *Hexaemeron* as its tenth and eleventh homilies. Some scholars do not think these are genuinely Basilian; see BBV ii.1201–7. Translations can be found in Nonna Verna Harrison, *St Basil the Great: On the Human Condition*, PPS 30 (Crestwood, NY: St Vladimir's Seminary Press, 2005).

The Moral Homilies as a Collection

The Moral Homilies are forty discourses by Basil on a variety of subjects.[17] The collection consists of two subsets: fifteen homilies on the Psalms and twenty-five homilies on diverse topics (this latter subset is basically all the homilies not devoted to interpreting a psalm, including several on the martyrs).[18] The label for the collection has an ancient pedigree. Since the fourth century Christians have identified a subset of Basil's homilies as Moral Homilies (ἠθικοὶ λόγοι or ἠθικά).[19] Unfortunately, it is not always clear in these ancient sources which homilies were included in this category. For example, while Gregory of Nazianzus speaks of Basil's "moral and practical homilies," he does not indicate which homilies he considers these to be, but he does seem to exclude Basil's homilies on the martyrs from this group.[20] The ninth-century Photius of Constantinople refers to some of Basil's homilies as "the so-called moral homilies" (οἱ λεγόμενοι ἠθικοὶ λόγοι), but does not give any hint about which homilies were included in this collection.[21] In the tenth-century

[17]Moral Homilies once ascribed to Basil but now considered spurious are excluded from this number.

[18]See BBV ii.xxxix n. 5.

[19]One could also translate this title as "Moral Discourses," "Moral Orations," or "Ethical Treatises," but the longstanding custom is to call these texts "homilies."

[20]In his panegyric on Basil (*Oration* 43), Gregory of Nazianzus supplies us with what must be the earliest description of the contents of Basil's literary corpus. After listing the homilies on the Hexaemeron, the polemical works (presumably the three books against Eunomius), and the treatise on the Holy Spirit, Gregory writes: "When I study his encomia on our athletes, I despise the body, and enjoy the society of those whom he is praising, and rouse myself to the struggle. When I study his moral and practical homilies (ἠθικοῖς λόγοις καὶ πρακτικοῖς), I am purified in soul and body, making me a temple fit for God, and an instrument struck by the Spirit, to celebrate by its strains the glory and power of God" (*Oration* 43.67.3; trans. NPNF 2.7, 418, slightly modified).

[21]*Bibliotheca* 142 (98b). That Photius refers to the Moral Homilies and not the *Moralia* (Moral Rules), see Józef Naumowicz, "Les oeuvres de St. Basile le Grand dans la *Bibliothèque* de Photius," in Waldemar Caren, ed., *Mélanges d'histoire byzantine offerts à Oktawiusz Jurewicz à l'occasion de son soixante-dixième anniversaire*, Byzantina Lodiensia 3 (Łódź: Wydawictwo Uniwersytetu Łódzkiego, 1998), 71–80 at 73–4.

Byzantine encyclopedia known as the *Suda*, the homilies on the martyrs are excluded from the Moral Homilies (as in Gregory), but the Moral Homilies themselves are equated with Basil's homilies on the Psalms.[22] In contrast to the lack of clarity in these sources, the medieval manuscripts of Basil's works supply us with the precise contents of the Moral Homilies collection. The *pinaxes* (tables of contents) of several manuscripts refer to *both* the homilies on the Psalms *and* the homilies on diverse topics (including those on the martyrs) as Moral Homilies.[23] It is the usage of the label in medieval manuscripts that is the basis for ours today.

We do not know who first gathered Basil's homilies into a collection of Moral Homilies, or when this happened. Nonetheless, scholars have been able to reconstruct what could be the primitive form in which the Moral Homilies circulated. The putative archaic form—for which Basil himself may be responsible[24]—contained thirty-five homilies in the following order: *Ps1, Att, Dest, Div, Ps14a, Ps14b, Iei2, Iei1, Ebr, Ira, Inv, Grat, Iul, Prov, Malo, Ps59, Ps61, Ps114, Ps115, Mart, Gord, Lak, Fam, Chr, Bapt, Fide, Verb, Ad virginem lapsam* (=*Ep.* 46), *Ep.* 243, *Ep.* 260, *Litt., Ps7, Ps28a, Ps29,* and *Ps32.*

---

[22]"He [i.e., Basil] wrote many works, among which those on the Hexaemeron stand out as the most remarkable. And he composed exceptional discourses against Eunomius, and a volume on the Holy Spirit, and nine homilies on the Hexaemeron, one ascetical volume, another on virginity, one panegyric on the forty martyrs, another on Gordius, another on Barlaam, another on Julitta, various moral homilies (ἠθικοὶ λόγοι) on various psalms. . . ." (*Suda* Beta 150 on Basil).

[23]The best example can be found in Vaticanus gr. 420 (Fedwick's **h74**, from the second half of the 14th century), which reads: "Pinax of what is written in this book, the moral discourses of Saint Basil the Great" (πίναξ τῶν ἐγγεγραμμένων τῇδε τῇ βίβλῳ ἠθικῶν τοῦ ἁγίου καὶ Μεγάλου βασιλείου λόγων); see BBV ii.47. Vaticanus gr. 411 (**h66**, from the 9th or 10th century) also uses title ἠθικοὶ λόγοι; see Édouard Rouillard, "L'édition des *Homélies morales* de Basile de Césarée," *Studia Patristica* 22 (1989): 75–78 at 77. Three other manuscripts—Vaticanus gr. 418 (**h72**, from the end of the 10th or the beginning of the 11th century), Escorial Ψ.II.12 gr. 447 (**h185**, from the 13th century), Patmos 29 (**h177**, from the end of the 9th or the beginning of the 10th century)—use the similar title ἠθικά; see BBV ii.107 and Rouillard, "L'édition des *Homélies morales*," 76–7.

[24]Édouard Rouillard, "Basile de Césarée a-t-il corrigé lui-même un premier état de texte de ses homélies?" *Studia Patristica* 22 (1989): 65–68; see also BBV ii.3 n. 12.

What is perhaps a slightly later edition added the following four homilies: *Ps33*, *Ps44*, *Ps45*, and *Ps48*.[25] Within this arrangement one can detect four groups. First, *Ps1* acts as a kind of preface to the entire collection.[26] The remaining three groups each consist of two blocks of homilies in sequence, some on diverse topics followed by some on the Psalms: (1) *Att*, *Dest*, *Div*, *Ps14a*, *Ps14b*; (2) *Iei2*, *Iei1*, *Ebr*, *Ira*, *Inv*, *Grat*, *Iul*, *Prov*, *Malo*, *Ps59*, *Ps61*, *Ps114*, *Ps115*; and (3) *Mart*, *Gord*, *Lak*, *Fam*, *Chr*, *Bapt*, *Fide*, *Verb*, *Ad virginem lapsam* (=*Ep*. 46), *Ep*. 243, *Ep*. 260, *Litt*., *Ps7*, *Ps28a*, *Ps29*, *Ps32*, *Ps33*, *Ps44*, *Ps45*, *Ps48*.[27] While no manuscript replicates this arrangement exactly, scholars judge the organization of the Moral Homilies into alternating blocks of homilies on diverse topics and homilies on the Psalms as indicative of the most archaic form of this homiletic corpus.[28]

Nonetheless, this primitive organization of Basil's Moral Homilies was slowly destroyed by scribes who began to rearrange the homilies into the two separate subsets. The homilies on the Psalms were copied together and sequenced according the number of the Psalm, and the homilies on diverse topics were copied together in an order somewhat preserving the sequence of the primitive form. The archaic form seems to have been supplanted for good in the ninth century when Studite monks in Constantinople produced a new recension of Basil's works that would in time become widespread and highly influential. In this so-called "vulgate" recension the primitive arrangement of Basil work's was abandoned. In manuscripts containing this recension, the homilies on the Psalms are presented first, followed by the homilies on diverse topics.[29] It is in

[25]See BBV ii.3–5. Note (1) that the following homilies are not included: *Sab*, *Mund*, *Hum*, *Trin*, and *Mam*; and (2) that the following are now not considered homilies: *Ad virginem lapsam* (=*Ep*. 46), *Ep*. 243, *Ep*. 260, *Litt*. Yet these texts seem to have been considered homilies in antiquity, as Rufinus' translation shows (it includes *Ad virginem lapsam*).

[26]See the comments on *Ps1* on p. 81 below.

[27]Édouard Rouillard has attempted to detect a rationale for this ordering; see his "L'édition des *Homélies morales*," 75–6.

[28]BBV ii.5

[29]See BBV ii.9–10.

this vulgate form that the European humanists of the Renaissance first encountered Basil's Moral Homilies. Therefore, this vulgate recension influenced the arrangement of Basil's homilies in the early printed editions of his works, and accordingly it continues to influence scholars today.

Unfortunately, this vulgate arrangement of Basil's Moral Homilies had a negative influence on the integrity the collection. Seeing the homilies on the Psalms separated from the homilies on diverse topics in the manuscripts, some scholars divided the Moral Homilies into two separate, unrelated collections: (1) the Homilies on the Psalms, and (2) the Homilies on Diverse Topics.[30] But this division obscures the fact that both the homilies on the Psalms and the homilies on diverse topics were considered a unified set in the years after Basil's death, or perhaps even by Basil himself. The two sub-groups within the Moral Homilies were not separated into two distinct collections, as if they differed in terms of origination or purpose. Basil did not preach a series of homilies on the Psalms (as Augustine would later do) whose character was somehow different from that of the homilies on diverse topics.[31] Some scholars have even gone so far as to classify the homilies on the Psalms among Basil's exegetical writings, completely separating them from his homiletic corpus, as if the genre or intention of each set

[30]E.g., Johannes Quasten, *Patrology, Vol. 3* (Westminster, MD: Newman Press, 1960), 216–220. Louis-Sébastien Le Nain de Tillemont, *Mémoires pour servir à l'histoire ecclésiastique des six premiers siècles* (Venice: Pitteri, 1732), ix.290 and 297–299. In the edition of Garnier the homilies on the Psalms are printed separately from the homilies on diverse topics. See also Prudentius Maran, *Vita Sancti Basilii Magni Archiepiscopi Caesariensis* 41.4–5 and 43.1–6 (De Sinner iii.ccxxxviii–ccxl and ccxlvi–cclii; PG 29.ccxiii–clxv and clxx–clxxiv). In this situation some scholars referred only to the homilies on diverse topics as the moral homilies; see e.g., L. Ellies Du Pin, *Nouvelle bibliothèque des auteurs ecclésiastiques* (Utrecht: Jean Broedelet, 1731), ii.183.

[31]The first half of Basil's homily on Psalm 1, which is a kind of introduction to the entire Psalter, was affixed as a preface, in the Latin translation by Rufinus, to Augustine's *Enarrationes in psalmos*. The first editors of Basil's works were surely aware of this, and it may have influenced them to view Basil's homilies on the Psalms along the lines of Augustine's. But it seems that Basil neither intended nor undertook a systematic homiletic commentary series on the Psalms in the manner of Augustine.

were fundamentally different.[32] This practice of disassociating the homilies on the Psalms and the homilies on diverse topics is mistaken. As we have seen, since the fourth century the homilies on the Psalms and the homilies on diverse topics were circulated together as the Moral Homilies. And furthermore, homilies from both subsets were mixed together in alternating blocks in the primitive form of the collection.

This unity of the homilies on the Psalms and on diverse topics as the Moral Homilies is also seen in the transmission of Basil's homilies in translation. Around the year 400 Rufinus translated "eight brief homiletic works of blessed Basil" (*octo beati Basilii breves istos homeliticos libellos*).[33] These eight homilies include some on the Psalms and others on diverse topics: *Ps1, Att, Dest, Inv, Prov, Fide, Ad virginem lapsam* (*Ep.* 46), and *Ps59*. Thus Rufinus clearly sees both the homilies on the Psalms and on diverse topics as part of a single collection. Unfortunately, Rufinus did not translate any of the homilies on the martyrs. So we cannot be certain whether he subscribed to Gregory's separation of the homilies on the martyrs from the Moral Homilies, or whether he included them with the others, as seen in Photius. Yet it is clear that for Rufinus the homilies on the Psalms and on diverse topics went together.

The fact that the homilies on the Psalms and on diverse topics have constituted the Moral Homilies from the fourth century justifies the inclusion of the eleven homilies translated in this volume: nine are homilies on diverse topics and two are homilies on the Psalms. Hence, taking the Latin translation of Rufinus as its inspiration, this volume contains a selection of the Moral Homilies.

[32] E.g., NPNF ii.8, xxxii–xxxiii, xliv, and lv; Edmund Venables, "Basilius of Caesarea" in DCB 1: 282–297 at 296.

[33] *Praefatio* (De Sinner ii.1012).

From Greek to English

In an Introduction it is customary to mention the edition of the original-language text used as the basis for the translation. Previous translations consulted are also noted in the same place. In this book, however, I have chosen to depart from this practice. There has not been a new edition of Basil's Moral Homilies since the 1720s—nearly 300 years ago. It would seem odd to list this edition as the basis for my translations without further explanation. In the course of this project, I have become keenly aware that my work on these translations is but the most recent episode in a history of Basilian textual scholarship that stretches back over 500 years. It is a story that is fascinating in its own right, one that is deeply intertwined with the history of Christianity itself, with the disintegration of the Byzantine Empire, with the rise of humanism in Europe, with the confessional polemics of the Reformation era, with monastic reform, and with the emergence of patristics as a modern academic discipline. Luckily, scholars now have available Paul Jonathan Fedwick's massive *Bibliotheca Basiliana Vniversalis*, which contains a detailed study of the complex history of the editions and translations of Basil's works from the late fourteenth-century onward.[34] Though a treasury of meticulous research, the sheer volume of the information provided by BBV can be daunting. Nonetheless, Fedwick's BBV has been indispensable for the account provided here of the most important developments in the textual scholarship on Basil's Moral Homilies.

The modern critical study of Basil begins in the Renaissance. Of supreme importance for humanist interest in Basil was his oration *To Young Men on How They Might Derive Benefit from Greek Literature*.

---

[34]Another invaluable resource is David Amand, "Essai d'une histoire critique des éditions générales grecques et gréco-latines de S. Basile de Césarée," *Revue Bénédictine* 52 (1940): 141–161; 53 (1941): 119–151; 54 (1942): 124–144; and 56 (1944/1945): 126–173. A shorter account can be found in Stig Y. Rudberg, "Manuscripts and Editions of the Works of Basil of Caesarea," in Jonathan Paul Fedwick, ed., *Basil of Caesarea: Christian, Humanist, Ascetic. A Sixteen-Hundredth Anniversary Symposium* (Toronto: The Pontifical Institute of Mediaeval Studies, 1981), 49–65.

It was translated into Latin by Leonardo Bruni (*c.* 1369–1444), one of the first humanists, in 1401 or 1402, printed for the first time in 1470, and reprinted more than 100 times thereafter.[35] Humanists appealed to it as one of the clearest expressions of the ideals of their own program of moral reform based on the classical authors. Bruni himself had learned Greek from the Byzantine nobleman and diplomat Manuel Chrysoloras (*c.* 1355–1415) when he taught in Florence in the years 1397–1400, the first time Greek had been taught in Italy in centuries. Born in Constantinople, Chrysoloras had come to Venice in 1390 at the head of an embassy sent by the Byzantine Emperor Manuel II Palaeologus to request aid from Christian rulers against the Ottoman Turks. He remained in Europe for the rest of his life as a Byzantine ambassador and teacher of Greek. And so, in Chrysoloras and Bruni we have a direct link between the Byzantine world in its final stages—the world in whose earliest stages Basil himself had lived—and European humanism.[36]

In 1515, the humanist Raffaello Maffei (1451–1522) published a Latin translation of some of Basil's works, including the Moral Homilies, which thus appeared in Latin for the first time.[37] Though born and educated in Rome, Maffei belonged to a prominent family from Volterra in northern Italy, so he was known as Il Volterrano. In 1466 he entered the Roman Curia as papal scriptor, and he remained in the Curia for the rest of his life. Unlike most other Roman humanists, Maffei was a student of Greek as well as of Latin. He had studied Greek with George of Trebizond (1395–1472/3). George was born in

[35]See BBV ii.819–835.

[36]On Bruni, see G. Griffiths, et al., *The Humanism of Leonardo Bruni* (Binghamton, New York: 1987); and Ronald G. Witt, *In the Footsteps of the Ancients: The Origins of Humanism from Lovato to Bruni* (Leiden: Brill, 2003), 392–442.

[37]*Opera Magni Basilii; per Raphaelem Volaterranum nup[er] in Latinum conversa* (Rome: Apud Iacobum Mazochium, 1515). On this edition, see BBV ii.842–843; this description supersedes BBV i.202–205. On Maffei himself, see John F. D'Amico, *Renaissance Humanism in Papal Rome: Humanists and Churchmen on the Eve of the Reformation* (Baltimore and London: The Johns Hopkins University Press, 1983), in which Maffei figures prominently. Maffei's life is sketched on pp. 82–85; his thought is explored on pp. 189–211; his translations of Basil are discussed on pp. 191–2.

Crete of parents originally from Trebizond on the southern shore of the Black Sea, who had presumably left the crumbling Byzantine Empire, as so many others were beginning to do, to seek a better life elsewhere. George rose to prominence and participated in the Council of Florence (1438–1439) and later became a papal secretary. Thus he arrived in the West on one of the earliest waves of Greek-speaking immigrants who sparked interest in the humanist studies that would inspire the Renaissance. And so, through George, Maffei was another Italian humanist with ties directly to the Byzantine world of Basil himself. It is not clear on which Greek text of Basil's Moral Homilies Maffei based his Latin translations. He probably used whatever texts were available to him locally in manuscripts, since a Greek edition of Basil's works had not yet been published. Maffei viewed Basil primarily as teacher of morality and the texts he chose to translate reflect this interest. Maffei's Latin translations are of abiding importance because they would be reworked by subsequent scholars for the next 100 years.

At the height of the Reformation, none other than Desiderius Erasmus (1466–1536), the most renowned Christian humanist of the Renaissance, published the *editio princeps*—the first Greek edition—of some of Basil's works in 1532, including the Moral Homilies.[38] In his introductory remarks Erasmus captures the momentous occasion by saying, "Behold, dear reader, we give you an invaluable treasure: the divine and truly great Basil speaking as eloquently as possible in his own language, who until this point you have only had stammering in Latin."[39] For this reason Erasmus did not provide Latin translations of these homilies.[40] In subsequent decades a number of scholars sought to correct this omission, though within the

---

[38]Published in Basel by Froben. On this edition, see Amand, "Essai d'une histoire critique," 52 (1940), 142–48; Rudberg, "Manuscripts and Editions," 56–7; BBV i.208–217; ii.849.

[39]*En amice lector, thesaurum damus inaestimabilem D. Basilum vere magnum sua lingua disertissime loquentem quem hactenus habuisti Latine balbutientem.*

[40]He had published Latin translations of *Iei1* and *Iei2* two years earlier; see BBV ii.849.

context of the confessional polemics emerging between Protestants and Roman Catholics. Basil became a kind of prize to be rescued by one side from the other. Scholars in both camps criticized each others' translations as inaccurate, or worse. Fedwick describes this controversy as one "in which mediocrity prevailed over scholarly discipline and love of learning."[41] "At issue," he writes, "was not so much accuracy as a desire to remove any possible obstacles to one's own 'pre-formed' opinions."[42]

On the Protestant side were Joannes Hahnpol or Hagnbut, also known as Ianus Cornarius (1500–1558), and Wolfgang Müslin or Musculus (d. 1563). Cornarius was a physician by profession and a friend of Erasmus who devoted his time to editing and translating ancient authors both pagan and Christian.[43] Musculus was a former Benedictine monk who had left his monastery in 1527 to join the Reformation.[44] Each published his own Latin translation of Basil's works in 1540. Both of their translations of the Moral Homilies were for the most part revisions of Maffei's translations to bring them into line with the edition of Erasmus.[45] On the Roman Catholic side was Godefridus Tilmann (d. 1561), who published an edition of Basil's works in 1547.[46] As a Carthusian monk, he was particularly critical of the ex-Benedictine Musculus, whose character as well as his skill as a translator he impugned. In his edition Tilmann himself translated the homilies on the Psalms, but his translations of the homilies on diverse topics are mostly reprinted from Maffei. These translations done in the heat of confessional controversy retain little value today. But they were highly influential on subsequent editors and translators of Basil's homilies, who both borrowed from them and criticized

[41]BBV i.221.

[42]BBV i.230.

[43]On Cornarius, see Amand, "Essai d'une histoire critique," 52 (1940), 159–60; and BBV i.225 n. 47.

[44]On Musculus, see BBV i.221 n. 34.

[45]On Cornarius' translation, see BBV i.221 and 225–229; ii.853–854; on Musculus', see BBV i.221–225; ii.855.

[46]On this edition, see BBV i.230–236; ii. 857–858. On Tilmann himself, see BBV i.230 n. 53.

them in their notes. I have not, however, consulted them for my own translations.

The next major of edition Basil's works was published by Fronton Du Duc or Ducaeus (1558–1624).[47] He was a Jesuit theologian who taught in the colleges of the Society of Jesus and engaged in the theological debates of the era. In 1604 he was appointed librarian at the Collège de Clermont in Paris and soon thereafter became involved in editing and translating various Greek Fathers, most notably Chrysostom. Ducaeus published his Greek-Latin edition of Basil's works in 1618 with the printer Fédéric Morel (1558–1630), himself a distinguished Greek scholar who had published many editions of the classics and the Fathers. The Greek text of the Moral Homilies which Ducaeus used for his edition was the 1532 Erasmian edition emended according to the corrections supplied by Richard Montague (1577–1641).[48] Montague had begun research for a critical edition of Basil's works in 1610, but soon learned of the edition being prepared by Ducaeus. He then sent the text-critical materials he had gathered to Ducaeus, who incorporated them into his edition. Ducaeus' Latin translations of these homilies were adaptations of those of Maffei, Erasmus, Cornarius, Musculus, and Tilmann. The abiding significance of Ducaeus' edition lies in the extensive notes on Basil's writings provided by both himself and Morel, which were published in an appendix.[49] These notes were reprinted by subsequent editors of Basil's works, and I consulted them with benefit when preparing my translations.[50]

[47] *Sancti Patris Nostri Basilii Magni Caesareae Cappadociae Archiepiscopi: Opera omnia quae reperiri potuerunt*, 2 vols. (Paris: Morel, 1618). On this edition, see Amand, "Essai d'une histoire critique," 53 (1941), 119–151; Rudberg, "Manuscripts and Editions," 57; and BBV i.259–270. On Ducaeus, see Amand, "Essai d'une histoire critique," 53 (1941), 143–6; and BBV i.259 n. 144.

[48] On Montague, see Amand, "Essai d'une histoire critique," 53 (1941), 141–3; and BBV i.265 n. 186.

[49] *Appendix ad Sancti Basilii Magni opera Graeco-Latina* (Paris: Morel, 1618).

[50] On these notes, see Irena Backus, "L'édition de 1618 des oeuvres de Basile de Césarée et sa fortune," in E. Bury and B. Meunier, eds., *Les pères de l'église au XVIIe siècle. Actes du colloque de Lyon 2–5 octobre 1991* (Paris: Cerf, 1993), 153–73.

The edition of Ducaeus represents the crowing achievement of the first stage of textual scholarship on Basil's Moral Homilies, which began with the Latin translations of Maffei, received great impetus with the *editio princeps* of Erasmus, and witnessed the gradual improvement of Maffei's translations over the course of a century, and culminated with the improved edition of Ducaeus. Yet as a greater number of Basilian manuscripts became available to European scholars, it became apparent that the Erasmian edition had served its purpose; a new edition independent of Erasmus' was needed, to be the basis for new Latin versions independent of the series of translations based on Maffei.

The first to undertake this task was the Dominican patrologist François Combefis (1605–1679). Initially a professor of theology, starting in 1640 he became involved in the editing of patristic texts. His first publications included editions of Amphilochius of Iconium, Methodius of Patara, and Andrew of Crete. He published a new Latin translation of most of Basil's homilies on diverse topics in 1674, along with notes—the first totally independent of Maffei's 1515 renditions.[51] Unfortunately, I have not been able to consult this translation. Combefis was preparing for a new edition of Basil's works to supersede those of Erasmus and Ducaeus when he died in 1679. Two volumes of his textual notes on Basil's works were posthumously published.[52] These textual notes were well utilized by subsequent editors. I too found them useful in crafting my translation, as Combefis sometimes provides translations and interpretations of difficult passages.

In 1618, the Benedictine Congregation of St Maur was founded to reform monastic life in France. The Congregation fostered scholarship, and soon these Benedictine monks—commonly known as the Maurists—produced a number of outstanding scholars who engaged in historical and text-critical work on patristic and medieval texts; the most renowned among them were Luc d'Achery (1609–1685),

[51]See BBV ii.895–896.

[52]*Basilius Magnus ex integro recensitus*, 2 vols. (Rome: Robert J.B. de la Caille, 1679). On these notes, see Amand, "Essai d'une histoire critique," 54 (1942), 128–136; Rudberg, "Manuscripts and Editions," 57–8; and BBV i.270–272.

Jean Mabillon (1632–1707), Edmund Martène (1654–1739), and Bernard de Montfaucon (1655–1741). In 1701 the Maurist Julien Garnier (1670–1725) was entrusted with the preparation of a critical edition of Basil's works. In this he was assisted by François Faverolles (1652–1724), who provided Garnier with collations of the Basilian manuscripts in Paris. The first two of the three volumes of the Maurist edition of Basil's works were published in 1721 and 1722. Garnier was responsible for the introductions, critical editions, notes, and fresh translations into Latin. Garnier died in 1725, and Prudentius Maran (1683–1762) brought the edition to completion. The third volume, containing Garnier's edition of Basil's letters (arranged by Maran), a *Life* of Basil by Maran, and Maran's *addenda et emendanda*, was published in 1730.[53]

The Maurist edition of Basil's works outshone all previous editions. It was reprinted numerous times, but only two of these deserve mention. Gabriel Rudolf Ludwig De Sinner (1801–1860) reprinted it in 1839 with minor alterations and additions.[54] Fedwick characterizes De Sinner's edition as "one of the better ones" due to "the much nicer layout and the almost complete absence of misprints."[55] Of the De Sinner reprint, Stig Rudberg said: "Technically this 1839 edition is of first-rate quality."[56] The Maurist edition was again reprinted with minor alterations and additions by Jacques-Paul Migne (1800–1875)

[53]*Sancti Patris nostri Basilii, Caesareae Cappadociae archiepiscopi, opera omnia quae exstant, vel quae sub eius nomine circumferuntur, ad manuscriptos Codices Gallicanos, Vaticanos, Florentinos et Anglicos, necnon ad antiquiores editiones castigata, multis aucta: Nova Interpretatione, criticis Praefationibus, Notis, variis Lectionibus illustrata, nova sancti Doctoris Vita et copioissimis Indicibus locupletata. Tomus Primus et Secundus: Opera et studio Domni Iuliani Garnier, Presbyteri et Monachi Benedictini, e Congregatione Sancti Mauri. Tomus Tertius: Opera et studio Monachorum Ordinis Sancti Benedicti, et Congregatione Sancti Mauri* (Paris: Coigard, 1721–1730). See Amand, "Essai d'une histoire critique," 54 (1942), 136–144; 56 (1944/1945), 126–149; BBV i.272–289.

[54]*Sancti Patris nostri Basilii, Caesareae Cappadociae archiepiscopi, opera omnia quae exstant, vel quae sub eius nomine circumferuntur . . . ,* Editio Parisina altera, emendata et aucta (Paris: Gaume Fratres, 1839). See BBV i.291–294.

[55]BBV i.291 n. 212.

[56]Rudberg, "Manuscripts and Editions," 58.

as part of his monumental *Patrologia Graeca* (PG), first in 1857 and again in 1886. Migne's PG is virtually ubiquitous in theological libraries, and it is the version of the Maurist edition most readily accessible. Unfortunately, the Migne edition is marred by a number of misprints, especially in the 1886 edition.[57] When I began translating Basil's Moral Homilies, I used Migne. But I soon became frustrated with its misprints and turned to De Sinner's edition. Therefore, the Maurist edition as reprinted by De Sinner is the basis for the translations contained in this volume.

The Maurist edition of Basil's works remained viable for scholarly use well into the early twentieth century. Indeed, writing in 1979 Stig Y. Rudberg called it a "complete success . . . that still today, 250 years later, remains unsurpassed."[58] Nonetheless, the late-nineteenth and early-twentieth centuries were a time of renewed interest in producing editions of the Fathers in the light of new discoveries, improved text-critical methodologies, and a better understanding of the history of the patristic era. In this period scholars began to gather and collate Basilian manuscripts in preparation for new editions of Basil's works to succeed the Maurist edition. There was no plan for a major edition of Basil's *opera omnia*—all of his works—like that of Ducaeus or Garnier. Instead, scholars focused on re-editing Basil's works on an individual basis.

The two scholars most closely associated with producing a new edition of Basil's Moral Homilies in the twentieth century are Stig Y. Rudberg (1920–2011) and Édouard Rouillard (1920–1992).[59] In 1953 the Swedish scholar Rudberg published a study of the manuscript tradition of Basil's Moral Homilies[60] and then tested his findings by producing a new edition of *Att.*[61] Édouard Rouillard, a monk of

[57] Rudberg, "Manuscripts and Editions," 58; and BBV i.274.

[58] Rudberg, "Manuscripts and Editions," 58.

[59] Yves Courtonne published new editions of *Dest* and *Div* in 1935, but based only on three manuscripts. See BBV ii.970; Rudberg, "Manuscripts and Editions," 60.

[60] *Études sur la tradition manuscrite de saint Basile* (Lund: Hakan Ohlssons Boktryckeri, 1953).

[61] *L'homélie de Basile de Césarée sur le mot 'Observe-toi-même.' Édition critique du*

the Abbaye de Wisques in France, began working on a new critical
edition of the Moral Homilies for the Sources Chrétiennes series
in 1947, publishing a series of articles on the manuscripts from
1958 onward.[62] In the late 1970s, Rouillard took on a collaborator,
Marie-Louise Guillaumin, but the edition never appeared. Rouillard died in 1992, and Guillaumin abandoned the endeavor. Sources
Chrétiennes, however, has recently revived a scaled-down version
of the project under the direction of Jean-Noël Guinot.[63] This will
be a new edition of the homilies on the Psalms based on a selection
of twenty-six manuscripts not used in the Maurist edition.[64] Guinot
reports, however, that, at least for the homilies on the Psalms, the
Maurist edition is basically sound and the new Sources Chrétiennes
edition will not differ from it in any substantial way.

   In the Anglophone world, Basil's Moral Homilies have been
one of the most untranslated portions of his corpus—that is, until
recently.[65] The first to be translated into English was *Iei1*, which was
published in 1569.[66] But there were no further English translations

texte grec et étude sur la tradition manuscrite (Uppsala: Almquist & Wiksell, 1962). See
BBV ii.1–10 and 977; Rudberg, "Manuscripts and Editions," 53–4.

   [62]"Recherches sur la tradition manuscrite des *Homélies diverses* de Saint Basile,"
Revue Mabillon 48 (1958): 81–98 and 57 (1967): 1–16 and 45–55; "La tradition manuscrite des *Homélies diverses* de Saint Basile," *Studia Patristica* 3 (1961): 116–121; "Peut-on
retrouver le texts authentique de la prédication de Saint Basile?" *Studia Patristica* 7
(1966): 90–101; "Basile de Césarée a-t-il corrigé lui-même un premier état de texte de
ses homélies?" *Studia Patristica* 22 (1989): 65–68; "L'édition des *Homélies morales* de
Basile de Césarée," *Studia Patristica* 22 (1989): 75–78; with Marie-Louise Guillaumin,
"Recherches à la Bibliothèque Nationale de Paris sur quelques manuscrits grec du Xe
siècle: leur intérêt pour l'édition des *Homélies morales* de Basile de Césarée," *Revue
d'histoire des textes* xiv–xv (1984–1985): 23–53.

   [63]Bernard Meunier (Directeur de l'Institut des Sources Chrétiennes et de la collection) to Mark DelCogliano, private e-mail, January 29, 2010.

   [64]Jean-Noël Guinot to Mark DelCogliano, private e-mail, September 11, 2010.

   [65]The information contained in this paragraph is summarized in tabular form
in Appendix 2.

   [66]Reginald Pole, *A Treatise of Iustification. Founde among the writings of Cardinal
Pole of blessed memory, remaining in the custodie of M. Henire Pyning, Chamberlaine
and General Receiuer to the said Cardinal, late deceased in Louaine. Item certaine
translations touching the said matter of Iustification, the Title whereof. see in the page
following. Namely, A Treatise of St Augustine, which he entitled: Of Faith and Workes.*

of any other Moral Homilies until the first half of the nineteenth century. In 1834 Hugh Stuart Boyd published English translations of *Fide*, *Gord*, and *Mart*,[67] and in 1843 Francis Patrick Kenrick published a translation of *Bapt*.[68] In the next one-hundred years, no further translations of the Moral Homilies were published until the Fathers of the Church series was launched in 1949. In 1950 a volume of Basil's "ascetical works" translated by Sister M. Monica Wagner was published in the series, in which was included *Att*, *Ira*, *Inv*, *Hum*, and *Mund*.[69] In 1963 Agnes Clare Way published a translation of Basil's "exegetic homilies" in the same series, in which she included the thirteen homilies on the Psalms considered genuine by Julien Garnier (thus omitting two now also considered genuine, *Ps14a* and *Ps115*).[70] Translations of *Dest*, *Fide*, *Hum*, *Inv*, and *Ira* were published in the late 1950s by M.F. Toal in his four volumes of patristic homilies on the gospels.[71] Thomas Halton published a translation of *Bapt* in a collection of patristic texts on baptism in 1967.[72]

Since the year 2000, great progress has been made in translating Basil's Moral Homilies into English: *Fam* by Susan R. Holman

Item, a Sermon of Chrysostome, of Praying unto God. Item, a Sermon of St. Basil, of Fasting. Item, certaine Sermons of St Leo the Great, of the same matter. Last of al, a notable Sermon of St Cyprian, of Almes dedes. Al newly translated into English, 2 vols. (Louanii apud Ioannem Foulerum. anno 1569. cum priuilegio); facsimile repr. Farnborough, Hants.: Gregg Press, 1967), vol. 2, 48–57; see BBV ii.867. Fedwick notes that the translation was probably done by Sir Thomas Copley, not Cardinal Pole.

[67]Hugh Stuart Boyd, *The Fathers not Papists; or Six Discourses by the Most Eloquent Fathers of the Church. With Numerous Extracts from Their Writings. Translated from the Greek. A New Edition Considerably Enlarged* (London: Samuel Bagster, 1834), 86–99, 44–69, and 21–43.

[68]Francis Patrick Kenrick, *A Treatise on Baptism; with an exhortation to receive it, translated from the works of St. Basil the Great. To which is added a treatise on confirmation* (Philadelphia: M. Fithian, 1843), 225–241.

[69]*Saint Basil: Ascetical Works*, FOTC 9 (New York: Fathers of the Church, Inc., 1950).

[70]*Saint Basil: Exegetic Homilies*, FOTC 46 (Washington, DC: The Catholic University of America Press, 1963); see BBV ii.977.

[71]M.F. Toal, *The Sunday Sermons of the Great Fathers*, 4 vols. (Chicago: Henry Regnery; London: Longmans, Green, 1957–1963).

[72]André Hamman, ed., *Baptism: Ancient Liturgies and Patristic Texts*, translated by Thomas Halton (Staten Island: Alba House, 1967), 75–87.

in 2001;[73] *Gord* and *Mart* by Pauline Allen in 2003;[74] *Att, Malo,* and
Ira by Nonna Verna Harrison in 2005;[75] *Iei1* and *Iei2* by Kent D.
Berghuis in 2007; [76] *Div* and *Malo* by Anna M. Silvas in 2009;[77] and
Dest, Div, and *Fam* by C. Paul Schroeder in 2009.[78] Translations of
Grat, Jul, Ebr, Mam, and *Chr* (which have never appeared in English
before) and fresh translations of *Iei1, Iei2,* and *Bapt* by Susan R. Hol-
man and me will appear in a forthcoming volume of the Popular
Patristics Series. The present volume contains translations of seven
Moral Homilies never translated into English before: *Prov, Verb, Sab,
Lak, Trin, Ps14a,* and *Ps115,* as well as fresh translations of *Inv, Fide,
Hum,* and *Mund.* When the volume by Holman and me appears, all
the Moral Homilies of Basil now considered genuine will finally be
available in English.

A Note to the Reader

The arrangement of the homilies in this volume does not seek to
replicate the primitive form in which the Moral Homilies circulated.
No single rationale is employed. The organization is partly topical,
partly chronological, and partly aesthetic. Homilies on Christian
practice (*Prov, Ps14a, Hum, Inv, Mund,* and *Lak*) precede homilies
on Christian doctrine (*Fide, Verb, Trin,* and *Sab*). *Ps115* is placed

[73] *The Hungry Are Dying: Beggars and Bishops in Roman Cappadocia* (Oxford:
Oxford University Press, 2001), 183–192.

[74] Johan Leemans, Wendy Mayer, Pauline Allen and Boudewijn Dehandschutter,
*Let Us Die That We May Live: Greek Homilies on Christian Martyrs from Asia Minor,
Palestine and Syria (c. AD 350-AD 450)* (London and New York: Routledge, 2003),
56–77.

[75] *St Basil the Great: On the Human Condition,* PPS 30 (Crestwood, NY: St
Vladimir's Seminary Press, 2005).

[76] *Christian Fasting: A Theological Approach* (s.l.: Biblical Studies Press, 2007),
184–201.

[77] "The Emergence of Basil's Social Doctrine," in Geoffrey D. Dunn, David Luckensmeyer, and Lawrence Cross, *Prayer and Spirituality in the Early Church. Volume 5.
Poverty and Riches* (Strathfield, Australia: St Pauls Publications, 2009), 133–176.

[78] *St Basil the Great: On Social Justice,* PPS 38 (Crestwood, NY: St Vladimir's
Seminary Press, 2009).

between these two sets as a transitional homily since it deals with both subjects. The volume opens with *Prov* not only because this is Basil's earliest extant homily (dated to late 362 or early 363), but also because it is a rhetorical tour-de-force and a superb introduction to Basil's preaching. This is followed by three homilies which can only be dated to the entire span of Basil's ecclesiastical career (362–378): *Ps14a, Hum,* and *Inv.* These are followed by *Mund* and *Lak,* which may have been preached in the early 370s. Firm dates cannot be fixed for the next three homilies, though *Fide* and *Verb* most likely should be assigned to the early 370s. These are followed by two homilies from the mid to late 370s, *Trin* and *Sab.* The volume concludes with *Sab* because it is a rhetorical and theological masterpiece and thus a fitting bookend to complement *Prov.*

The translation of each homily is preceded by an Introduction that aims to be informative and helpful for both the general reader and academic specialists. Each Introduction begins with a discussion of the homily's main theme or other points of interest. This segues into a section-by-section summary of the homily. Some summaries are short, others more detailed. But in all cases the summary is intended to help the reader understand the homily's structure and Basil's flow of thought, as well as to clarify the meaning of passages and sections that may be difficult to grasp. Noteworthy features of the homily are also pointed out. Following the summary sometimes there is a discussion of a more technical point about the vocabulary of the homily, about Basil's sources, or about something similar. What follows next are three labeled sections: (1) *Authenticity*, (2) *Date and Context*, and (3) *Translation*. These sections are meant particularly for academic specialists since they discuss points of technical interest and weigh in on academic debates over individual homilies. The general reader can skip these sections without detriment, though of course he or she can read them with benefit. In the last of these specialized sections (*Translation*) I state the edition on which the translation of the homily is based and list the previous translations I consulted when crafting mine. I have structured the Introductions in this way in an attempt to be useful for a diverse audience, consisting of scholars, students who are assigned this material, and non-academics who want to read Basil for their own spiritual edification.

This concern to benefit a diverse audience carries over into my philosophy of translation. I aim to satisfy two distinct audiences at opposite ends of the reading spectrum. The first is the general reader without knowledge of Greek who reads these translations without recourse to the original. The second is the academic reader who knows Greek and reads these translations constantly comparing them to the original. For the first reader, I strived to produce English prose that is not only understandable and idiomatic, but also conveys a sense of the power of Basil's rhetorical skill. As an accomplished public speaker, Basil knew when to use less formal language to good effect, and in the translation I have tried to reproduce his use of informal diction where it seemed appropriate. In addition, I have included explanatory footnotes to help when Basil is less clear than one would like. For the second reader, I tried not to stray into paraphrase so that the words of the translations could be matched with the Greek on which they are based. Even though the second reader may not always agree with my choices, I believe that he or she will understand them. I hope that the combination of these principles satisfies readers at both ends of the spectrum as well as the majority who fall somewhere between these two extremes.

A few words on the style and format of the translations are necessary. The division of the homilies into numbered sections is found in Julien Garnier's edition. Since these numbered sections are often quite long, however, they are divided into unnumbered paragraphs whose scope is determined by modern English practice. *Italics* are used in the translations for scriptural citations or reminiscences; these are always followed by the scriptural reference in square brackets, for example [Jn 1.1]. References to scriptural allusions are given in the footnotes. Note that the Psalms are referenced according to the Septuagint version. On rare occasions words are inserted in square brackets to improve the sense.

Homily on the Beginning of Proverbs (Prov 1.1–5)

[1] *The proverbs of Solomon, son of David,*
  who was king in Israel:
[2] *To know wisdom and discipline,*
  and to understand words of prudence,
[3] *and to grasp the twists and turns of arguments,*
  and to understand true justice and to direct judgment,
[4] *that he might give shrewdness to the innocent,*
  and both perception and insight to the young child,
[5] *for by hearing these things the wise man will become wiser,*
  and the man of discernment will acquire the ability to steer.

Introduction

Basil's homily on Proverbs 1.1–5 is most likely the earliest homily of his that we possess. In the opening lines Basil relates that his bishop, in whose presence he is speaking, has chosen these difficult lines from Proverbs as the subject-matter for the homily, as a kind of oratorical test for his new cleric. Since Basil was ordained as a presbyter by Eusebius of Caesarea around late 362 or early 363, this homily can probably be assigned to this early period of Basil's ecclesiastical ministry.[1] Basil had of course established a reputation for rhetorical

---

[1] Jean Bernardi, *La prédication des pères cappadociens* (Paris: Presses universitaires de France, 1968), 56; Elena Cavalcanti, "Dall'etica classica all'etica cristiana: il commento al prologo del libro dei Proverbi, di Basilio di Cesarea," *Studi e materiali di storia delle religioni* 56 (1990): 353–378 at 353–8 (her dating is also corroborated through a comparison of *Prov* with some of Basil's early works); Mario Girardi, "Basilio di

prowess long before he entered the ranks of the Caesarean clergy. One gets the sense that in setting Basil upon this task Eusebius wanted to showcase the talents his new presbyter, and perhaps to see if he could live up to the hype.

Basil met the challenge with gusto. He subjected the first five verses of Proverbs to such an exhaustive analysis that it resulted in his longest extant sermon. The meaning of each verse is examined in detail, and the significance of nearly each word in each verse is explored. At the same time, he does not treat each verse in isolation from its context, but discerns a logic in their sequence. One of the most remarkable features of this homily is Basil's ability to a draw a coherent teaching from the apparently unconnected sayings collected in Proverbs.[2] Here Basil musters the full resources of his superb education and oratorical skill for his exegesis. Rhetorical figures abound; he employs vivid metaphors and memorable comparisons not only to convey his point but also to delight his audience. He puts his wide-ranging knowledge on display, not always lightly. His familiarity with the Scriptures is exhibited by his frequent cross-references and citations. Called upon to impress, Basil strove to produce a homily that would take his audience's breath away. In this homily we see the young Basil, the newly-ordained presbyter filled with novice-zeal, showing off his considerable talents as he seeks to put them in the service of the Caesarean church, trying to establish a place for himself within it as he integrates his past into the present.[3]

Cesarea esegeta dei *Proverbi*," *Vetera Christianorum* 28 (1991): 25–60 at 25. This study of Girardi appears in a slightly altered form in his *Basilio di Cesarea interprete della Scrittura. Lessico, principi ermeneutici, prassi* (Bari: Epipuglia, 1998), 41–68.

   [2]Bernardi, *La prédication*, 56.

   [3]Bernardi, *La prédication*, 57, claims to have detected in this homily a certain lack of enthusiasm on Basil's part because he was compelled to discourse on the beginning stages of the Christian life when he was used to advising monks about spiritual and ascetical perfection. In this reconstruction, Eusebius would have chosen Proverbs 1.1–5 to reorient his new presbyter away from his elitist ascetical pursuits toward the humble tasks of sacerdotal ministry. But Girardi, "Basilio di Cesarea esegeta dei *Proverbi*," 58 (=*Basilio di Cesarea interprete della Scrittura*, 66), finds no trace of this reluctance in the homily, but on the contrary maintains that "his youthful enthusiasm

Ostensibly the homily interprets Proverbs 1.1–5 for beginners in the Christian life, perhaps for the newly baptized (see §13).[4] At one level it is an exhortation to read the Book of Proverbs, so that one can acquire the virtues it promises to those who follow its teaching. Basil provides a solid and detailed understanding of those virtues promised in verses 1.1–5: wisdom, discipline, prudence, grasping the twists and turns of arguments, justice, judgment, innocence, shrewdness, perception, insight, and the ability to steer (i.e., navigate through life's reversals of fortune). All these are essential for the Christian life. At another level, however, the homily is about the nature of virtue itself and the human capacity to learn and practice it. For Basil, virtue is more a matter of acquiring particular knowledge and the rational application of this knowledge by the mind than strenuous efforts by the will. Basil believes that every person has the capacity to be educated in virtue, to acquire the knowledge of what each virtue is and how to practice it. Thus the Book of Proverbs is a privileged resource for Christians to gain knowledge about the practice of virtue. Or to use Basil's language, Proverbs provides many "benefits" and "goods" for the moral life.

The ethical teaching that Basil draws from Proverbs 1.1–5 betrays some Stoic influence. For example, his definitions of some virtues— wisdom (§3), prudence (§6), and justice (§8)—repeat Stoic formulations. Some of his ideas are Stoic, e.g., his use of "proper function" (§4) and "impulse" (§14), and his appeal to natural "notions" (§9). But Basil is not beholden to Stoic ethics, as he adapts his sources for a specifically Christian presentation of the moral life rooted in the teaching of the Scriptures. Indeed, Mario Girardi has noted the pervasive influence of Origen on Basil in this homily.[5] Throughout

in applying himself to the utmost before the bishop and the faithful led him to accumulate verses, definitions, and examples in the desire to attain an exhaustive comprehensiveness through an undeniable effort of synthesizing the material and explaining it clearly." I agree with Girardi's judgment.

[4]Bernardi, *La prédication*, 57; Girardi, "Basilio di Cesarea esegeta dei *Proverbi*," 26 (=*Basilio di Cesarea interprete della Scrittura*, 41–2).

[5]Girardi, "Basilio di Cesarea esegeta dei *Proverbi*," 25–60 (=*Basilio di Cesarea*

the homily Basil implies that the Book of Proverbs corrects, deepens, complements, and perfects any ethical instruction based solely on human or philosophical sources. Elena Cavalcanti has argued that in this homily Basil is endorsing a Christian version of the Stoic position taken against Epicureans and Skeptics, that there is a supreme law dictated by reason that guides personal and social ethics and is the foundation of an objective and universal ethics.[6]

Basil begins his exposition by noting that he is delivering this homily in obedience to his bishop, whom he compares to an expert hunter testing one of his puppies (§1).[7] The use of this metaphor should not be taken as a sign of unwillingness on the part of Basil, but rather it seems that Basil, the new presbyter, employed it to emphasize his humility and obedience before his bishop.[8] Basil reminds his audience of the well-known difficulty of understanding the literal meaning of the Book of Proverbs, but nonetheless, he says, he will make an attempt to understand it, trusting in the prayers of his bishop. In this comment Basil signals the exegetical method he will employ: a literal and moral interpretation.[9] There is no allegorical exegesis here.

Next Basil brings up the connection of Proverbs with Ecclesiastes and the Song of Songs, which are the three biblical books of so-called "Solomonic corpus," i.e., the three books traditionally ascribed to Solomon (§1). While all three were written for our benefit, asserts Basil, each has a specific purpose (σκοπός). Proverbs provides ethical instruction, whereas Ecclesiastes teaches the transistoriness of natural goods and the Song of Songs discourses on intimacy of the bride and bridegroom, that is, on the soul's affinity with the Word.

interprete della Scrittura, 41–68). Girardi notes a number of precedents in Hippolytus and Didymus too.

[6]Cavalcanti, "Dall'etica classica all'etica cristiana," 359.

[7]Girardi, "Basilio di Cesarea esegeta dei *Proverbi*," 25–60 (=*Basilio di Cesarea interprete della Scrittura*, 41–68), provides an excellent summary of the homily.

[8]Girardi, "Basilio di Cesarea esegeta dei *Proverbi*," 27–28 (=*Basilio di Cesarea interprete della Scrittura*, 42–43).

[9]Girardi, "Basilio di Cesarea esegeta dei *Proverbi*," 28–29 (=*Basilio di Cesarea interprete della Scrittura*, 43).

Here Basil follows a typical Greco-Roman reading practice. Laying out the main theme or purpose (σκοπός) of a work was considered the necessary prelude to interpreting it. The meaning of difficult passages could be more easily determined by interpreting them in the light of the book's overall theme. For a book of notorious difficulty like Proverbs,[10] articulating its main theme was essential before any attempt to interpret its individual verses. At the same time Basil indicates the subject of his homily, ethical instruction.

His interpretation of Proverbs 1.1 is paradigmatic for his methodology (§2). He begins with a definition of the word "proverb." He notes its secular usage, but is more interested in its Christian meaning. It is a useful saying containing great insight but expressed obscurely. Throughout this homily Basil provides precise definitions for many of the scriptural terms encountered in the verses he is interpreting. He often notes the multiple senses of the term, both secular and Christian, to be as clear as possible about how the term is being used in the verse. Only after the meaning of the terms has been established can the verse itself can be properly understood; only then can the obscure proverb be made plain. Basil adds that the author of Proverbs is mentioned—Solomon, son of David—not merely to distinguish him from others of the same name, but also to indicate the authority of the book and to attract readers.

The next major section of the homily is devoted to an interpretation of Proverbs 1.2, *to know wisdom and discipline, and to understand words of prudence* (§3–6). Basil enumerates the forms of wisdom. First of all there is theology, which is acquired when the sapiential structure of creation is contemplated, and passing from visible to invisible realities one comes to know the Creator (§3). And this

[10]In *Against Eunomius* 2.20, written only a few years after this homily, Basil writes: "In this book [i.e., Proverbs] a great deal of the meaning is hidden and on the whole it proceeds by means of proverbs, parables, dark sayings, and enigmas [cf. Prov 1.6], such that no one may take anything from it that is either indisputable or crystal-clear" (trans. Mark DelCogliano and Andrew Radde-Gallwitz, *St. Basil of Caesarea: Against Eunomius*, FOTC 122 [Washington, DC: Catholic University of America Press, 2011], 160).

divine wisdom is personified in the Scriptures as that by which God made the world and that which is manifested in creation. But there is also a human wisdom which is expertise in specific practical and ethical spheres of human life (§4). Proverbs is more concerned with this kind of wisdom, exhorting Christians to it, praising the benefits it bestows upon all, and teaching the ways to acquire it. But in order to receive wisdom, notes Basil, one must first be purified through the fear of God (§4–5). The powers of reasoning can only operate when the mind is cleansed from wickedness. Offering wisdom to someone whose mind has not been purified through fear of God is, according to Basil, like pouring a costly perfume into a dirty vessel. And so, the reception of wisdom requires mental preparation.

Basil then turns to discipline, which is first described as the kind of training that benefits the soul and removes its stains of wickedness through suffering (§5). It is by means of this divine disciplining that God taught the people of Israel to be attentive to his commandments: their sins provoked the wrath of God and they were released from their sins only by accepting and submitting to the divine punishments inflicted upon them. Here Basil employs a memorable, though perhaps somewhat disturbing, metaphor: just as students learn their lessons more eagerly when they are beaten by their teachers, so too do Christians learn the divine precepts more readily when they are disciplined by God. Great exertions and pains are required and must be endured as God brings us from vice and sin to virtue and holiness through discipline. Hence another good that Proverbs teaches is discipline, which is to be valued more than riches. Once it is acquired, the Christian can endure any unfavorable circumstance, accepting the divine blows with patience as he is purified of sins.

But there is another meaning of discipline, namely, the acquisition of learning in a particular branch of knowledge (§6). Since there are many disciplines, some unprofitable and harmful, others beneficial and useful, one must take care to pursue the latter and avoid the former. The discipline that is most useful is the one which contributes to salvation, that is to say contemplating the Scriptures to gain knowledge of God. This discipline is to be preferred to all others. This capacity to choose the beneficial discipline and avoid the harmful discipline provides a transition to the next "good" taught by Proverbs, prudence.

After defining prudence as the virtue which enables one to know what is good, bad, and neutral (a typical Platonist-Stoic definition), Basil notes that there are disconcerting scriptural exemplifications of prudence, namely, the serpent (Gen 3.1; Mt 10.16) and the dishonest steward (Lk 16.8). This leads him to distinguish two senses of prudence: (1) self-interested scheming, and (2) discernment regarding what should and should not be done (another Platonist-Stoic definition). The serpent and the dishonest steward exemplify the former, whereas the latter is the "true prudence" which enables the Christian to be constant in virtue and avoid sin and vice, to be steadfast in the face of temptation, and to prepare properly for eternal life. Here Basil offers the approved moneychanger, the man who built his house on the rock (Mt 7.24–25), and the wise virgins (Mt 25.10–13) as counter-examples to the two exemplifications of the perverse kind of prudence mentioned above.

Basil next takes up the first section of Proverbs 1.3, *to grasp the twists and turns of arguments* (§7). Here he criticizes rhetoric, the subject to which he had committed himself in his youth, or rather, the devious use of rhetoric. Perhaps he is railing against current practices in the law-courts.[11] He deplores complex arguments of great stylistic ornateness which seek to persuade that the facts of the matter are other than they really are, as well as to delight the audience. Such discourse is, according to Basil, nothing but the twists and turns of arguments (στροφαὶ λόγων), that is, "distortion of the truth through argument" (§7). Instead he prefers simple and straightforward arguments aimed at clarifying the truth. But as Basil's critiques in this section continue, they seem to be aimed more

[11]Girardi, "Basilio di Cesarea esegeta dei *Proverbi*," 42–44 (=*Basilio di Cesarea interprete della Scrittura*, 55–56).

at the advocates of heretical doctrines, who reject the simplicity of
the Spirit's teaching through "the plausible arguments of sophisms"
(τῇ πιθανολογίᾳ τῶν σοφισμάτων), who make what is true appear
false. Basil assures his audience that those who have been trained
by Proverbs will not be confounded by the logical conundrums, the
scheming arguments, and the specious sophisms of the heretics,
even when they seem very plausible. Perhaps here Basil is alluding
to Eunomius, whose teaching he surely was already aware of when
he delivered this homily.[12] In his *Against Eunomius*, Basil accuses
Eunomius of rejecting the simplicity of the faith,[13] of teaching
falsehoods,[14] of using plausible arguments (ἐν πιθανολογίᾳ),[15] and
of employing the twists and turns of arguments to delight his audience.[16] It is likely that we see in this homily the earliest version of
the anti-Eunomian rhetoric he developed more fully in the treatise
directed against his principal theological opponent.[17] So then, Proverbs provides the resources for detecting the fallacious arguments of
heretics and not being tricked into falling for them.

Basil then turns to the subject of the second half of Proverbs
1.3, *to understand true justice* (§8). He defines justice as distribution
according to merit (a typical Platonist-Stoic definition). He emphasizes that it is difficult to achieve, both individually and collectively.
First of all, some people have distorted notions of justice. They may
lack the necessary prudence it requires, or be so prejudiced that they
disregard the poor and keep silent when the rich and powerful act

[12]*Against Eunomius* is dated to 364–365, two or three years after *Prov*; see DelCogliano and Radde-Gallwitz, *St. Basil of Caesarea: Against Eunomius*, 33.

[13]*Eun.* 1.1 and 1.4. See also Mario Girardi, "«Semplicità» e ortodossia nel dibattito
antiariano di Basilio di Cesarea: la raffigurazione dell'eretico," *Vetera Christianorum*
15 (1978): 51–74.

[14]*Eun.* 1.1, 1.2, and 1.4.

[15]*Eun.* 1.1.

[16]*Eun.* 1.5 (SChr 299: 174 Sesboüé): "He takes pride in how his arguments take
twists and turns (τῇ τῶν λόγων στροφῇ), and so puts on a fine show . . . " (trans. Del-
Cogliano and Radde-Gallwitz, *St. Basil of Caesarea: Against Eunomius*, 93).

[17]For a fuller discussion of Basil's anti-Eunomian rhetoric in *Against Eunomius*,
see DelCogliano and Radde-Gallwitz, *St. Basil of Caesarea: Against Eunomius*,
38–46.

unjustly. Others merely pay lip service to justice and equitable treatment. But Proverbs teaches the true meaning of justice, exposing the spuriousness of these false notions of justice as well as sophistical philosophical accounts of justice. Justice is also hard to achieve collectively, as is demonstrated by the skewed and contradictory notions of justice embodied in the various legal codes and customs of nations. In contrast Proverbs teaches true justice and reveals the irrationality of such laws and customs. True justice is nothing less than equal distribution. But there is another kind of justice taught by Proverbs, namely, divine justice, which is corrective and retributive, and very hard to understand. Nonetheless, Proverbs also manifests divine justice.

Furthermore, true justice also recognizes that there is no single rule for applying justice since sin arises from diverse conditions, some involuntary, others deliberate (§9). Basil endorses the idea that a sin ought to be judged with due regard not only to circumstances beyond the control of the one who sinned but also to the diverse social and educational factors that could have played a determining role in the sin, and might lessen or increase moral responsibility and thus culpability. Basil gives concrete examples of how the degree of culpability for the exact same sin depends upon the preceding circumstances. For example, a man raised in wickedness from birth is less responsible for a sin than a man who was provided with every inducement to virtue from his youth but yet chose to commit the same sin. This attentiveness to preceding circumstances is part of the true justice that Proverbs teaches.

The understanding of true justice learned from Proverbs is therefore the prerequisite for rendering judgments (§9). In the famous case about the two prostitutes and the child (1 Kings 3.19–28), Solomon could not render a decision based on the external testimony and so had to rely on his understanding of true justice. Like Solomon, those who render judgments in courts of law should act out of true justice, not out of partiality, bias, or vindictiveness, nor should they take bribes. But applying true justice when rendering judgments is applicable not only to judges, but to all of us. For all of us render important judgments in the hidden court of justice within ourselves, where we must distinguish good from evil, and choose virtue over vice every time (§9–10). Here Basil offers an elaborate metaphor in which our intellect is described as a judge hearing the arguments of a virtue and its opposing vice, each pleading its case. We are exhorted to render an unbiased and impartial judgment, every time choosing the law of God over against sin. If we do so, we will receive those crowns of justice (2 Tim 4.8) promised to the just on the day of the final judgment.

Basil next turns to the interpretation of the first part of Proverbs 1.4, *that he might give shrewdness to the innocent.* Once again, the key terms are defined (§11). There are two kinds of innocence: (1) the state achieved when sin is overcome through reason, and (2) the lack of experience of wickedness which characterizes such people as children or country bumpkins. The former is innocence in the proper sense of the term and results from a choice, whereas the latter does not. David and Jacob are scriptural examples of the true kind of innocence, of removing evil from the soul through the practice of virtue, simplicity, and lack of artifice. As for shrewdness, it is the resourcefulness which complements innocence. For without shrewdness the innocent man is liable to succumb to evil. But while shrewdness is neutral in itself, it also has two senses and thus can be used in a way that merits blame when it is used to harm others, or in a way that merits praise when it is used to pursue good for oneself and others. Scripture is filled with examples of both kinds (§12). For instance, the midwives who spared the lives of the Hebrew boys against the order of Pharaoh (Ex 1.17) exhibited praiseworthy shrewdness, whereas Absalom displayed a shrewdness worthy of condemnation in his plot against his father, King David (2 Sam 15.1–12). Since innocence is prone to deception, it must be joined to shrewdness so that the latter can protect the former. While Eve was innocent, she lacked shrewdness, and so was deceived by the serpent.

Furthermore, Proverbs gives *both perception and insight to the young child* (Prov 1.4). Basil first asks who this young child is, and what sort of perception Proverbs gives to him (§13). Basing himself on the Pauline distinction between an inner and an outer nature, Basil affirms that this verse surely cannot refer to an infant receiving sensory perception from Proverbs. That would be ridiculous. Rather, the verse refers to the interior nature, whose age is a function of spiritual intelligence. Those who are interiorly infants still need the milk of the introductory teachings of the gospels; those who are interiorly in their prime of life practice virtue with fervor and strength; those who are interiorly old and venerable exercise wisdom, even if young in body like Daniel. Therefore, when Proverbs says that perception and insight are given to the young child, it means that the newly baptized who are young in their faith are given perception into the true nature of present realities lest fleeting pleasures be pursued, and insight into what is to come so as to inspire belief in what God has promised. Here Basil makes a connection between the perception taught by Proverbs and the spiritual senses, that is, in what way the faculties of the soul hear, see, taste, and touch (note that the sense of smell is omitted) (§14). Basil concludes this section with a description of the insight given to the young child, which is a fear of those things with which sinners are threatened and a desire for those things prepared for the just.

The next section of the homily is devoted to the first half of Proverbs 1.5, *for by hearing these things the wise man will become wiser* (§14). Basil first enumerates the many senses in which a person can be called "wise" in order to determine how Proverbs makes the wise man wiser. Both those knowledgeable in the wisdom of the world and those who "have received the true wisdom, our Lord Jesus Christ, by believing in him" are called "wise" (§14). If this is the sense of "wise" in Proverbs 1.5, then it means that those wise with worldly wisdom will become wiser if they learn the teaching expounded in Proverbs. But people are also called "wise" if they are either desirous of wisdom, or progressing in wisdom, or perfect in wisdom. In this case, Proverbs 1.5 refers to those in the first two categories: Proverbs will bring such people to the perfection of wisdom, which brings an aversion to evil and a yearning for good.

The homily concludes with a lengthy discussion of the second half of Proverbs 1.5: *And the man of discernment will acquire the ability to steer* (§15–17). Basil conceives of steering (κυβέρνησις) as a craft or skill that needs to be learned. It is defined as "the knowledge of the soul that deals with navigating the instable nature of human circumstances in an appropriate manner" (§15). Just as the wrestler and runner must have the physical endowments of nature to participate successfully in their crafts (i.e., sports), so too the steersman must have certain mental endowments and be a man of discernment, that is, his mind must be sharp and perspicacious. For life is charting one's course through the waters of the sea. Each of us is like the pilot of a ship sailing through waters, now serene, now rough, trying to keep from sinking. Thus no situation in life is permanent; all is fleeting and transitory.

In fact, there are three kinds of steering that Proverbs teaches. The first navigates through the unexpected changes that life inevitably brings, neither growing complacent in good fortune nor despondent over strokes of bad luck. Yet it is not only external circumstances which bring instability, but also the interior passions of the soul. So there is a second kind of steering whereby the mind is like a steersman seated high above the violent storm of the passions in the soul, who uses the rudders of our thoughts to steer the ship of the soul without being submerged by the waves of passion. The metaphor of piloting a ship is extended when Basil compares the Christian to a merchant who is transporting his goods over the sea and speaks about a third kind of steering (§16). Just as a merchant acquires earthly goods through commerce, so too the Christian acquires heavenly goods by following the commandments. Just as the merchant seeks to steer his ship laden with goods through the storms so as to reach safe harbor and receive recompense for his wares, so too the Christian must protect the virtues he has acquired throughout life to receive rewards from God. Just as merchant can lose all his goods in a single shipwreck brought on by a sudden squall, so too the Christian can lose all the goods acquired throughout life in a single sin brought on by an attack of a demon.

Therefore, in all three cases we must hold the rudder of our life steady and steer ourselves through all the storms of misfortune, passion, vice, and sin that could sink us. We must be in control of our senses and beware of disturbing emotions. Just as sailors guide their ships using the light of the constellations high in the sky, so too the Christian must guide his life by the light of the lofty commandments of the Lord. Only in this way will we be transported safe and sound to the peaceful harbor of God.

Authenticity. The authenticity of this homily is certain and has never been doubted. It is one of the eight homilies of Basil translated into Latin by Rufinus of Aquileia in the early 400s.[18] It is also widely attested in the best manuscripts of Basil's homilies.[19] Nothing within the homily itself suggests that Basil is not its author.

Context and Date. As mentioned above, this homily can probably be assigned to the early period of Basil's ecclesiastical ministry, that is, late 362 or early 363, when he was given the opportunity prove and showcase his oratorical talents.[20] Le Nain de Tillemont had spoken of *Prov* as Basil's first homily delivered before the people after he was ordained a presbyter.[21] Prudentius Maran more correctly said that it was Basil's earliest extant sermon, the only one that seems to have be delivered in the presence of his bishop. "The reason for

---

[18]PG 31.1761–1781.

[19]See BBV ii.1118–1120.

[20]Raymond Van Dam, *Families and Friends in Late Roman Cappadocia* (Philadelphia: University of Pennsylvania Press, 2003), 31–2, see this homily, in places, as "quietly subversive of Eusebius' standing and authority" (32). In particular, Van Dam sees *Prov* 15, where Basil expounds upon "steering," as offering unsolicited advice to Eusebius about how to govern the church. But *Prov* 15 has nothing to do with church governance. Hence, Van Dam's speculations about the subversiveness of this homily seem unwarranted.

[21]Louis-Sébastien Le Nain de Tillemont, *Mémoires pour servir à l'histoire ecclésiastique des six premiers siècles* (Venice: Pitteri, 1732), ix.69 and 291.

this," writes Maran, "is not obscure and obtuse. For Basil withdrew [from Caesarea] not long after his ordination; when he returned to Caesarea, he undertook the administration of one church which the bishop was not accustomed to visit."[22] After being ordained in late 362 or early 363, a few months later in late 363 Basil withdrew to his family estates in Annisa because of some disagreement with Eusebius and did not return to Caesarea until shortly before October, 365. He returned to add rhetorical and theological heft to the leadership of the Caesarean church as it prepared for the synodical examination to be conducted by emperor Valens and his agents in October, 365.[23] Therefore, Maran dates *Prov* to the period shortly before October, 365, when Basil was preparing for Valens' visit, not late 362 or early 363, when Basil was first ordained. But this reconstruction seems unlikely because surely when Basil was recalled by Eusebius he soon become occupied with preparing for the imperial visit. There was neither the need nor the time to put Basil to the test. And so, *Prov* is more plausibly dated to late 362 or early 363.

Translation. The following translation is based on Julien Garnier's edition as reprinted in De Sinner ii.136–158 (=PG 31.385–424).[24] In crafting my translation, I benefited from the Latin translations of Rufinus and Garnier, as well as from the excerpts translated into English by Blomfield Jackson[25] and James Marshall Campbell,[26] and into Italian by Mario Girardi and Elena Cavalcanti in their articles.

[22]Prudentius Maran, *Vita S. Basilli* 9.3 (De Sinner iii.lxxxi; PG 29.xxxix) and 43.4 (De Sinner iii.ccxlviii–ccxlix; PG 29.clxxii). The quotation is from the latter.

[23]On these dates, see Philip Rousseau, *Basil of Caesarea* (Berkeley: University of California Press, 1994), 67; Paul Jonathan Fedwick, "A Chronology of the Life and Works of Basil of Caesarea," in idem, ed., *Basil of Caesarea: Christian, Humanist, Ascetic. A Sixteen-Hundredth Anniversary Symposium* (Toronto: The Pontifical Institute of Mediaeval Studies, 1981), 3–19 at 7–11; and John A. McGuckin, *St Gregory of Nazianzus: An Intellectual Biography* (Crestwood, NY: St Vladimir's Seminary Press, 2001), 131–2 and 140–3.

[24]CPG 2856.

[25]"Prolegomena. Sketch of the Life and Works of Saint Basil," NPNF 2.8, lviii–lix.

[26]*The Influence of the Second Sophistic on the Style of the Sermons of St. Basil the Great* (Washington, DC: Catholic University of America Press, 1922).

TRANSLATION

1   A good reward is given for ready obedience.[1] So let us obey our kind father, who proposes contests based on the oracles of the Spirit.[2] He is like an expert hunter who wants to test how one of his puppies runs in places hard to traverse. He has proposed that we give an interpretation of the beginning of Proverbs. Everyone who is even slightly acquainted with this text is well aware how difficult it is to grasp its literal meaning.[3] Nonetheless, we must not recoil from making an attempt, placing our hope in the Lord who, through the prayers of our shepherd, will give speech to us when we open our mouth.[4]

We know all three books of the most wise Solomon: Proverbs, Ecclesiastes, and the Song of Songs. Each was composed for a particular purpose,[5] but all three were written for the benefit of human beings. Proverbs instructs us in ethics and corrects our passions; and in sum, it teaches us how to live, giving wise advice about what we ought to do. Ecclesiastes touches upon the study of nature and reveals to us the vanity of things in this world, so that we do not think of transient realities as objects of great desire, nor let our soul become consumed with concern for vanities. The Song of Songs sketches the way in which souls are perfected. For it deals with the concord of the bride and bridegroom, that is, the soul's intimacy with God the Word.[6] But let us return to the task set before us.

2   *The Proverbs of Solomon, son of David, who was king in Israel* [Prov 1.1]. Those outside[7] use the term *paroimia* (proverb) for

[1]The language here is scriptural; cf. Mt 5.12; Prov 21.28; Eccl 4.9; 4 Macc 8.6; 15.9.
[2]That is, based on the Scriptures.
[3]Gk. δυσθήρατος τῆς λέξεως ταύτης ὁ νοῦς.
[4]See Eph 6.19.
[5]Gk. πρὸς ἴδιον σκοπόν.
[6]Basil has probably derived his understanding of the "Solomonic" corpus from Origen, *Commentary on the Song of Songs* prol. 3. In this section Origen also gives a summary of Prov 1.1–6 which in many ways is a kind of blueprint for Basil's homily.
[7]That is, non-Christians outside the church.

common expressions and particularly for those used in the streets. For one of their words for "street" is *oimos*, and based on this they define a *paroimia* as an expression used in the streets which has become clichéd through overuse and which can be transferred from a few cases to a multitude of similar cases.[8] But as for us, we view a proverb as a beneficial saying expressed with moderate obscurity, containing great usefulness within itself but also concealing great meaning in its deeper sense. Hence the Lord said: *I have spoken these things to you in proverbs; the hour is coming when I will no longer speak in proverbs but plainly* [Jn 16.25]. For a proverbial saying does not have a meaning that is obvious and easily known, but discloses its true intent in an oblique manner to those with the requisite skill. Therefore, *The Proverbs of Solomon*, that is, his exhortatory sayings, are useful for every path of life.

He added the author's name to attract readers by the renown of his person. After all, when a teacher has a trustworthy reputation, it makes his lessons easier to accept and his students more attentive. So then, *the Proverbs of Solomon* are by that Solomon to whom the Lord said: *Behold, I have given you a prudent and wise heart; like you there has not been anyone before you, and after you there shall not arise anyone like you* [1 Kg 3.12]. And again: *And the Lord gave wisdom and very great understanding to Solomon and largeness of heart like the sand by the sea. And the wisdom of Solomon was multiplied, surpassing the understanding of all ancient peoples and surpassing all the sages of Egypt* [1 Kg 5.9–10 LXX = 4.29–30 MT]. Thus it was necessary to add his name.

The Proverbs of Solomon, son of David [Prov 1.1]. He also adds his father so that you may know that Solomon was wise, that he was from a father who was wise and a prophet, that he was educated from boyhood in sacred literature, that neither by lot did he obtain dominion, nor by force did he seize a kingdom which did not belong to him, but rather that he received his father's scepter by

[8]As was the custom in antiquity, Basil explains the meaning of the word "proverb" (*paroimia*) through etymology: *para* ("on") + *oimos* ("road").

the just judgment of his father and the decision of God. This is the man who became king of Jerusalem. These details are not without significance, in particular for distinguishing him from others with the same name, but also with regard to the construction of the celebrated temple, that you may know that he was its builder and that he was responsible for every aspect of the administration of the city, its laws, and its good order.

Now the very fact that a king wrote this book greatly contributes to the acceptance of its exhortations. For if kingship is a legitimate authority, it is clear that the counsels given by a king—at least if he is truly worthy of this designation—have great legal force, since they look out for the common good of all and are not prescribed for the sake of individual benefit. After all, there is a difference between a tyrant and a king: the former looks after his own interests in every way, but the latter seeks to benefit his subjects. And so, what useful teachings does this book offer to its disciples? How many are there? Let us now enumerate them.

3 The first of the Proverbs is *to know wisdom and discipline* [Prov 1.2]. Wisdom is "the systematic knowledge of divine and human things and their causes."[9] So then, the one who successfully engages in theology knows wisdom,[10] as the blessed Paul also said: *We speak wisdom among the perfect; yet not the wisdom of this world, nor of the princes of this world who are doomed to pass away. Rather, we speak God's wisdom in a mystery, a hidden wisdom which God decreed before the ages* [1 Cor 2.6–7]. And the one who considers the Artificer in the structure of the world comes indeed to know God through the wisdom of the world: *From the creation of the world his invisible things have been clearly perceived, understood by the things that have been made* [Rom 1.20]. This brings us to recognize God,

---

[9]This is a widely-quoted Stoic definition of wisdom; see SVF 2.35–36; LS 26G; Origen, *Against Celsus* 3.72.

[10]For Basil, theology is contemplating God in abstraction from his works; cf. *Eun.* 2.3 and 2.15.

as is shown by: *God by wisdom founded the earth* [Prov 3.19], and: *When he prepared the heaven, I was present with him* [Prov 8.27], and: *I was by his side governing; I was the source of his delight* [Prov 8.30]. For all this is said from wisdom, who has been personified for us in order to clearly communicate knowledge of it. And in sum: *The Lord created me the beginning of his ways* [Prov 8.22]. This is said about the wisdom manifest in the world, which all but sends forth a voice through visible things, proclaiming that the world was made by God and that the great wisdom seen in created things is not spontaneous. For just as *the heavens proclaim the glory of God, and the firmament declares the work of his hands* [Ps 18.2] (now this is proclaimed without the use of a voice, for *no speech, no word, no voice is heard* [Ps 18.4]), so too there are also certain words of the primal wisdom, which was established before all else along with the created order at the creation of the world. It is this wisdom that silently announces its Creator and Lord, so that through it you may go back to the notion of wisdom alone.

4   Yet there is also a human wisdom: the expertise needed in the concrete realities of life. This is what enables those skilled in each of the beneficial arts to be called "wise." Therefore, the writer devotes most of the book to exhortations to this sort of wisdom. *Wisdom sings at the gates, and in the squares she speaks boldly, and on the top of the walls she cries out* [Prov 1.20–21]. Seeing how human beings love honor and knowing that all of us by nature would gladly welcome the dignity that wisdom confers, he praises wisdom to rouse souls to strive for it, but not in a manner that is either lazy or perfunctory. He says that wisdom's message can be found almost everywhere: at the gates,[11] in the marketplaces, in the high citadels. He speaks of gates, squares, and walls for a reason: by the gates and squares he indicates the dignity that wisdom confers, and by the walls he points to the benefit that it bestows, and how it is sufficient for all well-being

---

[11]Here I read ἐν ἐξόδοις instead of ἐν ὁδοῖς. The word ἔξοδος is used as a synonym for the πύλη ("gate") of Prov 1.20–21 in the next sentence.

in life. And he wants us to associate with wisdom, saying: *Say that wisdom is your sister* [Prov 7.4]. And again: *Love her, and she will guard you* [Prov 4.6].

Then he points out that wisdom benefits all in common, and that the benefit it bestows is extended to all alike. He says: *She slaughtered her own sacrificial victims* [Prov 9.2]. In other words, she prepared *solid food* for *those who have the faculties* of their soul *trained by practice* [Heb 5.14].[12] *In a mixing bowl she mixed her own wine* [Prov 9.2]—the wine which gladdens the human heart.[13] Now what he calls the "mixing bowl" is the common and universal participation in the goods,[14] whereby everyone is equally permitted to drink of them according to each individual's capacity and need. *And she prepared her own table* [Prov 9.2]. All this he says by implication,[15] signifying spiritual truths to us through corporeal realities. For what he calls the "table" is the rational nourishment of the soul, to which he summons us with *a loud proclamation* [Prov 9.3]—that is, with teachings in which there is nothing lowly or abject. *He who is a fool, let him turn aside to me* [Prov 9.4]. For just as the sick need healing, so too do fools need wisdom. And: *for it is better to trade in her than in treasures of gold and silver* [Prov 3.14]. And: *She is more precious than precious stones, and every precious thing is not worthy of her* [Prov 3.15]. And: *My son, if you become wise for yourself, you will be wise for your neighbors as well* [Prov 9.12]. And: *a wise son will have prosperous business* [Prov 9.13]. And in sum, you will be able to know the true meaning of these statements if you read through what Solomon said about wisdom in your leisure.

But *wisdom will not enter a soul that plots evil* [Wis 1.4]. Therefore, the souls of those who are going to converse with wisdom are first purified through the fear of God. For if one were to throw the mysteries of salvation to anyone who happens to be around, so that they were equally received by all those whose life is impure and

[12]Basil similarly connects Prov 9.2 and Heb 5.14 in *Iei2* 8.
[13]Ps 103.15.
[14]That is, the goods bestowed by wisdom.
[15]Gk. δι' ἐμφάσεως, that is, using figurative language.

whose use of reasoning is still untested and imprecise, it would be as if someone poured a very expensive perfume into a filthy bottle. Therefore, *the beginning of wisdom is fear of the Lord* [Prov 1.7]. Fear is purification of the soul according to the entreaty of the prophet who said: *Pierce*[16] *my flesh with fear of you* [Ps 118.120]. Where fear dwells, there resides every purity of soul, every wickedness and unholy action retreats, and the parts of the body, since they are pierced with fear, are unable to move toward any immoral activity. For just as a person who is pierced with real nails is prevented from doing anything because of the pain, so too the person who is seized with the fear of God is able neither to use an eye for what is inappropriate, nor to move his hands toward forbidden actions, nor to do anything small or great, except for the proper function,[17] since he is transfixed by the expectation of that with which he has been threatened, as if by a kind of pain.[18]   **5**   And he[19] banishes those who are profane and vulgar from the divine teachings, saying: *Those without fear will stay by the gates* [Prov 19.23+12.13a].[20] And: *You may seek wisdom among the wicked, but you will not find it* [Prov 14.6]. And again: *Wicked people will seek me, but they will not find me* [Prov 1.28]. For divine fear has not purified them. Hence anyone who is about to advance to the acquisition of wisdom should move forward purified by a salutary fear from the disgrace that comes from evil. So then, we derive another good from the teaching of Proverbs, the acquisition of fear, which is generated in us through wisdom.

The second of the precepts was: *to know discipline* [Prov 1.2]. Discipline is a kind of training that benefits the soul, which it purifies of the stains of wickedness, though most frequently not without considerable suffering; *for the moment it does not seem pleasant but*

---

[16]Gk. καθήλωσον, literally, "nail down, pierce with a nail."

[17]Gk. καθῆκον. This is a Stoic ethical term which refers to an action which is appropriate given the nature of an individual and the constraints placed upon him or her; see LS 59.

[18]Basil gives a similar interpretation of Ps 118.120 in *Ps33* 6; see also *Ep.* 22.3.

[19]That is, Solomon.

[20]Here Basil conflates and alters these two verses.

rather painful, yet later it yields for salvation *a peaceful fruit to those educated by it* [Heb 12.11]. Therefore, not just any random mind can know this discipline. For many people grow weary of experiencing suffering and out of ignorance do not wait for the benefit it obtains. Rather, they become exasperated by how harsh the experience is and remain mired in the sicknesses of their ignorance. For this reason the voices of the just are worthy of admiration when they say: *Lord, do not rebuke me in your anger; do not discipline me in your rage* [Ps 6.1]. Now it is not discipline that they refuse, but rage. Another is quite similar to this: *Discipline us, Lord, but yet in just measure and not in anger* [Jer 10.24]. And: *The discipline of the Lord opens my ears* [Is 50.5]. For just as young children negligent in their studies become more attentive and understand their lessons only after they have been whipped by their teachers or pedagogues; and just as the same material, which was not listened to before the blows, is accepted by their ears and retained in the memory only after the pains inflicted by the whipping, as if their ears are now opened; so too it is for those who disregard the divine teachings and are contemptuous of the precepts. After God lays discipline upon them, only then do they accept God's commandments, which were always articulated and always disregarded, as if they have reached their ears for the very first time. For this reason he says *the discipline of the Lord opens my ears* [Is 50.5].

So then, discipline admonishes the idle man;[21] for example, Paul did so when he delivered certain men *to Satan*, as if to a kind of executioner who tortures and flogs, *so that they could be disciplined and learn not to blaspheme* [1 Tim 1.20]. And discipline restores the rebellious person; for example, one rebel said that after his captivity he repented.[22] It is necessary to be aware of the power of discipline with respect to its great usefulness. So then, knowing the benefit that comes from discipline, Solomon exhorts: *Do not refrain from disciplining a child, for if you beat him with the rod, he will not die;*

[21]See 1 Thess 5.14.
[22]See Jer 38.19 LXX = 31.19 MT.

for you shall beat him with a rod and deliver his soul from death [Prov 23.13–14]. *For what son is there whom a father does not discipline?* [Heb 12.7]. Those who judge things correctly consider this discipline more precious than great riches. Therefore, Solomon says: *Take discipline, and not silver* [Prov 8.10]. Thus in a time of crisis or bodily sickness or when things are not going well in the home, you will never think a wicked thought about God. Rather, you will be able to accept his blows with great patience, being disciplined for your sins, and now you too, because you know discipline, will be able to say: *The wrath of the Lord I will endure because I sinned against him* [Mic 7.9]. And: *It was good for me that you humbled me* [Ps 118.71]. Paul was in this state of mind when he said: *Disciplined but not killed* [2 Cor 6.9]. And: When we are rebuked *by the Lord, we are disciplined so that we may not be condemned along with the world* [2 Cor 11.32].

6   Discipline is also a name for the acquisition of learning, according to what was written about Moses: *He was disciplined*[23] *in all the wisdom of the Egyptians* [Acts 7.22]. Therefore, it is not applying oneself to just any kind of learning, but rather it is knowledge of that discipline which is the most useful of all that makes a not insignificant contribution to salvation. For at present some people are devoted either to geometry, which the Egyptians discovered, or to astrology, which is esteemed by the Chaldaeans, or are wholly engaged in debates about the shapes and shadows of astronomical phenomena, and thus they overlook the discipline of the divine oracles.[24] Others occupy their time with poetry, rhetoric, and the invention of sophistical arguments; however, the subject matter of all of these pursuits is false. For you cannot have poetry without myths, nor rhetoric without oratory, nor sophistry without fallacies. So then, since many in their eagerness for these pursuits neglect knowledge of God and grow old as they inquire into vanities, the knowledge of discipline is

[23] Gk. ἐπαιδεύθη, literally, "instructed." The translation above is intended to demonstrate the etymological connection this verb has with παιδεία, "discipline."

[24] That is, the Scriptures.

needed both for choosing the beneficial discipline and for avoiding the one that is unprofitable and harmful.

It is also possible for anyone who is attentive to the Proverbs and is not indifferent to receiving benefit from them *to understand words of prudence* [Prov 1.2]. We know that prudence is one of the principal virtues, that by which we become people who have knowledge of things that are good and bad and neutral.[25] Now the adjective "prudent" is clearly derived from "prudence." So then, why is there testimony that the serpent was *the most prudent of all beasts* [Gen 3.1]? And again: *Be prudent as serpents* [Mt 10.16]. And the dishonest steward was prudent.[26] Or is it the case that the term "prudence" has a double meaning? On the one hand, prudence is the protection of one's own interests coupled with scheming against one's neighbor. Such was the prudence of the serpent, who was saving his own head. This sort of prudence appears to be a perversity of character and habits, which swiftly discovers what is profitable for itself and snatches it away from the innocent. Such was the prudence of the dishonest steward. On the other hand, true prudence is discerning what should and should not be done.[27] Whoever is attentive to true prudence will never depart from the works of virtue and will never be pierced with the destructive spear of vice. So whoever "understands words of prudence" knows that some people are sophistical and fallacious, and some people give us the best advice about what we ought to do in life. And like an approved moneychanger, he will retain what is approved, but will abstain from every form of evil.[28] This is the prudence which was given to the man who built his own

[25]This is a widely-quoted Platonist-Stoic definition of prudence; see Plato, *Definitions* 411d; LS 61H1 (=SVF 3.262), SVF 3.266, 3.274; Cicero, *On Invention* 2.53; Augustine, *Eighty-Three Different Questions* 31.1. The four principal or primary virtues are prudence, moderation, courage, and justice; see LS 61H6.

[26]See Lk 16.8.

[27]This is another widely-quoted Platonist-Stoic definition of prudence; see Plato, *Definitions* 411d; LS 61D2 (=SVF 3.280), LS 61H1 (=SVF 3.262), SVF 3.268.

[28]Here Basil alludes to a widely-quoted agraphon (i.e., non-scriptural saying) of Jesus, which was first cited by Clement, *Stromata* 1.28: "Become approved moneychangers, rejecting the [evil] things, and embracing the good." Cf. 1 Thess 5.21–22.

house by setting its foundation upon the rock—that is, by relying upon faith in Christ.[29] Hence it remained unmoved when the rains and the winds and the floods assaulted it.[30] For what the Lord shows us in the words of this parable is steadfastness in the face of temptations, both those of human origin and those brought down on us from above. He teaches us, moreover, not to neglect necessities, but rather to prepare provisions for life[31] beforehand and to await the arrival of the bridegroom in readiness of heart. For he related that because the prudent virgins had oil in their lamps, they went in with the bridegroom, but because the foolish virgins were not ready, they were excluded from the joy of the bridal chamber.[32]

7   Next, let us see what it is *to grasp the twists and turns of arguments* [Prov 1.3]. An argument that is true and proceeds from a sound mind is simple and straightforward, saying the same things about the same arguments on every occasion. But an intricate and scheming argument of great complexity and stylistic ornateness assumes a myriad of forms and takes countless twists and turns, transforming itself for the delight of the audience. So then, our ability to make a strong stand against the attack of scheming arguments is greatly benefited by the Proverbs. For anyone who is attentive to them and does not idly receive their exhortations, as if fully armed with expertise, grasps the twists and turns of arguments without harm to himself, neither toppled by them nor ever departing from the truth. Now when the facts are by nature one way and arguments are used to persuade that they are otherwise, it is nothing but twisting and turning, or rather distortion of the truth through argument. And the person who seems to be one thing, but in reality is otherwise, uses twists and turns of arguments, deceiving those with whom he converses. He acts as hares and foxes do with dogs, giving signs of movement in one direction but then going in another. Surely *the objections of*

[29]See 1 Cor 10.4.
[30]See Mt 7.24–25.
[31]That is, eternal life.
[32]See Mt 25.10–13.

what is falsely called knowledge [1 Tim 6.20] are a kind of twisting and turning of arguments. Since those who have been whetted for counter-arguments by dialectic do not accept the simplicity of the Spirit's teaching,[33] often they use the plausible arguments of sophisms to overturn the strength of the truth. So then, anyone who is fortified by the Proverbs grasps these twists and turns of arguments. Even if at some point he encounters logical conundrums which have equally strong dialectical arguments for each alternative, and it is hard to judge which of them has discovered the more plausible argument, nonetheless because of his training in the Proverbs, he will not be confounded in his intellect, even if the disputants seem to pummel each other with blows of dialectical arguments that are as evenly-matched as possible.

8 The Proverbs also enable us *to understand true justice* [Prov 1.3]. So then, justice is the state of mind that distributes according to merit.[34] But this is hard to do. There are some who lack prudence and accordingly do not discover how to distribute an equal portion to each. There are others who are prejudiced by human passions and accordingly lose sight of justice when they spurn the poor and do not rebuke the powerful if they act unjustly. Therefore, the Book of Proverbs promises to give to its disciples knowledge of true justice. There are many who pursue the adulation of the masses: in their actions they prefer injustice and avarice, as if these were beneficial, whereas in outward appearance and in their conversations they express great admiration for equality and justice. Not even these sorts of people does the one who has been instructed in the Proverbs ignore, but he knows which justice is fraudulent and spurious, and which is true and sincere. Indeed, even the external sages[35] have written many

[33]On simplicity, p. 46 above.

[34]This is a widely-quoted Platonist-Stoic definition of justice; see Plato, *Definitions* 411e; LS 61D5 (=SVF 2.280); 61H3 (=SVF 3.262); SVF 3.263, 3.266; cf. Aristotle, *Nicomachean Ethics* 5.5 (1134a). The same definition is attributed to Aristotle in Diogenes Laertius 5.21.

[35]That is, non-Christian philosophers external to the church.

treatises on justice, and by using plausible arguments they mislead those unable to follow the true account of this subject. Therefore, this book promises knowledge of true justice so that we may avoid the harm that comes from sophistical arguments.

Furthermore, at present the laws of the nations, which differ so much from one another, produce confusion in the minds of those who do not comprehend the precise account of justice. For some of the nations maintain that parricide is just, whereas other nations abhor every murder as horrendous. And some value moderation above all else, whereas others fall madly in love with their mothers, daughters, and sisters. And in sum many who abide by ancient customs do not realize how abominable these acts are. But this book, which teaches what pertains to true justice, rescues human beings from their irrational passions. There is one kind of justice which is found among us, namely, equal distribution. Even if we are not entirely successful in this endeavor, and yet we act with a most just intention, then we do not fall from the goal. But there is another kind of justice which is sent down from heaven by *the just judge* [2 Tim 4.8]. It is both corrective and retributive. Yet it is very hard to understand because the teachings stored up in it are so sublime. I think this is what the Psalmist was talking about when he said: *Your justice is like the mountains of God* [Ps 35.7]. So then, he promises that this really true and divine justice will be manifested to those trained in the teaching of the Proverbs.

9 In addition, since some sins are involuntary and others arise from a wicked intention, there is no single rule for applying justice in both cases. Let us suppose that we are judging an instance of prostitution, and there are two prostitutes. One woman was sold to a brothel and thus compelled into this evil, giving what she earns from her body to her wicked master. The other woman gave herself to this sin voluntarily because of the pleasure she derived from it. So then, in the first case the involuntary actions are pardoned, and in the other case the actions which arose from a despicable choice are condemned. Another example: a man sinned who was raised in wickedness from birth. Indeed, he was brought into life by unjust parents and brought up in an environment of illicit words and deeds. Another man had many inducements to virtue: a nurturing of the most noble sort, the admonition of parents, the strictness of teachers, instruction in divine discourses, a sparse diet, and the other things which educate the soul in virtue. But then he fell into a similar sin. How is it not just that the latter is worthy of a more serious punishment? For the first man will be charged only with misusing the salutary resources implanted among our notions.[36] But in addition to this charge, the other man will also be blamed because he forsook every assistance given to him and through inattention was drawn into a wicked life. So then, it belongs to a great mind of the highest perfection *to understand true justice.*[37]

Perhaps this book also promises that anyone who has been educated in the Proverbs will thereafter be capable of applying his mind to theology with precision.[38] For the true justice is Christ, *who was made for us wisdom, and justice, and holiness, and redemption* [1 Cor 1.30].

To understand true justice is joined with *to direct judgment* [Prov 1.3]. Anyone not first educated in justice cannot correctly adjudicate

[36]Here Basil is talking about the naturally-implanted notions that each human being has innately in virtue of being a human being. In Stoic and Epicurean epistemology, a "common notion" (κοινὴ ἔννοια) or a "natural notion" (φυσικὴ ἔννοια) is any ordinary, naturally well-founded concept that is available to the mind as a "preconception" (πρόληψις). A preconception is the innate concept of a thing that makes discussion, investigation, and understanding of it possible. Preconceptions are the necessary foundations and principles of all further knowledge that arises from rational inquiry. Human beings were thought to be "pre-programmed" with a number of preconceptions and common or natural notions. For ancient testimonies, see Cicero, *On the Nature of the Gods* 2.43 and *On Academic Skepticism* 2.30 (=LS 40N); Diogenes Laertius 7.54 (=LS 40A); Epictetus, *Discourses* 1.22; and Sextus Empiricus, *Against the Mathematicians* 8.331a-332a (=LS 40T).

[37]The idea that judgment ought to take into account the preceding circumstances is also found in *Ps7* 5, a passage which exhibits even verbal parallels with this one.

[38]"Applying his mind to" translates ἐπιβαλεῖν, a key epistemological term for Basil; the cognate noun, ἐπιβολή is used in *Eun.* 1.6–7. On Basil's understanding of theology, see n. 10 on p. 55 above.

disputes. Unless even Solomon had had within himself the precise accounts of justice, he would not have been able to pronounce that celebrated verdict about the two prostitutes and the boy with such rectitude and accuracy.[39] For when the testimony of each could not be corroborated by witnesses, he appealed to nature and thereby discovered the unknown facts of the case. While the phony mother cold-heartedly would have allowed the death of the boy, the true mother could not even bear to hear of his suffering, because of natural affection. So then, anyone who knows true justice and has been taught by it to distribute to each what is proper is able *to direct judgment*. For just as the archer directs his arrow straight to the target, not straying from the art of archery either by overshooting, or by falling short, or by deviating to either side, so too the judge aims at justice neither by showing partiality (for *it is not good to show partiality in judgment* [Prov 24.23]), nor by showing favoritism, but rather by pronouncing judgments which are fair and unbiased. And when he judged the two women, the one had more than what she should and the other had less. So when acting as judge he made them equal to one another and took away from the one who had more as much as he discovered that the wronged party had been deprived of.

But as for someone without true justice first stored up in his soul, and who instead is corrupted by money or partial to friendship or vindictive out of hatred or in the pocket of the powerful: such a person cannot direct judgment. The Psalm speaks against such a person: *Do you then truly speak justice? Do you judge fairly, O sons of men?* [Ps 57.2]. For rectitude in judging is the proof of a state of mind that is just. Hence further on he gives a prohibition, saying: *A large and a small weight are abominations to the Lord* [Prov 20.10]. Here he uses the word "weight" as proverbs customarily do to intimate unfairness in judging. This is useful not only for judges, but also when making any choice in life. After all, we have within ourselves a kind of natural court of justice where we distinguish good from evil. Therefore, when we choose what we ought to do we must judge the

[39]See 1 Kg 3.19–28.

matter before us rightly; like a judge choosing between opponents with an equitable and just mind, we must be convinced by virtue and condemn vice. For example, imagine that you are judging fornication and moderation, and your lofty intellect has been entrusted with presiding over the court of justice. Pleasure pleads the case of fornication, and the fear of God advocates for moderation. So then, if you condemn the sin and grant victory to moderation, you have rendered a fair verdict in the case. But if you tip the scale in favor of pleasure, declaring that sin is to be preferred, then you have given an unfair judgment and are liable to the curse uttered by the one who said: *Woe to those who call bitter sweet and sweet bitter, who call darkness light and light darkness* [Is 5.20].[40]

10   According to the same Solomon *the thoughts of the just are judgments* [Prov 12.5]. So then, within our thoughts' hidden court of justice we must be eager to render unbiased judgments about the matter at hand; our intellect should be like a scale, weighing each course of action impartially. Whenever anything which has been commanded and the vice opposite it are submitted to your judgment, grant the victory to the law of God over against sin. Are avarice and equity being judged? Denounce the desire for what belongs to another, give the favorable decision to virtue. Are verbal abuse and patience pitted against one another? Hold verbal abuse in contempt, and patience in esteem. Hatred and love? Treat the former as ignominious and despise it as much as possible, but honor love and make it your own. Are pretence and simplicity, bravery and cowardice, prudence and foolishness, justice and injustice, moderation and intemperance, and in a word every virtue and every vice submitted to your judgment? Then indeed put rectitude in judging on display in your soul's hidden court of justice. And once you have taken what has been commanded as your assessor, show hatred for every wickedness, turning away from the sins and valuing the virtues above all else. In every course of action to be judged, if you give victory within

[40]The idea of the inner court of law is also found in *Ps61* 4.

yourself to the better way, you will be blessed *on that day when God judges the secrets of men in accordance with our gospel, and their conflicting thoughts accuse or even defend them* [Rom 2.16+15]. Nor will you depart a condemned man because you tipped the scale toward the bad course of action. Instead you will be honored with *the crowns of justice* [2 Tim 4.8] with which you crowned virtue throughout your entire life. Since the Book of Proverbs teaches *true justice* and *to direct judgment*, how many goods will it obtain for you?

11 So then, what else is there in addition to this? He says: *That he might give shrewdness to the innocent, and both perception and insight to the young child* [Prov 1.4]. We can understand innocence in two ways. One kind of innocence is the estrangement from sin achieved through reason. After we have given sustained attention to the goods[41] and practiced them for a long time in order to extirpate, as it were, the root of wickedness from ourselves, insofar as it has been completely taken away from us we receive the designation "innocent." Another kind of innocence is still not having any experience of wickedness. Because they are still young, as is most often the case, or because they have cultivated a certain kind of life, some people continue to lack experience of certain vices. For example, a child does not know arrogance; he does not know deceit and fraud. Again, some who live in the country do not know the malpractices of commerce, nor the crooked ways of the law courts. We do not call such people innocent because they made the choice to separate themselves from wickedness, but we do so because they have still not experienced an evil state of mind. Now David was innocent in the proper sense of the term, saying: *I have walked in my innocence* [Ps 25.11]. For he who has removed all evil from his own soul through the practice of virtue is worthy of inheriting the goods. Therefore *the Lord will not withhold the goods from those who walk in innocence* [Ps 83.12]. Such a person confidently says: *Judge me, O Lord, because I have walked in my innocence* [Ps 25.1]. And again: *Judge me, O*

[41]That is, the virtues.

Lord, according to my justice and according to my innocence in me [Ps 7.9]. Now innocence is characterized by simplicity in behavior, high-mindedness, and lack of artifice. Such was Jacob. It says: *He was a simple man, living at home* [Gen 25.27]. In other words, by using his natural simplicity, he did not give a false impression of himself through artifice, as if putting on a mask, in order to deceive those whom he met.

Yet here in this verse[42] he seems to say that the innocent man lacks experience of evil. He also says that he needs a shrewdness that is praiseworthy, so as to acquire, in addition to his natural purity, the astuteness born of experience, and also to become immune from the attacks of his enemies by being strengthened by good shrewdness as if by a shield. Now it is appropriate, I think, that the perfect man be prudent with respect to the good and pure with respect to evil.[43] Hence it is as if from a kind of spring that the innocent draw salutary shrewdness.[44] *A shrewd person is a throne of perception* [Prov 12.23]. And: *A shrewd person hid when evils approached* [Prov 27.12]. And: *Whoever heeds reproof is shrewder* [Prov 15.5 Aq]. So then, shrewdness is the activity of doing everything with skillful resourcefulness, just as wickedness is doing only what is wicked.[45] So then, since the shrewd person is concerned with all works, and among all works are included bad works, the word "shrewdness" has two meanings. On the one hand, a person is evil if he uses his ingenuity for works that harm others. On the other hand, a person is shrewd in a praiseworthy way if he seeks what is good for himself with acuity and intelligence and flees the harm which others have prepared for him out of deceit and treachery. So then, be attentive to the precise meaning of the term "shrewdness." Understand that it is a

---

[42]That is, Prov 1.4.

[43]Cf. Mt 10.16.

[44]Cf. Is 12.3.

[45]Basil's wordplay here is impossible to capture in English: "shrewdness (*panourgia*) is the activity (*energeia*) of doing everything (*pan*) with skillful attention, just as wickedness (*kakourgia*) is doing (*ergasia*) only what is wicked (*kakon*)." The root *ergon*, which appears as *ourgia* in *panourgia* and *kakourgia*, means "work."

neutral state of mind, according to which a person is either praised
or condemned: praised, if shrewdness is used with sound aims for
the benefit of both himself and his neighbor, but condemned, if it is
exercised to harm his neighbors, since he uses his resourcefulness
as a means of destruction.

12   The historical narrative is full of the use of resourcefulness in
both ways. The shrewdness used by the Hebrews was good when
they deceived the Egyptians: they received the reward for their
labor of building cities and procured for themselves materials for
the tabernacle.[46] The midwives who saved the lives of the male
children of the Hebrews acted shrewdly in a praiseworthy way.[47]
The shrewdness of Rebecca was good when she procured the great
blessing for her son.[48] Rahab acted shrewdly in a good way, and
Rachel also in a good way: the one saved the life of the spies,[49] and
the other deceived her father and extricated him from idolatry.[50]
But the Gibeonites employed shrewdness against the Israelites in an
evil manner.[51] The shrewdness used by Absalom was evil when he
beguiled his subjects under the pretence of fairness and assembled
a great crowd of rebels in the plot against his father.[52] And some
are denounced because they intentionally employed shrewdness
against the people of God.[53] Yet here in this verse[54] Scripture
approves the shrewdness that is used for benefit, like a shield against
life's misfortunes which protects the souls of simpler people. For if
Eve had had this shrewdness, she would not have been susceptible
to the deceitfulness of the serpent.[55] So then, since innocence is

[46]See Ex 12.35–36.
[47]See Ex 1.17.
[48]See Gen 27.1–28.5.
[49]See Josh 2.1–24; 6.17–25.
[50]See Gen 31.34–35.
[51]See Josh 9.3–27.
[52]See 2 Sam 15.1–12.
[53]See Ps 82.4.
[54]That is, Prov 1.4.
[55]See Gen 3.1–20; 2 Cor 11.3.

prone to having its thoughts corrupted because it believes every word, it is protected by the teaching discussed above. This teaching furnishes innocence with the benefit of shrewdness as a defense against life's misfortunes.

13 Next we must investigate how he gives *both perception and insight to the young child* [Prov 1.4]. Now human nature is two-fold, as the Apostle says: one nature is exterior and the other is interior.[56] The one corresponds to what is seen and the other to what is understood in secret. Therefore we must determine whether the age of this child is to be understood according to the exterior or the interior nature. So then, it is not far from ludicrous to say that this newborn child receives corporeal perception. For what sort of perception can this book provide? Not sight and hearing and smell and taste and touch! For we have these from the moment we are born and we do not acquire them through our education; rather, nature perfects the living being[57] through them. So then, this "child" must not be understood as corporeal, nor should this "perception" be taken as one of the senses just enumerated. Instead, the child's age must be understood according to the inner nature.

We have been taught in many passages of Scripture that there is one state of the soul which is like a child, another which is like a man in his prime, and another which is like a man who is already old and venerable. For example, as we have learned from Paul, the Corinthians were babes; therefore they still needed milk—that is, the introductory and simpler teaching of the gospel—because they could not yet master the solid food of doctrine.[58] That person is young in soul who is perfectly taught in all the branches of virtue,[59] who is *fervent in spirit* [Acts 18.25], who is eager for the practices of piety, and who being in his prime is vigorous in every way for the performance of goods works. Such a person the gospel also calls "a man of violence"

[56]See 2 Cor 4.16.
[57]Gk. τὸ ζῷον. Basil means the animate life within a person.
[58]See 1 Cor 3.1–2.
[59]Cf. Lk 6.40.

who can seize the kingdom of heaven by force.[60] In addition, such a person the Holy Spirit sees as suited for hymns of praise, for he says: *Let young men and maidens praise the name of the Lord* [Ps 148.12–13]. And in Joel it is promised that *the young men shall see visions* [Joel 2.28]. But that person is old and venerable in soul who has been perfected in prudence. Such was Daniel, who while young in body showed that the honor which intelligence obtains is more respectable than every grey hair. Therefore, the men who were full of wicked days said to him: *Come, sit among us, and tell us, for God has given you the right of a venerable elder* [Dan 13.50].

Thus here in this passage,[61] by "young child" is meant that person who is reborn *by the washing of regeneration* [Titus 3.5], who turns[62] and becomes like a child,[63] and who by such a state *is fit for the kingdom* of heaven [Lk 9.62]. Therefore, after being trained by the Book of Proverbs, the newborn babe, who longs for rational and guileless milk,[64] is given *perception and insight*: perception of what is present, insight into what is to come. For on the one hand, this book teaches human truths and makes the true reality of things perceptible, so as to prevent both enslavement to disgusting pleasures and excitement about the vainglorious things of this world. On the other hand, it confers insight into the age to come, and through what it says brings one to belief in its promises.

14   Since we have interpreted these differences in age as pertinent to the interior nature, it is logical furthermore to transfer the names of the sense-perceptions to the faculties of the soul. Hence, when he says: *Incline your ear to my words* [Prov 4.20; 5.1], we should understand that he asks for the soul's obedience, as when the Lord said: *He who has ears, let him hear* [Mt 13.9]. And: *A wise word to an*

---

[60]See Mt 11.2

[61]That is, Prov 1.4.

[62]Here I prefer the mss reading στραφέντα to Garnier's τραφέντα because Basil seems to be using scriptural language here (see the next note).

[63]See Mt 18.3; cf. Mt 18.4; Mk 10.15; Lk 18.17.

[64]See 1 Pet 2.2.

obedient ear [Prov 25.12]. So then, through these passages and others like them he gives a sound sense of hearing *to the young child*. And when he says: *Pay no attention to a worthless women* [Prov 5.3], and again: *Do not fix your eye upon her* [Prov 9.18a], and: *Let your eyes look straight* [Prov 4.25], he is clearly giving the child a kind of sense of sight within the soul. And when he exhorts: *Eat honey, my son, that your palate may be sweetened* [Prov 24.13]—here "honey" is used figuratively for divine teaching; for he says: *how sweet are your sayings to my throat, beyond honey to my mouth!* [Ps 118.103]—through this exhortation he whets the soul's spiritual sense of taste, about which it is said: *Taste and see that the Lord is good* [Ps 33.9]. And there is a kind of sense of touch within the soul, according to which wisdom lays hold of the soul, as if embracing her own lover.[65] For he says: *love her, that she may embrace you* [Prov 4.6+8]. And again Ecclesiastes: *a time to embrace and a time to be far from embracing* [Eccl 3.5]. Now bodies become defiled by impure embraces, but when the soul is embraced by wisdom and becomes wholly united to her, it is filled with holiness and purity. So then, this is the way in which he bestows *perception on the young child.*

Now, how does he confer *insight*? When he says: *Riches will not benefit on the day of evil* [Prov 11.4 MT].[66] For riches weigh down your heart with scruples about that day on which abundant wealth will neither be of help to you nor deliver you from everlasting punishment. Or when he says: *The innocent will inherit the earth*[67]—that earth of which the meek are heirs, according to both the Psalm which says: *The meek will inherit the earth* [Ps 36.11] and the beatitude of the Lord, who says: *Blessed are the meek, for they shall inherit the earth*

[65]Here I read ἐραστήν instead of ἀρετήν, which makes better sense in the context.

[66]This verse is not found in the LXX. In his Hexapla, Origen placed it between asterisks, indicating that it was included by either Aquila, Symmachus, or Theodotion.

[67]This verse is not found in the LXX. It may be a conflation of Prov 2.21 (*The kind will be inhabitants of the earth, and the innocent will be left in it, because the upright will dwell on the earth and the holy will be left in it*) with either Ps 36.22 (*Those who bless him will inherit the land*) or Ps 36.29 (*The just will inherit the land*).

[Mt 5.5]. And again: *The wise shall inherit glory* [Prov 3.35]. He stirs the soul to desire these promised goods. This is the *insight* which he gives *to the young child*: to fear those things with which sinners are threatened and to desire those things prepared for the just.

For by hearing these things the wise man will become wiser [Prov 1.5]. Scripture ascribes great power to the Proverbs because they surpass the wisdom of the wise, because this book hands on something superior to the teaching found among the wise. Hence, the disciples of the other teachers are ignorant, but the students of this book are wise. On the one hand, the term "wise" is homonymous, in that some called "wise" are of this world,[68] but others called "wise" have received the true wisdom, our Lord Jesus Christ, by believing in him.[69] In this case, Scripture promises those who are outside of our doctrine[70] that they will be wiser if they have recourse to the sound teaching of the Proverbs, if they scorn the knowledge of vanities and come to admire the truth. On the other hand, "wise" is said in many ways, in that the person who desires wisdom, the person who has already made progress in the contemplation of wisdom, and the person who is habitually perfected in wisdom are all similarly designated "wise." In this case, *by hearing these things the wise man*—either the lover of wisdom or the one already deeply rooted in it—*will become wiser.* Such a person will learn many things about the divine teachings and be taught many things about human truths. This book will banish wickedness in various ways and inculcate virtue by various means. It bridles the unjust tongue, disciplines the eye that sees evil, does not permit unjust hands to rule, chases away idleness, chastises disgusting desires, teaches prudence, teaches fortitude, extols moderation. So then, when a person has been taught these things, he has within himself the strong prejudice against what is bad and has gained the appetite for what is good by a better impulse as if given a shout of encouragement. And so, while he is wise because of his own impulse,

---

[68]See 1 Cor 1.20.
[69]See 1 Cor 1.24, 1.30.
[70]That is, non-Christians outside the church.

he has become even wiser because of the perfection he has received from this teaching.[71]

15 *And the man of discernment will acquire the ability to steer* [Prov 1.5]. Anyone is who is going to take up a particular craft must have the endowments of nature needed to practice it. The wrestler must have a body that is in shape and strong. The runner must have legs that are well-suited for racing and nimble. Likewise, the steersman must have a mind that is sharp and perspicacious. It is for this reason that Scripture does not call just any random person to steering, but *the man of discernment.* Now what is steering? Surely it is nothing other than the knowledge of the soul that deals with navigating the instable nature of human circumstances in an appropriate manner. For in many passages we find that Scripture has used the words "waters" and "sea" to indicate the present life, as in the Psalm: *From on high he reached down and seized me; he drew me forth from the mighty waters* [Ps 17.17]. Here he clearly calls life's upheavals "waters." For the prosperity greatly desired by many is instable and impermanent. Adverse and gloomy situations are not firmly established. Rather, all things are subject to a kind of rocking by the sea, turmoil, and unexpected changes. So then, just as it is impossible for the sea to remain the same for long (for now it is serene and calm, but a little later you will see it agitated by the force of the winds, and yet when the sea is wild and violently shaken by the waves, quickly a deep tranquility sets in), so too life's circumstances easily take a turn in either direction.

Therefore, a steersman is needed so that when life is tranquil and everything is going with the flow, you may expect changes to happen and not be complacent with the present circumstances as if they were immortal, and when the situation is gloomy, you may neither despair nor *be overwhelmed by excessive sadness* [2 Cor 2.7]

---

[71]Basil's language of "impulse" (ὁρμή) here is of Stoic provenance; see LS 57. It refers to innate capacity of human beings to actualize themselves; as such, impulses are foundational for the virtuous life.

so as to be dragged underwater. For neither the health of the body, nor the flower of youth, nor the prosperity of the family, nor any of the other strokes of good fortune in life remains for a long time. When life is tranquil, expect stormy circumstances to arise at some point. Sickness will come. Poverty will come. The wind does not always fill the sails.[72] Even the person who is circumspect and zealous in all things is frequently overtaken by unexpected situations of a disgraceful sort. Unwanted circumstances have arisen like storms to wreak havoc upon all the good fortune in life. The constant evils are like waves for you: one after another makes life rough for you, and your life is caught in the midst of a terrible storm. At some point you will see even these things subside, and your life will be changed to cheerfulness and truly joyful tranquility. So then, the discerning steersman deals with what happens with careful attention to its underlying nature, and remains self-consistent at all times, neither elated by joys, nor dejected by misfortunes.

Furthermore, the good of steering provides us with something else that is useful. For I know another kind of waves, that terrible storm that rises up against the soul from the passions of the flesh. For when anger and fear and pleasure and sadness arise suddenly from *the mind of the flesh* [Rom 8.6] as if from a violent storm, they frequently sink a soul that is without a steersman. So the mind as if a steersman, seated high above the passions and mounted on the flesh as if it were a ship and expertly turning the disturbing thoughts in the right direction as if they were rudders, must quell the waves in a vigorous manner. Remaining high above and being impregnable to attack by the passions, the mind must never become filled with their bitterness as if with seawater, but must always pray, saying: *Rescue me from those who hate me and from the waters of the deep. Do not let a tempest of water overwhelm me, nor the deep swallow me* [Ps 68.15–16].

---

[72]Literally, "rise against the stern."

16 Do you want me to talk about another ship for which we also need the gift of steering? *The kingdom of the heavens is like a merchant* [Mt 13.45]. So then, all of us who travel the path of the gospel are merchants, being in the business of acquiring heavenly goods through the profits we earn by keeping the commandments. So then, we must collect heavenly riches in great numbers and of various sorts, if we do not want to be shamed when we report our profits, as those who received the talents were, and hear: *You wicked and lazy servant!* [Mt 25.26]. We must put our goods on board, and try to pass through this life safely. For there are many people who have accumulated many goods from their youth, and when they reached middle age and were attacked by temptations from the spirits of wickedness, they could not bear the burden of the storm because they lacked the ability to steer, and so suffered the loss of all their goods. Hence, while *some have made shipwreck of their faith* [1 Tim 1.19], others lost the moderation they acquired in their youth when it was assaulted by wicked pleasure as if by an unexpected tempest. Here is a most wretched sight: after fasting, after living an austere life, after intense prayer, after abundant tears, after continence for some twenty or even thirty years, through the soul's inattention and negligence, to be stripped of all things. Such a person who once abounded in the profits we earn by keeping the commandments is like a filthy rich merchant who rejoices[73] in the abundance of his goods while his ship is carried by a fair wind, but then passes over the terrifying seas and in the harbor itself his ship is dashed to pieces, and he is deprived of all his goods in one fell swoop. If indeed what he came to possess through innumerable toils and much sweat he has lost in a single attack of a demon, he has been sunk by sin as if by a wild tempest. The following utterance is appropriate for whoever has made shipwreck of every virtue all at once: *I have entered the depths of the sea, and a tempest overwhelmed me* [Ps 68.3].

---

[73]The word is ἐπαγγελλόμενος, "promises," which makes little sense in the context. Garnier translated this as *laetus*, which is followed here.

17   So then, hold the rudder of your life steady. Steer your eye, lest a fierce wave of desire ever crash upon you through your eyes. Steer your ear, your tongue, lest you hear something harmful, lest you utter something forbidden. Do not let the storm of anger capsize you. Do not let the buffets of fear overwhelm you. Do not let the burden of sadness sink you. The passions are our waves. If you raise yourself above them, you will be a trusty steersman of your life. But if you do not steer clear of each of these waves with skill and steadfastness, then like a ship without ballast tossed about by their constant assaults you will be lost in the sea of sin.

So listen how you too can acquire the skill of steering. It is the custom of sailors to gaze up at the sky in order to receive guidance for their voyage from it (in daytime from the sun and at night from Ursa Major or another of the constellations which are always above the horizon). And under the guidance of these they always chart the right course. As for you, then, direct your eye to heaven, according to the one who said: *To you have I lifted up my eyes, you who dwell in heaven* [Ps 122.1]. Look upon the sun of justice.[74] Guided by the commandments of the Lord as if by bright stars, keep your eye sleepless, giving no sleep to your eyes nor slumber to your eyelids,[75] so that the commandments may guide you forever more. For he says: *Your law is a lamp for my feet and a light to my paths* [Ps 118.105]. If you never fall asleep at the tiller, then as long as you are in this life, in the midst of the instable nature of mundane realities, you will also receive assistance from the Spirit, who will propel you ever onward and transport you safely by gentle and peaceful breezes, until you are brought safe and sound to that waveless and calm harbor of the will of God, *to whom be glory and might* endlessly *for ever and ever. Amen* [1 Pet 4.11].

---

[74]See Mal 3.20.
[75]See Ps 131.4.

First Homily on Psalm 14
(Ps 14.1–4)

[1]*Lord, who shall sojourn in your tent?*
And who shall dwell on your holy mountain?
[2]*He who walks without fault and he who acts with justice.*
He who speaks the truth in his heart,
who has not practiced deceit with his tongue.
    [3]*He who has not wronged his neighbor in any way,*
    Nor taken reproach with regard to his neighbors.
In his sight a worker of wickedness is held in disdain,
    [4]*but he honors those who fear the Lord.*
He who swears an oath to his neighbor and does not
    repudiate him.

INTRODUCTION

In early Christianity the Psalms played a central role in worship and piety. Psalms were included among the readings from Scripture at the Synaxis (or Liturgy of the Word) and sung at the Sunday Eucharist. Psalms were also employed at other liturgies, such as baptisms, funerals, and the celebrations of martyrs. The use of the Psalms in prayer was especially popular among monks, whose daily offices consisted largely of a certain number of psalms, either recited or sung. No doubt the Psalms were also used by Christians in their private devotions as well.[1]

---

[1]On the early Christian use of the Psalms, see John Alexander Lamb, *The Psalms in Christian Worship* (London: Faith, 1962), 23–45; and W. Holladay, *The Psalms through Three Thousand Years: Prayerbook of a Cloud of Witnesses* (Minneapolis: Fortress, 1993), 113–33 and 161–74.

Since the Psalms were originally composed in Hebrew for use in a Jewish religious milieu, one of the main challenges of incorporating them into Christianity was finding specifically Christian meaning in them.[2] To this end Christian commentators on the Psalms took a number of approaches to extract Christian significance from them. For example, they saw the Psalms as prophecies about Christ and the church, as a summation of salvation history, both looking back to the story of Israel and forward to the redemption in Christ; and they even identified Christ as the speaker of the Psalms or the one spoken about. The Psalms were considered to offer a mirror for the whole range of human attitudes, emotions, affections, feelings, experiences, and needs, as well as remedies for their transformation and conversion for the salvation of the soul. And commentators otherwise drew from the Psalms a treasury of spiritual wisdom.[3] When viewed in this light, the Psalms were seen as offering a superabundance of liturgical, devotional, christological, ethical, and theological resources for the Christian life.

The frequent use of the Psalms in a variety of contexts, coupled with the difficulty of appropriating and understanding them, resulted in the production of commentaries or sets of homilies dedicated to explicating the Psalms for a Christian audience. Basil was one of the Church Fathers who participated in the this project, along with many others, the most prominent of whom are Origen, Eusebius of Caesarea, Athanasius of Alexandria, Hilary of Poitiers, Diodore of Tarsus, Theodore of Mopsuestia, and Augustine of Hippo.[4] There are

[2]See O. Linton, "Interpretation of the Psalms in the Early Church," *Studia Patristica* 4 (1961): 143–56; and Balthasar Fischer, "Zum Problem einer christlichen Interpretation der Psalmen," *Theologische Revue* 67 (1971): 6–12.

[3]A classic effort in this regard is Athanasius' *Letter to Marcellinus on the Interpretation of the Psalms*. See the translation of Robert C. Gregg, *Athanasius: The Life of Antony and the Letter to Marcellinus* (New York: Paulist Press, 1980), 101–29.

[4]See Aimé Solignac, "Psaumes V: Les commentaires" in DSpir 12: 2562–2568; and David L. Balás and D. Jeffrey Bingham, "Patristic Exegesis of the Books of the Bible. VI. Wisdom and Poetry: Psalms," in Charles Kannengiesser, *Handbook of Patristic Exegesis: The Bible in Ancient Christianity* (Leiden: Brill, 2006), 297–301 and 307–309.

fifteen of Basil's homilies on the Psalms still extant.[5] His homily on Psalm 1 begins with a prologue in which he praises the Psalms; therefore, it is a good introduction to his perspective on the role of the Psalms in the Christian life.[6] The Psalms, according to Basil, gather together the most beneficial parts of the Old Testament: historical narrative, prophecy, law, moral instruction, and so forth. In a sense the Psalms are a summation and epitome of the entire Old Testament. They offer beneficial teaching for the cure of souls, delivering them from passions and afflictions. There is something useful for all people, regardless of their stage in the spiritual life, from beginners to the perfect, no matter what their current emotional state. The Psalms are conducive to calmness and peace, to friendship, unity, and charity. They offer protection from the forces of evil and provide weapons against them. They bring rest and repose from toils, and consolation to the disheartened. The Psalms confer countless benefits. They also instruct in the virtues, such as courage, justice, self-control, prudence, and patience. They contain the fullness of theology, including prophecies about Christ, the hope of resurrection, the threat of punishment, and the promise of glory. One of the unique features of the Psalms is that they instruct and train the soul using song and pleasant melodies, which makes their teaching more palatable and easier to apply. But above all, says Basil, the Psalms provide deep insight into Christian practice and doctrine.

Therefore, Basil's main goal in his homily on Psalm 14 is to explain its Christian meaning, to make it relevant for Christians. Psalm 14 opens with a question about who will sojourn in God's tent and dwell on his holy mountain. The remainder of the verses present various moral characterizations of the kind of person who will do so. Basil considers the initial question to be asked by the Christian seeker desiring eternal life with God and the remainder of the Psalm

[5]See p. 21 above.

[6]*Ps1* 1–2; see the translation of Agnes Clare Way, *Saint Basil: Exegetic Homilies*, FOTC 46 (Washington, DC: The Catholic University of America Press, 1963), 151–4. The relevant portion is also translated by Blomfield Jackson, "Prolegomena. Sketch of the Life and Works of Saint Basil," NPNF 2.8, xlv–xlvi.

to be the Lord's answer (§2). Hence he views Psalm 14 as the Lord's description of the different virtues which characterize the perfect Christian.[7] At the same time Basil takes Psalm 14 as an exhortation for those Christians who still fall short of perfection, that they too may acquire these virtues. Therefore Psalm 14 is viewed as a kind of program for spiritual advancement.[8]

It took Basil two homilies to interpret Psalm 14, even though it has only five verses. In his first homily, which is translated below, he manages to cover only the first four verses, discussing the various virtues of the perfect man. Apparently he resumed his interpretation of the same Psalm the next day.[9] In his second homily he finally deals with the fifth verse, *He who does not lend money at interest*, producing a diatribe against the practice of usury, seen as inimical to Christian charity. This second homily is considered one of the classics of Basil's preaching on social justice.[10] These two homilies of Basil are among the earliest extant Christian interpretations of Psalm 14.[11]

---

[7]Basil's view of Psalm 14 appears to be traditional; commenting on the same Psalm Athanasius had said: "And then, if you wish to learn what sort of person the citizen of the kingdom of heaven is, chant Psalm 14" (*Letter to Marcellinus* 16; trans. Gregg, *Athanasius*, 115).

[8]A similar view of Psalm 14 as a program of spiritual advancement can be found in *The Rule of Saint Benedict* prol. 22–34.

[9]See *Ps14b* 1.

[10]There is an excellent, recent translation: C. Paul Schroeder, *St Basil the Great: On Social Justice*, PPS 38 (Crestwood, NY: St Vladimir's Seminary Press, 2009), 89–99. An older translation can be found in Way, *Saint Basil: Exegetic Homilies*, 181–91.

[11]Hilary's *Tractatus in Psalmum xiv* (CSEL 22.84–96 Zingerle) is roughly contemporary with Basil's two homilies. The commentary on Psalm 14 attributed to Eusebius of Caesarea (PG 23.147–154) is not genuine; see p. 90 below. A few fragments of Origen on Psalm 14 are extant (PG 12.1207–1210), but they are of doubtful authenticity. But we also possess what is probably a more or less intact homily of Origen on Psalm 14 among the *Tractatus lix in Psalmos* attributed to Jerome (CCSL 78.2 Morin). A compelling case has been made by Vittorio Peri that these fifty-nine homilies on the Psalms are Jerome's Latin translations and adaptations of authentic homilies of Origen; see *Omelie origeniane sui Salmi: Contributo all'identificanzione del testo latino*, Studi e Testi 289 (Vatican City: Biblioteca Apostolica Vaticana, 1980). There are a few parallels between Origen/Jerome's *Tractatus in Psalmum xiv* and Basil's *Ps14a*, but on the whole Basil does not appear indebted to Origen's interpretation (if indeed it is recoverable from Jerome's homily on Psalm 14).

Basil begins the first homily on Psalm 14 by noting that the perfect man is described using "a particular order and method" (§1). In other words, Basil detects a precise progression in the sequence of the ideas in the first verse of Psalm 14, *Lord, who shall sojourn in your tent? And who shall dwell on your holy mountain?* Sojourning in God's tent must precede dwelling on God's holy mountain. Basil explains that sojourning is living this life as a transition to eternal life, not attaching oneself to earthly, temporary goods. It is living in exile from our true, heavenly home. Such is how David and Abraham lived. The tent in which we must sojourn is the body, with whose care we have been entrusted so that it can be returned to God fruitful, like farmland leased under a contract. All this is a prerequisite to dwelling on the holy mountain, that is, in the heavenly country. But residing on the holy mountain is also possible in this life if one sojourns in the tent of his body undisturbed by the passions of the flesh, living in the flesh as if an exile in a foreign land (§2). Basil admits that this happens only rarely. Only the perfect Christian is capable of this dual-residency, sojourning in the tent of the body and at the same time dwelling on the mountain of God.

The remainder of the homily is devoted to a description of the virtues of the perfect Christian who simultaneously sojourns in the tent of his flesh and dwells on the holy mountain. Psalm 14.2 says that the perfect Christian walks without fault and acts with justice. Basil rejects the idea that these two descriptions are merely parallel, each denoting the person who possesses all the virtues and is free from all vices; rather, each description has a distinct meaning. The person who walks without fault has the perfection of virtue within, while the person who acts with justice has the perfection of virtue in external works. So the verse suggests that a Christian is perfect when just deeds flow from an interior disposition of justice. Basil adds that the present tense of the verbs in this verse indicates that perfection is not achieved by a single good deed, but by the continual performance of good deeds throughout life (§3).

The two clauses of the next verse (Ps 14.2–3) bear a relation to each other similar to that of the two clauses in the previous verse: speaking the truth in the heart refers to the perfect Christian's truthful inner disposition, whereas not practicing deceit with the tongue signifies truthfulness in spoken words. In this context, Basil elaborates on the two senses of truth: (1) comprehension of realities conducive to the blessed life, i.e., salvific-moral truth, and (2) understanding of temporal realities, i.e., scientific truth. The second kind of truth is not essential; the Christian does not need a purely intellectual knowledge of scientific truths as a condition for salvation. All that really matters for Christians is the first kind of truth because it alone, according to Basil, is "the co-worker of salvation" (§3). This salvific-moral truth must in every case be transmitted without deceit, i.e., without being falsified or distorted. At the same time, this salvific-moral truth, or "the mystical doctrines" as Basil calls it (§3), should not be divulged to just anyone, but only to baptized Christians. In this comment Basil sees Psalm 14.2–3 a prefiguration of the *disciplina arcani*, the practice among early Christians of concealing the "mysteries" of the Christian faith from non-Christians and even catechumens.[12] At any rate, the idea that this salvific-moral truth should not be proclaimed in a deceitful way is buttressed by the frequent scriptural reproaches against deceit as the enemy of God. Just as wine and gold should not be adulterated by mixing them with water or copper, so too, says Basil, the truth should not be adulterated by mixing it with blasphemy.[13]

Next Basil turns to Psalm 14.3, *He who has not wronged his neighbor in any way, nor taken reproach with regard to his neighbors* (§4). He first clarifies who is our neighbor by using the Lukan parable of the man coming down from Jerusalem to Jericho (Lk 10.29–37):

---

[12]On the *disciplina arcani*, see Edward Yarnold, *The Awe-Inspiring Rites of Initiation: The Origins of the R.C.I.A.*, 2nd ed. (Collegeville: Liturgical Press, 1994), 55–9. Basil famously speaks of the *disciplina arcani* in *Spir.* 27.66.

[13]On Basil's discussion of truth here, see Mario Girardi, *Basilio di Cesarea interprete della Scrittura. Lessico, principi ermeneutici, prassi* (Bari: Epipuglia, 1998), 89–90.

every human being. Basil admits that treating every human being as our neighbor is difficult. But as the first clause of the verse teaches, it is a mark of the perfect Christian to take great pains not to mistreat our neighbor in any way, not verbally, not wishing him evil, not even being jealous of his successes. Though Basil thinks that the second clause of the verse is ambiguous, he finds meaning in each of the senses in which it can be taken. Either the perfect Christian does not do anything to deserve the reproach of his neighbors, or he himself does not reproach his neighbors when misfortune strikes them. While the latter is the more common interpretation of the clause—indeed modern translations render it something like *he has not taken up reproach against his neighbor*—Basil may have acknowledged the former possibility because it might have been Origen's interpretation.[14] At any rate, in this context, and in line with the latter interpretation, Basil notes that not even a sinner ought to be reproached, corroborating this claim by the fact that Paul exhorted Timothy to rebuke, encourage, and reprove sinners, but never to reproach them. For while rebuke aims to correct the sinner, reproach seems intended to disgrace the sinner. Basil concludes his interpretation of this verse with the observation that it is "utterly irrational" to reproach people for involuntary circumstances like poverty and physical disability. The better response is mercy.

According to the following verse, *In his sight a worker of wickedness is held in disdain, but he honors those who fear the Lord* (Ps 14.4), the perfect Christian, says Basil, is the embodiment of justice: apportioning to each what he is due (§5).[15] In other words, the perfect Christian disdains the wicked and honors the pious regardless of their external circumstances, that is, even if the wicked are rich and powerful, and high and mighty, even if the pious are poor and weak, and unimportant and uneducated.

---

[14]This is the interpretation found in the Origenian *Tractatus in psalmum xiv* of Jerome.

[15]On Basil's understanding of justice, see *Prov* 8–10.

Basil next launches into a discussion of oaths since what follows is: *He who swears an oath to his neighbor and does not repudiate him* (§5). It is first noted that there seems to be discrepancy between this verse and the injunction of Jesus not to swear oaths at all (see Mt 5.34). The apparent contradiction is resolved by noting that the Lord has the same intention (σκοπός) throughout the Scriptures, namely, guarding against sin before it arises and cutting it off as soon as it arises. In support of this view, Basil compares the Decalogue with the Sermon on the Mount. While the former forbids adultery and murder, Jesus prohibits lust and anger. In other words, the old law seeks to forestall acts of sin, whereas the more perfect law of Jesus guards against sin before it arises by focusing attention on extirpating the internal disturbances which lead to sin. It is the same with oaths. The overall goal is to avoid the sin of perjury. While Psalm 14 allows the swearing of good oaths, the injunction of Jesus precludes the very possibility of perjury by disallowing all oaths. For even the person who swears a good oath is not immune from perjury if he is betrayed against his will.

The attempt to reconcile the injunction of Jesus against oaths with scriptural evidence in favor of oaths continues when Basil notes that sometimes what Scripture calls an oath is really a confirmation of some fact. So Psalm 14.4 can be taken in the same way: the perfect Christian confirms the facts in support of his neighbor and never repudiates him, that is, he never denies the facts, never compromises his trustworthiness. Elsewhere in Scripture expressions which have the form of oath are actually signs of respect for the audience. There is nothing wrong with this. And so, in this section of the homily Basil has attempted to rescue many instances of scriptural oath-swearing from seeming to contradict the injunction of Jesus.

Rather than dealing with Psalm 14.5, which is deferred to the second homily on Psalm 14, the last section of the homily comments on Matthew 5.42, *Give to everyone who begs from you, and do not refuse anyone who wants to borrow from you* (§6). While this may seem like a non-sequitur, it is possible that Basil chose to discuss this verse as an implicit interpretation of the first clause of Psalm 14.5, *He who does not give his money at interest*, or perhaps as a prelude to its full interpretation in the next homily. Indeed, both verses are plausibly seen as concerned with the care of the poor and needy, and there is even a verbal connection between them (the verb *give*).[16]

Basil begins his interpretation of Matthew 5.42 by noting that this verse and other passages of Scripture exhort Christians to community and mutual charity because human beings are by nature social creatures, even alluding to Aristotle (*Pol.* 1253a2). Hence, the support of those in need, suggests Basil, is not merely a Christian virtue, but a basic human virtue. But Basil's interest in the present context is more with outlining the proper Christian way to care for the poor and needy. Basil acknowledges that not every one who begs really has a genuine need. There are many swindlers, conmen, and cheats who would exploit the good intentions of those who distribute alms out of Christian charity. Accordingly, a certain expertise is needed in distinguishing between the true need born of affliction and the feigned need contrived out of greed. When donations are made to the poor, continues Basil, it is like giving them a loan. Since showing mercy to the poor is lending to God (see Prov 19.17), it is God who repays the loan given to the poor. But the repayment is not in kind, but the kingdom of heaven. Having broached the subject of loans, Basil abruptly concludes the homily, apparently planning to resume the theme the next day.

In two different contexts in this homily Basil employs a metaphor about giving medicine to the sick. In the first case, he is discussing Psalm 14.2, which Basil interprets as teaching that perfection in doing just deeds must flow from a just inner disposition (§2). Here Basil makes a distinction between a layman and a physician making medicine for a sick person. Only the physician, because he has been trained in the art of medicine, knows how to make truly effective medicine. The implication is that nothing guarantees that

---

[16]On *Ps14a* 6, see Susan R. Holman, *The Hungry are Dying: Beggars and Bishops in Roman Cappadocia* (Oxford: Oxford University Press, 2001), 111–4.

a layman's medicine will be truly effective since he is unschooled in the art of medicine. So it is too with just deeds: in order to perform just deeds perfectly, they must be motivated by true interior justice. The interior knowledge of the art of medicine or justice is required for its perfect application in external works. In the second case, Basil is discussing Matthew 5.42 and the discerning care of the poor (§6). When people are sick, they know they need medicine and ask for it. But not every person is qualified to give medicine. Only a physician can discern the precise need of the patient: its frequency, quantity, and quality. So it is too with caring for the poor and needy. Only experts in Christian charity can determine the true need of the poor who ask for help and give accordingly. Note that in both cases the use of the metaphor is informed by the concept of justice: in the first case this is obvious, but in the second it is implicit. In other words, Basil's understanding of discerning Christian charity is based on his understanding of justice, giving to each what they deserve. The repetition of this metaphor not only demonstrates the rhetorical skill of Basil in making the same metaphor so versatile, but also ties the homily together.

For one of the hazards of a patristic homily devoted to a line-by-line interpretation of a psalm is that it seems to jump from one topic to the next as the homilist attempts to derive Christian meaning from it. The structure of the homily is dictated by the sequence of the verses in the psalm. But Basil connects the potentially unconnected verses of this Psalm by identifying its overall theme as Christian perfection. The various virtues of the perfect Christian are detachment from the body and earthly goods (§1–2); justice both interior and exterior, in judging others regardless of external circumstances, and in discerning true need (§2–3, §5–6); truthfulness both interiorly and exteriorly, and in avoiding perjury (§3, §5); and mercy toward the neighbor, the sinner, and the needy (§4, §6). It is not likely that Basil intends to teach that detachment, justice, truthfulness, and mercy are the only virtues of the perfect Christian. In this homily he is not presenting a complete profile of Christian perfection, but using Psalm 14.1–4 to discourse on some of its typical and essential characteristics.

Authenticity. Though it was accepted as a genuine homily of Basil by previous editors and scholars, Julien Garnier placed *Ps14a* among the works falsely ascribed (*falso adscripta*) to Basil.[17] He discovered that several passages of this homily were in fact paraphrased or borrowed verbatim from a commentary on the same Psalm attributed to Eusebius of Caesarea. Assuming that Basil was a brilliant and original writer of impeccable style, Garnier could not fathom that Basil might have borrowed from a previous ecclesiastical writer whose style he deemed far inferior. And so, he relegated this homily to the Basilian *spuria*.

Prudentius Maran concurred with Garnier's decision. Speaking in general of the homilies on the Psalms that Garnier considered spurious, he said: "Without timidity I will affirm that nothing is read in them which is unworthy of Basil or alien to his doctrine."[18] But he agreed with Garnier that "in these homilies there is nonetheless a dissimilarity with the style of Basil, which does not permit us to attribute them to him with certainty."[19] Specifically regarding the first homily on Psalm 14, Maran noted a number of parallels with Basil's genuine works. But the poor style was still, for Maran, an impediment to the homily's authenticity.

But determining authorship based on perceived lapses in style is a flawed methodology.[20] After citing a few of Garnier's specious "stylistic" arguments, Jean Gribomont made a comment that captures the astonishment that today's scholars feel upon reading them: *Ineluctabilem vide subjectivismum criticae internae, apud optimos quoque viros!*[21] Furthermore, recent scholarship has demonstrated

[17]"Praefatio," §VI, 33 (De Sinner i.xxvi–xxix; PG 29.cxcvi–cxcix).

[18]Maran, *Vita. S. Basilii* 41.5 (De Sinner iii.ccxxxix; PG 29.clxv).

[19]Maran, *Vita. S. Basilii* 41.5 (De Sinner iii.ccxl; PG 29.clxv).

[20]For further comments on Garnier's "stylistic" arguments against authenticity, see pp. 190–191, 216, and 267.

[21]*In Tomum 29 Patrologiae Graecae ad editionem operum Sancti Basilii Magni Adnotationes* (Turnhout: Brepols, 1959), 11. The sense is that, though Garnier was a great scholar, his criteria were inescapably subjective.

that the commentary on Psalm 14 which Garnier thought belonged to Eusebius of Caesarea actually belongs to someone else who lived after Basil and in fact borrowed from him.[22] Therefore, as Gribomont said, Garnier's arguments "retain little usefulness today."[23] Nonetheless, since Garnier's opinion about *Ps14a* is frequently found in older but common handbooks, it has persisted until the present.[24]

When J.-P. Migne reprinted Garnier's edition, he placed *Ps14a* among Basil's genuine works, for two reasons.[25] First, it was ascribed to Basil in ancient manuscripts. Second, the opening words of *Ps14b* (which is indisputably genuine) allude to his earlier homily on the same Psalm. Gribomont, Bernardi, and Fedwick have agreed with Migne's assessment of the homily's authenticity.[26] More recently, it has been shown that *Ps14a* is widely attested in the best manuscripts of Basil's homilies.[27] And so, today nothing within the homily itself nor within the manuscript tradition suggests that Basil is not its author.

Context and Date. The homily itself does not contain any details that would allow us to reconstruct its original context and date with any certainty. Nonetheless, the inquiry into the context and date of *Ps14a* must proceed in tandem with those of *Ps14b*, since they were preached on consecutive days. Jean Bernardi thought that most of the homilies on the Psalms could be dated to the years just before

[22]*In Tomum 29*, 8 and 10.

[23]*In Tomum 29*, 8.

[24]E.g., J. Tixeront, *A Handbook of Patrology* (St Louis / London: Herder, 1920), 171; Berthold Altaner, *Patrology* (Freiburg: Herder, 1960), 339; Johannes Quasten, *Patrology, Vol. 3* (Westminster, MD: Newman Press, 1960), 218. Furthermore, *Ps14a* was omitted in the only English translation of the homilies on the Psalms: Agnes Clare Way, *Saint Basil: Exegetic Homilies*, FOTC 46 (Washington, DC: The Catholic University of America Press, 1963).

[25]PG 29.249 note (a).

[26]*In Tomum 29*, 10; Jean Bernardi, *La prédication des pères cappadociens* (Paris: Presses universitaires de France, 1968), 22–3; Paul Jonathan Fedwick, "A Chronology of the Life and Works of Basil of Caesarea," in idem, ed., *Basil of Caesarea: Christian, Humanist, Ascetic. A Sixteen-Hundredth Anniversary Symposium* (Toronto: The Pontifical Institute of Mediaeval Studies, 1981), 3–19 at 10.

[27]BBV ii.1008–11.

and just after Basil became the bishop of Caesarea, that is, 368–372. His method was to detect in certain passages veiled or at least vague allusions to current events or Basil's current situation. Once these historical circumstances in which the homily was preached were discerned, they could then be used to assign a date.

Bernardi found ample material for this methodology in the two homilies on Psalm 14. At *Ps14b* 3, Basil says: "We poor men differ from the rich in this one thing: freedom from care."[28] Bernardi endorsed Maran's view that this line indicates that Basil was still a presbyter since he seems still not burdened with distributing sustenance to the needy, as he would be as a bishop.[29] Bernardi clarified the situation more concretely: Basil was yet to be involved in either raising funds for the Basiliad or the quarrels that ensued because of this. In addition, based on the passage about the distribution of alms and the care of the needy in *Ps14a* 6, Bernardi suggested that the processes described by Basil do not exhibit the level of organization that would later characterize the Basiliad. According to Bernardi, then, both homilies on Psalm 14 should be dated to before Basil's episcopacy, or at least before 372, when land was granted to build the Basiliad.

As can be seen from this example, Bernardi's arguments for dating are tenuous. Jean Gribomont has pointed out that Basil himself makes no clear reference to external events, and that the statements of Basil used by Bernardi as evidence do not require the specific historical circumstances adduced. In other words, nothing in the homily is specific enough to warrant detecting an allusion to a current event or personal situation. These statements of Basil are too vague and general to bear the evidentiary weight that Bernardi wants to impose on them.[30] They remain possible but are ultimately unprovable conjectures. Paul Jonathan Fedwick appears to agree

[28]PG 29.273.

[29]Maran, *Vita S. Basilii* 41.4 (De Sinner iii.ccxxxviii; PG 29.clxiv); Bernardi, *La prédication*, 24–5.

[30]Jean Gribomont, "Notes bibliographiques s. Basile le Grand," in Fedwick, *Basil of Caesarea: Christian, Humanist, Ascetic*, 21–48 at 29–30.

with Gribomont in this regard, as he assigns *Ps14a* broadly to 363–378.[31] Hence all that can be said with confidence is that *Ps14a* was delivered at some point during Basil's ecclesiastical ministry, either as a presbyter or as a bishop.

Translation. The following translation is based on Julien Garnier's edition as reprinted in De Sinner i.499–507 (=PG 29.249–264).[32] In crafting my translation, I benefited from Garnier's Latin translation and the excerpt translated into English by Blomfield Jackson.[33]

Translation

1 *Lord, who shall sojourn in your tent? And who shall dwell on your holy mountain?* [Ps 14.1]. Scripture, when it wished to describe for us the perfect man who would attain blessedness, employed a particular order and method in the treatment of the points about him to be observed, starting with those most pertinent and primary: *Lord, who shall sojourn in your tent?* [Ps 14.1]. Sojourning means staying someplace as a temporary resident. It does not indicate living someplace permanently, but rather transitionally in the hope of migrating to a better place. Now a holy man lives this life transitionally and hastens to live the other life.[1] Thus even David says of himself: *I am a sojourner in your house, a pilgrim, like my fathers* [Ps 38.13]. For Abraham was a sojourner. Not even a foot's length of his own land did he possess. But when he needed a tomb for himself, it appears that he bought one with silver.[2] Here Scripture shows that it is fitting for a person to be a sojourner so long as he lives in the flesh, but he rests in his very own place when he passes from this life. Therefore,

[31]"A Chronology," 10.
[32]CPG 2836.
[33]Blomfield Jackson, "Prolegomena. Sketch of the Life and Works of Saint Basil," NPNF 2.8, xlvi–xlvii.

[1]That is, eternal life.
[2]See Gen 23.16; Acts 7.16.

in this life he sojourns with foreigners, but in the tomb the plot of land he bought for himself to receive his corpse is his very own.

Blessed indeed it is neither to grow attached to what is on earth as if it were our very own, nor to cling to things here as if they belonged to our natural homeland! Blessed instead it is to be aware that we have fallen away from better things and, weighed down by our condemnation to life here, to sojourn like those whom judges have exiled from the land of their birth into foreign lands because of their crimes. It is rare however for someone to relate to present goods as if they were not his very own, to know that the enjoyment of riches is temporary, to realize that the body's health lasts for but a short time, to know that the flower of human renown quickly fades away.

So then, *who shall sojourn in your tent?* What is here called God's tent is the flesh given by God to the soul of a human being as a place of habitation.[3] "Who shall relate to this flesh as if it were foreign?"[4] Just as sojourners hired in a foreign land cultivate the field according to the wishes of the lessor, so too are we entrusted with the care of our flesh under a contract, whereby we are obligated to care for it properly through a labor of love so that we may return it to the Giver fruitful. And if the flesh is worthy of God, it truly becomes a tent of God insofar as it is his place of habitation in the saints. Such then is the sojourner's flesh. Therefore, *Lord, who shall sojourn in your tent?*

Then comes the way of advancing forward to what is more perfect: *And who shall dwell on your holy mountain?* Now when an earthly Jew hears the word "mountain," he runs off to Zion. *Who shall dwell on your holy mountain?* He who has sojourned in the flesh shall dwell on the holy mountain. This mountain is the heavenly country, splendid and radiant, of which the Apostle says: *You have come to*

---

[3]See *Ps28* 1, where Basil gives the same interpretation of the tent as the human body.

[4]This interrogative sentence seems to be Basil's interpretive paraphrase of the question, *Who shall sojourn in your tent?*

Mount Zion and to the city of the living God, the heavenly Jerusalem, in which there is a festal gathering of angels and the assembly *of the firstborn, who are enrolled in heaven* [Heb 12.22].[5]

2   So then, if someone transcends this flesh, sojourning undisturbed by the passions as if this flesh were foreign to him, and if he is not attached to it as if it were his very own, then on account of the mortification of his members upon the earth[6] and his acquisition of holiness he is worthy of dwelling on the holy mountain. Desiring to dwell there the Psalmist said: *I shall go over to the place of the wonderful dwelling-place* [Ps 41.5], and: *How lovely are your dwelling-places, Lord of hosts!* [Ps 83.2]. Both friendship with neighbors for the sake of dwelling on the mountain and friendship born of the mammon of iniquity enable us to dwell there. *Make friends for yourself of the mammon of iniquity, so that when you fail they may receive you into the eternal dwelling-places* [Lk 16.9].[7] While praying, the Lord spoke of the way of life there: "Holy Father, grant that where I am they too may be."[8] It is rare for someone to both sojourn in the body and dwell on the mountain. Therefore, Scripture says as if puzzled: *Who shall sojourn? Who shall dwell?*, just as it does in these passages: *Who has known the mind of the Lord?* [Is 40.13], and: *Who shall tell you that the fire is kindled? Who shall tell you of the eternal place?* [Is 33.14], and: *Who then is the faithful and prudent steward?* [Lk 12.42].

Now the *who* is interrogative, as if perhaps someone is seeking an answer from the holy Lord, to whom the question is directed. What does the divine voice say to him in reply to the question? *He who walks without fault and he who acts with justice* [Ps 14.2]. If he who

[5]The distinction between the transitoriness of sojourning in the tent and the permanence of dwelling on the holy mountain is also found in the Origenian *Tractatus in psalmum xiv* of Jerome. But here the "tent" is not interpreted as the human body, but as the church.

[6]See Col 3.5.

[7]Basil has altered the scriptural text from *it fails* to *you fail*.

[8]See Jn 17.11; 14.3.

is *without fault* lacks none of the goods[9] and passes his life free from every vice without ever stumbling, how is he different from the one who *acts with justice*? So then, is the same sense conveyed by both clauses: *He who walks without fault and he who acts with justice*? Or does each of the clauses communicate a distinct meaning? It is the latter: he who is *without fault* has achieved every perfection of virtue in his inward man, but he who *acts with justice* perfects his active life through corporeal works. For it is fitting not only to perform just deeds, but also to act from a just inner disposition. This is in line with the saying: *Pursue what is just with justice* [Deut 16.20]—that is, "Perform deeds based on the principle of justice." For example, when a layman makes a medicine conducive for helping the sick, he does not make it as a physician would, a consequence of his not knowing anything about the art of medicine when he did it. So then, *he who walks without fault* is perfect in his mind, whereas *he who acts with justice* is, according to the voice of the Apostle, *a workman of the Lord who has no need to be ashamed* [2 Tim 2.15].   **3**   Now be attentive to the precision of the wording. It did not say, "he who walked without fault," but *he who walks without fault*. Nor did it say, "he who acted with justice," but *he who acts*. For it is not a single deed that perfects the good man, but he must perform virtuous actions throughout his entire life.

He who speaks the truth in his heart, who has not practiced deceit with his tongue [Ps 14.2–3].[10] Here again the two phrases, "to speak the truth in the heart" and "not to practice deceit with his tongue," have the same connection with each other that "to be without fault" has with "to act with justice." Just as in the previous passage Scripture is speaking of the person who is both inwardly perfect and does good in the active life, so too it is in this passage. Since what a person says comes *from the abundance of the heart* [Mt 12.34; Lk 6.45], given

[9]That is, the virtues.

[10]Elsewhere Basil defines "deceit" (δόλος) as "contrived plotting, whenever one puts on a show of something good and sets this before another as bait, and thereby achieves the goals of his plot" (*Reg. brev.* 77), and "hidden wrongdoing done to the neighbor under the pretense of better things" (*Ps33* 9).

that the spoken word flows from one's inner disposition as if from a spring, this passage first speaks about the truth in the heart, then about lack of deceit in the speech effected through the tongue.

We will find that there are two meanings of truth. On the one hand, truth is the comprehension of the realities conducive to the blessed life. On the other hand, truth is the sound understanding of whatever pertains to this life. So then, that truth which is the co-worker of salvation in the heart of the perfect man[11] must be transmitted to the neighbor without deceit in every circumstance. But as for that truth which pertains to realities in this life, if the good man were ever to fall away from it, nothing would hinder him from pursuing the goal set before him. For how many miles are there of land or sea? How many stars move? By how much does one speed ahead of the other? If we were not to know the truth about these things, it would be no hindrance to us in attaining the promised blessedness.

And perhaps Scripture also declares these things to us because it is not appropriate for what pertains to the truth—that is, the mystical doctrines—to be told to just anyone, but only to the neighbor.[12] In other words, it is not appropriate to divulge them to whoever happens to be around, but only to those who have come to share in the mysteries. For if our Lord is truth,[13] each of us should have this truth impressed and as it were sealed upon his heart; speaking to ourselves about it in our hearts, we should not practice deceit when announcing and proclaiming the word of the gospel to our neighbors. *He who has not practiced deceit with his tongue.* In many passages of Scripture deceit is reproached as the enemy of God. It says: *May the Lord destroy all deceitful lips* [Ps 11.4]. And: *Deceit is in the heart of those who devise evil* [Prov 12.20]. Now we are said to be deceived about any good thing when it is mixed with something worse. Just as we are deceived about wine when it is adulterated with something worse or diluted with water, and we are deceived about gold when

[11]Cf. Rom 8.28.
[12]Cf. Eph 4.25.
[13]See Jn 14.6.

it is alloyed with silver and copper, so too we are deceived about the truth when blasphemies are mingled with holy words.

4 *He who has not wronged his neighbor in any way* [Ps 14.3]. Whom does Scripture say is our neighbor? No one doubts the reply given in the gospel to the person who asked: *And who is my neighbor?* [Lk 10.29]. It was to this person that the Lord told the parable of the man coming down from Jerusalem to Jericho. The Lord asked him: *Which of these seems to you to have been the neighbor?* [Lk 10.36]. And he responded: *The one who showed mercy to him* [Lk 10.37]. By these words in fact he taught that every human being is to be thought of as our neighbor. Now this is something hard to do. And we must take great care not to mistreat our neighbor in matters small and great, not to hurt him by our words, not to deprive him of any of his possessions, not to wish him evil, not to be jealous of the successes of our neighbors.[14]

Nor taken reproach with regard to his neighbors [Ps 14.3]. The wording here is ambiguous.[15] Either he did not do anything that merited being reproached by his neighbors and thus "he has not taken reproach from them,"[16] or he did not reproach any of his neighbors when human misfortune came upon them, when they were stricken by corporeal disabilities or some other deficiencies of the flesh. Indeed, not even the sinner ought be reproached, according to what is written: *Do not reproach a man who is turning away from sin* [Sir 8.5]. Nor have we ever known of a case when reproach benefited the sinner. For in his instructions to his disciple Timothy,

[14]The use of the Lukan parable of the man coming down from Jerusalem to Jericho to clarify who is our neighbor is also found in the Origenian *Tractatus in psalmum xiv* of Jerome.

[15]Gk. καὶ ὀνειδισμὸν οὐκ ἔλαβεν ἐπὶ τοὺς ἔγγιστα αὐτοῦ. The ambiguity of this sentence, which the translation tries to capture, seems in Basil's mind to result from the question whether the verb ἔλαβεν plus the preposition ἐπὶ should be taken in a passive or an active sense. In other words, either he has not *taken* (i.e., received) reproach *from* his neighbors, or he has not *taken up* reproach *against* his neighbors.

[16]This is the interpretation found in the Origenian *Tractatus in psalmum xiv* of Jerome.

the Apostle turned to rebuke and encouragement and reproof, but nowhere did he resort to reproach as if it were contrary to these.[17] And it seems that while rebuking has the goal of correcting the sinner, reproach is meant to disgrace the fallen sinner. Now as for reproaching poverty, low birth, ignorance, or physical disability, this is utterly irrational and alien to the virtuous man. For whatever we did not choose to happen to us is involuntary. And in the case of involuntary disadvantages, it is appropriate to show mercy to the unfortunate rather than to mistreat them.

5   *In his sight a worker of wickedness is held in disdain, but he honors those who fear the Lord* [Ps 14.4]. Apportioning to each what he is due is a trait of a noble mind unfettered in any way by human necessity and in possession of the highest state of justice possible for a man. He holds workers of wickedness in disdain, even if they have acquired positions of great power, even if they abound in riches, even if they belong to a distinguished family, even if they claim to be high and mighty. Based solely on whether he detects wickedness in them does he hold such people in disdain, that is, he counts them as nothing. In contrast, those who fear the Lord, even if they are poor, even if they are low born, even if they are untrained in proper speech, even if they have physical disabilities, he honors and exalts and considers blessed, since the Spirit taught him to call such people blessed: *Blessed are all who fear the Lord* [Ps 127.1]. It is a trait of one and the same mind both to hold the worker of wickedness in disdain, even if he is exalted to a high and mighty position, and to honor the one who fears the Lord, even if he is unimportant, even if he is poor in life, even if he is contemptible, even if he owns nothing that would elicit admiration.

He who swears an oath to his neighbor and does not repudiate him [Ps 14.4]. Why does swearing good oaths here in this passage find a place among the brave deeds appropriate for the perfect man, but in the gospel such a thing is altogether forbidden? *Who shall sojourn,*

17See 2 Tim 4.2; cf. 1 Tim 4.13; 5.20.

and who shall dwell? He who swears an oath to his neighbor and does not repudiate him. But in the gospel it says: *But I say to you, do not swear an oath at all* [Mt 5.34]. So then, what do we say? We say that the Lord has the same intention[18] everywhere, guarding against sins before they are committed and cutting off wickedness from the moment it arises. For example, the ancient law said, *You shall not commit adultery* [Ex 20.13], but the Lord said, "You shall not lust."[19] Similarly, it said, *You shall not murder* [Ex 20.15], but he prescribed something more perfect, saying, "You shall not get angry."[20] The same situation obtains in the present case too: the first passage is happy with good oaths, but the other eliminates the very possibility of perjury. For he who swears a good oath may still at some point be betrayed against his will, whereas he who does not swear an oath at all completely eliminates the danger of perjury.

Now in many passages what he calls an oath is the unwavering confirmation of some fact. For example: *I have sworn an oath and made up my mind to obey the ordinances of your justice* [Ps 118.106]. And: *The Lord has sworn an oath and he will not change* [Ps 109.4]. Here David did not bring in God to testify to his statements and remove doubts about his reliability, but rather God confirmed the grace promised to David with unshakeable and unalterable decrees. So then, this passage can also be taken in the same way: *He who swears an oath to his neighbor.* In other words, he provides confirmation for his neighbor and does not repudiate him. And this agrees with what the Lord said: *Let what you say be "Yes, yes", "No, no"* [Mt 5.37]. Confirm facts such as these with a gesture of assent. Never let yourself be persuaded, even if everybody were to urge you, to confirm what is not the case in contradiction to the truth of the matter. What is not fact must be followed by a denial; what is fact must be confirmed with assent. Try to speak the very truth of the matter without entangling it in something else, using simple confirmations.

[18]Gk. σκοπός.
[19]See Mt 5.27–28.
[20]See Mt 5.21–22.

Let the untrustworthy person have the damage incurred by his untrustworthiness. For it is altogether disgraceful and foolish to accuse yourself of being unworthy of trust and to assert that security comes from oaths.

Now there are certain expressions which have the form of oaths but are not actually oaths; rather, they are meant to show respect to the audience. For example, when Joseph was trying to win over the Egyptians, he swore an oath *by the health of Pharaoh!* [Gen 42.15]. And when the Apostle was telling the Corinthians about his love for them, he said: *By my pride in you which I have in Christ Jesus our Lord!* [1 Cor 15.31].[21] Now he who believed the gospel did not contravene the gospel's teaching. Rather, he used a simple statement in the form of an oath to show his pride in them, as if he valued them most of all.

6   *Give to everyone who begs from you, and do not refuse anyone who wants to borrow from you* [Mt 5.42]. Scripture exhorts us to community, mutual charity, and what is proper to our nature. For a human being is a civic and social animal.[22] Because our life is communal and we pass our lives with one another, generosity in improving the lot of those in need is necessary. *Give to everyone who begs from you.* He wants you, out of charity, to give liberally to those who beg, but then again, to reckon and discern the need of each one who begs. And in Acts we learned how to do this successfully from those experts in fulfilling the goal of piety: *As many as were possessors of lands or houses sold them, and brought the proceeds of what was sold and laid it at the apostles' feet; and they distributed to each as any had need* [Acts 4.34–35]. Many people who consume necessities in excessive amounts see begging as an opportunity for exploiting others and an excuse for shameless self-indulgence. Accordingly those entrusted with the care of the poor had to gather funds, so that from

[21]Both Gen 42.15 and 1 Cor 15.31 employ νή ("by"), an adverb of asseveration commonly used in oaths.
[22]See Aristotle, *Politics* 1253a2.

these resources necessities could be distributed in a prudent and well-regulated manner according to the needs of each. The sick often have a need for wine, but not everyone can estimate the frequency, amount, and quality of the wine needed. So it is the physician who needs to dispense the wine. Likewise, not everyone can provide care for those in need in a beneficial manner. Indeed, there is absolutely no benefit in giving generous aid to those who compose songs of woe to deceive women and display the body's mutilated limbs and sores as an opportunity for exploiting others. For the abundance given to them will become an opportunity for doing wrong. Instead we must drive away the barking of such people by giving in small amounts, and we must show compassion and brotherly love to those who have been taught to bear affliction with patience.[23] To any who do this it will be said: *I was hungry and you gave me something to eat* [Mt 5.35], and the rest.[24]

And do not refuse anyone who wants to borrow from you [Mt 5.42]. This instruction is in line with the previous one. Indeed, whoever begs in this life because he is poor is begging you to give him a loan; he is showing you the riches in heaven and absolves you of your debt on his own behalf. For *whoever shows mercy to the poor lends to God* [Prov 19.17]. The kingdom of heaven is the security for the loan.[25] May all of us be worthy of this, by the grace of our Lord Jesus Christ and his love for humanity, with whom, to the Father, and to the Holy Spirit *be glory and might for ever and ever. Amen* [1 Pet 4.11].

[23]See Rom 5.3; 2 Cor 1.6 and 6.4; 2 Thess 1.4.

[24]Similar advice about cautious almsgiving can also be found in *Reg. brev.* 100–101 and *Ep.* 150.3.

[25]On the theme of almsgiving as "loans" to the poor, see also *Fam* 6 and *Ps14b* 5.

Homily on Humility

INTRODUCTION

Humility is a quintessential Christian virtue, but not all humility is virtuous. Humility characterizes those who are dependent upon others, such as the poor, the needy, the suffering, and the oppressed. Living thus in humble conditions is not in itself a virtue. Humility becomes virtuous when dependence on God is acknowledged and indeed rejoiced in, when God is praised as the giver and sustainer of all that we have received and will receive. On the spectrum on Christian virtue and vice, humility stands diametrically opposed to pride. At its core, pride is egocentricity, viewing ourselves as the source of all that is good in our life and seeing in our achievements the proof that we are better than others. The proud person lacks the capacity recognize God's gifts in his or her life.[1]

Humility is also a uniquely Christian virtue. In the Greco-Roman world, humility was considered a sign of weakness or a personal flaw, and the humble were easily scorned and ignored. In contrast, Christianity placed great value on humility. In the gospels Jesus is often depicted as exhorting to humility and denouncing any form of pride.[2] One of the most famous sayings attributed to Jesus on this topic is: *Whoever exalts himself will be humbled and whoever humbles himself will be exalted.* This saying is found (with slight variations in the wording) in both Matthew and Luke, but not in

---

[1]On the Christian concept of humility, see G. Gilleman, "Humility" in NCE 7: 205–207; B. Dolhagaray, "Humilité," DThC 7:321–329; Pierre Adnès, "Humilité" in DSpir 7:1136–87; A. Dihle, "Demut" in RAC 3:735–778; Karl-Heinz zur Mühlen, "Demut" in TRE 8:459–483.

[2]E.g., Mt 5.5, 18.4.

Mark; thus advocates of the Two-Source Hypothesis claim that Matthew and Luke derived this saying from Q, the now-lost collection of Jesus' sayings. Whether this saying records the actual words of Jesus or not, the teaching it contains is related to, and may be based upon, Proverbs 3.34: *God resists the proud but he gives grace to the humble.* This proverb was later cited in James and 1 Peter, where it is used as the basis for an exhortation to humble yourself so that God may exalt you.[3] In the gospels, however, the saying is employed as a summation of the reasons why Jesus censures the Pharisees (Mt 23.12; Lk 14.11; 18.14). Perhaps the saying is most memorably employed in the parable of the Pharisee and tax-collector (Lk 14.7–11). Here the repentant tax-collector's humble begging for mercy and acknowledgement of his need for God, rather than the Pharisee's proud piety, is presented as bringing righteousness in God's sight. Yet in the New Testament, Jesus is depicted as a teacher of humility not only in word but also in deed.[4] Matthew even portrays Jesus as calling himself *meek and humble of heart* (Mt 11.29). Paul presents Jesus as the exemplar of Christian humility, of humbling oneself in order to be exalted by God, in the christological hymn of Phil 2.5–11: though Christ *was in the form of God . . . ,* he *emptied himself, taking on the form of a servant . . . ,* and he *humbled himself and became obedient unto death, even death on a cross. Therefore God has highly exalted him and bestowed on his the name which is above every name . . . .* Paul's words here express the paradox at the heart of the Christian notion of humility: it is the only pathway to true greatness. As for Christ, so for the Christian: only voluntary humility brings true exaltation. This centrality of humility for a life of Christian virtue and the exemplary humility of Jesus himself is a constant theme of patristic literature.

Though this homily is entitled *On Humility*, it is as much, if not more, about pride.[5] But this should come as no surprise, since it is

[3]Jas 4.6, 10; 1 Pet 5.5–6.

[4]E.g., Jesus' washing of his disciples' feet (Jn 13.5).

[5]Gk. περὶ ταπεινοφροσύνης. In some mss there is an alternate title, *How one must be self-controlled* (πῶς δεῖ σωφρονεῖν). Other mss combine the two, e.g., *On*

a perennial pedagogical technique to exhort to a particular virtue by contrasting it with its opposite vice.[6] In this homily Basil situates humility and pride within the economy of salvation, both rhetorically and theologically. He opens and closes his discourse with the idea that humility restores fallen human beings to the glory they once possessed from God but lost through pride. And so, humility is presented not as one virtue among others that characterizes the Christian life, but as the supreme virtue necessary for salvation, which is achieved by imitating the humble Christ in his saving economy.

Basil views pride as the cause of the fall of Adam and Eve in the Garden of Eden, when they forsook the true glory which they possessed from God and sought to win glory through themselves (§1). But in seeking to attain this false glory, they lost their true glory. Hence humility is the remedy for the human pride that precipitated the fall, whereby humanity can return to true glory. The devil, however, thwarts this pathway to restoration by continuing to entice human beings with the same hope for false glory, with the same temptations to pride. Basil then reviews the various temptations employed by the devil: money and the sumptuous lifestyle that it enables, privileged rank in the community, and even one's physical capacities and beauty (§1–2). Even those human gifts which would seem to be most immune to pride—wisdom and prudence—can lead to it (§2). Here Basil provides several scriptural examples of demonic and human wisdom fostering pride, backfiring, and ultimately bringing destruction: the devil himself, Pharaoh, Abimelech, and the Jews who killed Jesus. Yet at the same time there is a proper way to be proud, namely, if one boasts in God and not in oneself (§3). True greatness lies not in self-exaltation but in recognizing God

humility and how one must be self-controlled. Nonetheless, the most primitive title is *On humility.* See BBV ii.1079.

[6]This technique is perhaps most memorably employed in St Bernard of Clairvaux's *The Steps of Humility and Pride.* See the translation of M. Ambrose Conway in *The Steps of Humility and Pride*, Cistercian Fathers Series 13A (Kalamazoo: Cistercian Publications, 1989).

as the giver of all our blessings. Once again Basil supplies several scriptural examples of the failure to acknowledge God thus (§4). His two most important examples are Peter's over-confidence, which led to his threefold denial of Jesus, and the Pharisee of Luke 18.11–14. The parable of the Pharisee and the tax-collector leads Basil to warn against exalting oneself above others (§5). Nothing we do, not even confessing Christ or enduring exile for the sake of his name in time of persecution, not even ascetical prowess, should be taken as an occasion for thinking ourselves greater than our neighbor. That was the trap into which devil and the Israelites fell.

After this, Basil turns his attention more explicitly to the theme of humility. He begins by connecting Proverbs 3.34 and Luke 14.11 as summations of the scriptural teaching about humility (§5). Basil admonishes his listeners to judge themselves humbly, that is, not to gloss over their misdeeds while exalting themselves on account of their accomplishments. Neither should the sins of our neighbors lead us to exalt ourselves over them. A more thorough examination often reveals that they have a habit of doing good and in fact are better than we are. Next, though Basil does not directly cite or allude to Paul's christological hymn, he considers every aspect of the Lord's earthly existence as an object lesson in humility (§6). The earliest disciples displayed a similar humility and therefore are also worthy of imitation. The homily concludes with concrete recommendations for the practice of humility (§7). While humility is a quality of the soul (an interior disposition), it is cultivated by manifesting it in our comportment and interactions with others. Only when humility is loved will it become the pathway that restores a person to that true greatness and glory which comes from God, which we lost in Adam through pride.

In Greek as in English, humility and pride are conceptualized in terms of "low" and "high." Humility connotes lowliness and abasement, whereas pride loftiness and grandeur. Basil employs a rich vocabulary for humility and pride rooted in these connotations. His preferred terms for "humility"—*tapeinotēs* and *tapeinophrosunē* (literally, "humble-mindedness")—are based on the adjective *tapeinos* ("low, humbled, humble") and cognate with the verb *tapeinoō* ("to lower, humble"). His typical terminology for pride is more varied: "to be haughty" and "haughtiness" (from the verb *epairō*, "to raise up"); "to exalt oneself" and "exaltation" (from the verb *hupsoō*, "to heighten, elevate"); "to be cocky" and "cockiness" (from the verb *thrasunō*, which when used in a bad sense means "to be rash, overconfident, presumptuous"); "arrogance" (*alazoneia*, "bragging, vain boasting"); and "pride" (*huperēphania*, "being conspicuous above others"). While most of this vocabulary has scriptural precedent (particularly the contrast between humbling oneself and exalting oneself; see Mt 23.12; Lk 1.52; 14.11; 18.14; Phil 2.8–9; Jas 4.10; 1 Pet 5.6), Basil also draws upon the wider resources available to him from Greek literature.

Authenticity. The authenticity of this homily is certain and has never been doubted.[7] It is widely attested in the best manuscripts of Basil's homilies.[8] Nothing within the homily itself suggests that Basil is not its author.

Context and Date. There is little in this homily that is helpful for determining its original context and date. It is clear enough that Basil's audience included local elites of Caesarea, not only the rich, but also dignitaries, as both riches and political power are identified as temptations to pride in the homily. Bernardi situates this homily in the period of Basil's presbyteral ministry (362–370), seeing it as typical of Basil's preaching of social justice, which won him great popularity among the masses but led to resistance to him on the part of elites when he was elected bishop.[9] Humility, however, was surely a topic on which Basil frequently preached, and nothing precludes this homily in its present form from being a final version attained through years of

[7]Jean Gribomont, *In Tomum 31 Patrologiae graecae ad editionem operum rhetoricorum, asceticorum, liturgicorum Sancti Basili Magni Introductio* (Turnhout: Brepols, 1961), 6.

[8]See BBV ii.1079–82.

[9]Jean Bernardi, *La prédication des pères cappadociens* (Paris: Presses universitaires de France, 1968), 66–7.

revision.[10] Therefore, this homily cannot be dated more precisely than to the entire span of Basil's ecclesiastical ministry, 362–378.

Translation. The following translation is based on Julien Garnier's edition as reprinted in De Sinner ii.220–228 (=PG 31.526–539).[11] In crafting my translation, I benefited from Garnier's Latin translation and Sister M. Monica Wagner's English translation of the homily in the Fathers of the Church series,[12] as well as from the excerpt translated into English by Blomfield Jackson.[13]

TRANSLATION

1   Man[1] ought to have abided in the glory he possessed from God. Indeed, he would have possessed an exaltation that was genuine rather than false, being magnified by God's power, made illustrious by divine wisdom, gladdened by everlasting life and its blessings. But since he set aside his desire for divine glory, looking for something better and striving for what he could not attain, he lost what he could possess. And so, the greatest salvation for him, both the remedy for his illness and the road back to his original state, is humility,[2] not imagining that the ornament of glory is attained through himself but seeking it instead from God. For in this way he will correct his fault; in this way he will be cured of his illness; in this way he will return to the sacred commandment which he forsook.

[10]See Paul Jonathan Fedwick, "A Chronology of the Life and Works of Basil of Caesarea," in idem, ed., *Basil of Caesarea: Christian, Humanist, Ascetic. A Sixteen-Hundredth Anniversary Symposium* (Toronto: The Pontifical Institute of Mediaeval Studies, 1981), 3–19 at 9 n. 31.

[11]CPG 2865.

[12]M. Monica Wagner, *Saint Basil: Ascetical Works*, FOTC 9 (New York: The Fathers of the Church, Inc., 1950), 475–486.

[13]"Prolegomena. Sketch of the Life and Works of Saint Basil," NPNF 2.8, lxv.

[1]Gk. ἄνθρωπος, literally, "human being." Here Basil speaks of Adam as the human being in whom the entire human race fell.

[2]Gk. ἀτυφία, literally, "not being self-conceited." This is the only occurrence of this term in this homily.

But the devil, having overthrown the man by getting him to hope for false glory, never rests from luring human beings by the same enticements and devising innumerable schemes for this purpose. For instance, he shows a person an enormous amount of money as something great, to get him to regard it as the means to personal greatness and make every effort to obtain it. Now doing this contributes nothing to his glory, but it does put him in great danger. For acquiring money lays a foundation for avarice and possessing it does nothing for a good reputation. On the contrary, it blinds without purpose, it causes vain haughtiness, and it brings about an affliction in the soul that is much like swelling. For a tumor is neither healthy nor beneficial to swollen bodies, but noxious and harmful, a source of danger, and even a cause of death. Such too is pride in the soul.

Indeed, it is not only money that causes haughtiness to arise. It is not only the fancy food and ostentatious clothing which money buys that causes people to become haughty, those who set their tables with feasts sumptuous far beyond necessity, who drape themselves with superfluous clothing, who build enormous houses and decorate them with beautiful objects, who retain for themselves a great throng of household servants to follow them around, and countless hordes of flatterers. But it is also being selected for positions of distinction that causes people to exalt themselves beyond what is natural. If the populace bestows upon them some distinguished position, if it deems them worthy of some privileged rank, and they are voted to be given some exceptional distinction, then they act as if they have transcended human nature. Not only do they start to think of themselves as seated upon the clouds and regard the people subject to them as their footstool, but they are also haughty to those who bestowed the honor upon them in the first place. Indeed, they are arrogant to those by whose actions they believe they have become persons of great importance! They get themselves involved in a situation which teems with foolishness, since the glory they have is more fleeting than a dream. They are wrapped with a splendor more unreal than the phantasms of the night, since it arose by the decision of the populace and can be dissolved by the decision of the same. Such was that deranged son of Solomon, young in years and in common sense even younger. When the people sought a more gentle rule, he threatened them with an even harsher one. But by making this threat he lost his kingdom. And so, by that very thing by which he expected to be looked upon as even more kingly he was deprived of the dignity that he had.[3]

Furthermore, a person can be cocky on account of the power of his hands and the swiftness of his feet and the elegance of his body—things which are ravaged by illness and plundered by time. Such a person does not realize that *all flesh is grass, and all the glory of man is like the flower of grass; the grass has withered and the flower has fallen* [Is 40.6]. Such was the arrogance of the giants on account of their power.[4] Such was the effrontery of the foolish Goliath, whereby he fought against God.[5] Such was Adonijah, who had a high opinion of himself on account of his beauty.[6] Such too was Absalom, who was haughty on account of his luxuriant hair.[7]

2   Of all the goods possessed by human beings, the one which appears to be the greatest and the most reliable is wisdom and prudence. Yet even this is liable to vain haughtiness and may not result in true exaltation. For these count for nothing when the wisdom that comes from God is lacking. After all, the devil's plot against the man backfired for him. He unwittingly launched against himself the scheme he planned to launch against the man. He did not so much injure the one whom he had hoped to alienate from God and everlasting life, as he betrayed himself, becoming a rebel against God and condemned to everlasting death. And though he set the snare for the Lord, he was caught in it, crucified by that by which he expected to

[3]Here Basil speaks of Rehoboam; see 1 Kgs 12.1–15.
[4]See Wis 14.6.
[5]See Sir 47.4.
[6]See 1 Kgs 1.5f.
[7]See 2 Sam 14.26.

crucify the Lord and put to death by that death by which he hoped to destroy the Lord.

Now if *the ruler of the world* [Jn 12.31, 14.30, 16.11], the primary, greatest, and invisible master of worldly wisdom, was caught in his own snares and brought to utter foolishness, so much more have his disciples and emulators also been. Even though they devised thousands of plots, *claiming to be wise, they became fools* [Rom 1.22]. Pharaoh devised a plot for the destruction of Israel, but unbeknownst to him his plot was foiled in an unexpected manner: an infant who was exposed at his command so that it would die was secretly raised in the royal household, and destroyed his power and that of his whole people, and led Israel out to safety.[8] Furthermore, the murderer Abimelech, the illegitimate son of Gideon, assassinated his father's seventy legitimate sons and, thinking that he had found a clever way to secure his grip on the kingdom, crushed his accomplices in the murder. But then he was crushed by them. For in the end he was destroyed by the hand of a woman and the throwing of a millstone.[9] In addition, all Jews devised a deadly plot against the Lord, saying to themselves: *If we let him go on thus, all will believe in him, and the Romans will come and destroy both our place and our nation* [Jn 11.48]. When they went from just plotting to actually slaying Christ on the supposition that this would preserve their nation and place, they lost both by setting their plan in motion: they were exiled from their place and became strangers to the laws and the worship of God. And in sum, from countless examples anyone can learn that whatever human wisdom achieves is flawed, being insignificant and lowly rather than great and exalted.

3   And so, no one who is prudent will have a high opinion of himself on account of either his own wisdom or the other things mentioned above. Instead, he will comply with the excellent advice offered by the blessed Anna and the prophet Jeremiah: *Let not the*

[8]Gk. σωτηρία. Or, "salvation."
[9]See Judg 9.1–57.

wise man boast in his wisdom, nor the powerful man boast in his power, nor the rich man boast in his riches [Jer 9.23].[10] But what is true boasting? And what makes a person truly great? He says: *Let him who boasts boast in this: that he understands and knows that I am the Lord* [Jer 9.24]. This is what truly exalts a person; this is what truly confers glory and majesty: to know in truth what is great and to cling to it, and to seek the glory which comes from *the Lord of glory* [1 Cor 2.8; Jas 2.1]. The Apostle says: *Let him who boasts boast in the Lord*, when he says: *Christ became for us the wisdom from God, righteousness and sanctification and redemption; therefore, as it is written, "Let him who boasts boast in the Lord"* [1 Cor 1.30–31]. For boasting in God is perfect and unstinting when someone is not haughty on account of his own righteousness, but has come to realize that he lacks true righteousness and is made righteous only by faith in Christ. Indeed, Paul boasts because he despises his own righteousness and seeks *that which comes through Christ,*[11] *the righteousness from God by faith, that he may know him and the power of his resurrection, and may share his sufferings by becoming like him in his death, if somehow he may attain the resurrection of the dead* [Phil 3.9–11].[12] By this is every exaltation of pride laid low.[13] Nothing is left to inflate your arrogance, O man, since your boasting and hope now lies in mortifying yourself in all things and seeking the life to come in Christ. When we have a foretaste of this life to come, we are already doing these things, living entirely by God's grace and his gifts. Indeed, *God is the one who works in us both to will and to work for his good pleasure* [Phil 2.13]. Through his own Spirit, God reveals his wisdom, which is ordained for our glory.[14] God grants efficacy to our toils; Paul says: *I worked harder than all of them, yet not I but the grace of God with me* [1 Cor 15.10]. God also delivers us from

[10]For Anna, see 1 Sam 2.3.

[11]Basil alters the standard text here: *through faith in Christ.*

[12]Basil has slightly altered the verbs in the passage from first-person to third-person singular.

[13]Cf. 2 Cor 10.5.

[14]See 1 Cor 2.7, 10.

dangers when all human hope is lost: *We felt that we had received the sentence of death so that we would not rely on ourselves but on God who raises the dead, who rescued us from so terrible a death and will continue to rescue us; on him we have set our hope that he will rescue us again* [2 Cor 1.9–10].

4 So then, tell me, why are you haughty as if the good things you possess come from yourself, instead of expressing gratitude to the Giver of these gifts? For *what do you have that you did not receive? If then you have received it, why do you boast as if you did not receive it?* [1 Cor 4.7]. You have not come to know God through your righteousness, but God has come to know you through his kindness. He says: *You have come to know God, or rather to be known by God* [Gal 4.9]. You have not embraced Christ through your virtue, but Christ has embraced you through his advent. He says: *I press on, so that I may embrace, since I have been embraced by Christ* [Phil 3.12]. *You did not choose me,* says the Lord, *but I chose you* [Jn 15.16]. Is it because you have been honored that you think highly of yourself and take these acts of mercy as occasions for pride? In that case, know yourself, recognize who you are: Adam banished from paradise,[15] Saul abandoned by the Spirit of God,[16] Israel severed from the holy root.[17] He says: *By faith you have stood firm, do not be proud but fear* [Rom 11.20].

After grace comes judgment, and the judge will examine how you have used the gracious gifts you have received. But if you do not understand that you have obtained grace, but instead through excessive stupidity make this grace into your own accomplishment, then you are acting no more honorably than the blessed Apostle Peter. Indeed, when it is a question of love for the Lord, you will not be able to surpass Peter, who loved the Lord so much that he even wanted to die for him.[18] But he uttered words which bespoke a high

[15]See Gen 3.24.
[16]See 1 Sam 16.14.
[17]Cf. Rom 11.16–18.
[18]See Mk 14.31; Jn 13.37.

opinion of himself, when he said: *Even if all should fall away because of you, I myself nonetheless will never fall away* [Mt 26.33]. Because of this he was delivered over to human cowardice and fell into denying the Lord.[19] Yet this was so that by his lapse he could be recalled to prudent caution and by coming to terms with his own weakness he could learn to be merciful to the weak. And clearly he came to understand that, just as he was lifted up by the right hand of Christ when he was sinking into the sea,[20] so too, when he was in danger of being destroyed by the waves of his falling away through lack of faith, he was protected by the power of Christ, who had told him earlier what would happen, when he said: *Simon, Simon, behold! Satan has demanded to sift you like wheat. But I have prayed for you, that your faith may not fail; and when you have turned again, strengthen your brothers* [Luke 22.31–32]. And thus rebuked Peter was rightly given help, learning to get rid of his arrogance and to be merciful to the weak.

Furthermore, that Pharisee, who was overbearing and excessively proud, who not only was cocky on account of his righteousness but also disparaged the tax-collector who was standing before God, lost the righteousness in which he could boast because of his sin of pride.[21] Indeed, it was the tax-collector rather than the Pharisee who went down [to his house] made righteous. For the tax-collector glorified the holy God and did not even dare to lift up his eyes, but sought only mercy, accusing himself by his posture, by beating his breast, and by seeking nothing other than mercy. So then, see and beware of this example of the painful loss incurred through pride. The Pharisee was deprived of his righteousness by being proud and lost his reward by being cocky. He made himself inferior to that humble and sinful man by exalting himself above him and not awaiting the judgment of God, but instead rendering his own judgment. But as for you, never exalt yourself above anyone, not even above

[19]See Mk 14.66–72; Mt 26.69–75; Lk 22.54–62.
[20]See Mt 14.30–31.
[21]See Lk 18.11–14.

great sinners. It is often the case that humility saves a person who has committed many serious sins. So then, do not make yourself righteous over against another, lest God decide to condemn you for deciding to make yourself righteous. Paul says: *I do not judge myself. For I am not aware of anything against myself, but I am not thereby made righteous. It is the Lord who judges me* [1 Cor 4.3–4].

5   Do you think you have accomplished something good? Give thanks to God lest you exalt yourself above your neighbor. He says: *Let each one test his own work, and then his reason to boast will be in himself alone and not in another* [Gal 6.4]. For how did you help your neighbor when you confessed the faith, or endured exile for the name of Christ, or persevered in the toils of fasting? These bring no benefit to another, but only to you. Beware of falling like the devil. After exalting himself above a human being, he fell by a human being and was delivered over to be trodden upon by the one upon whom he had trodden.[22] Another example is the fall of the Israelites. When they exalted themselves above the nations whom they regarded as unclean, they in fact became unclean, but the nations were made clean: the righteousness of the Israelites became like the rag of a menstruating woman, but the wickedness and impiety of the nations was wiped away through faith.[23]

In general, remember that true proverb: *God resists the proud but he gives grace to the humble* [Prov 3.34]. Keep this word of the Lord near: *Everyone who humbles himself will be exalted and everyone who exalts himself will be humbled* [Lk 14.11].[24] Do not judge yourself with prejudice, nor examine yourself with partiality. If you think you possess some good, do not count this to your credit while purposely overlooking your misdeeds, extolling yourself on account of the good things you accomplished today and pardoning yourself for the bad things you did yesterday and long ago. Instead, whenever the

[22]Cf. Gen 3.14–15.
[23]See Is 64.6.
[24]Note that Basil has reversed the order of the two clauses.

present causes you to exalt yourself, recall the past, and you will put an end to any stupid self-inflation.

And if you see your neighbor sinning, do not take only his sin into consideration. Reflect upon all that he has done or continues to do rightly. It is often the case, when your examination goes through every detail and you do not judge based on partial information, that you will discover that he is better than you. Indeed, not even God examines human beings based on partial information. For he says: *I am coming to gather together their works and thoughts* [Is 66.18]. And when he rebuked Josaphat one time for a sin committed in an unguarded moment, he also remembered the good things he accomplished, saying: *Nonetheless, good words have been found in you* [2 Chr 19.3].

6 These passages, and the others like them, let us always recite to ourselves in order to combat our pride. Let us lower ourselves to exalt ourselves, imitating the Lord who descended from heaven into extreme humility and in turn was raised up from humility to an appropriate exaltation.[25] Indeed, we find that everything the Lord did is a lesson in humility. As an infant, at first he lay in a cave, and not even in a bed but in a manger.[26] In the home of a carpenter and a poor mother, he was subject to his mother and her betrothed.[27] As a student, he listened to what he did not need to learn; even still, he asked questions, and the questions he asked led people to marvel at his wisdom.[28] He submitted to John, and the Master received baptism from his servant.[29] He offered no resistance to anyone who rose up against him, nor did he make use of the indescribable power that he possessed; instead, he yielded to them as if they were more powerful and allowed the temporal authorities to exercise the power given them. He stood before the high priests

[25]Cf. Phil 2.6–11.
[26]See Lk 2.7.
[27]See Lk 2.51.
[28]See Lk 2.46–47.
[29]See Mk 1.9; Mt 3.13–15.

as a condemned criminal,[30] and was led to the governor and subjected to his judgment.[31] And even though he could have rebuked
those who made false accusations against him, he bore their false
accusations in silence.[32] He was spit upon by slaves and worthless
louts.[33] He was delivered up to death—the most shameful death to
be found among human beings. Thus he experienced every stage of
human existence, from birth to death. And after such great humility, only then did he manifest his glory, giving a share of his glory
to those who had glorified him. First among these are his blessed
disciples, who passed through this world poor and naked, without
eloquent wisdom [1 Cor 1.17], without a throng of followers, alone,
and wandering, and solitary, traveling on land and sea, scourged,
stoned, persecuted, and finally killed.[34] These are for us divine
lessons passed down by our fathers. Come, let us imitate them, so
that out of our humility there may arise for us everlasting glory, the
perfect and true gift of Christ.

7   So then, how shall we descend to saving humility and be rid of
the malignant tumor[35] of pride? If we practice humility in everything and do not neglect anything as if no harm could come to us
from it. For the soul grows like what it pursues, and is molded and
shaped according to what it does. Your appearance, and your garments, and your transportation, and your table, and your chairs,
and the style of your meals, and your bed and bedding, and your
house, and the furnishings in your house: all of these should reflect
thrift. And your speaking, and your singing, and your conversations
with your neighbor: these too should look to modesty rather than
to pretentiousness. Please, let there be no sophistical bombast in
your speaking, no cloying sweetness in your singing, no proud and

[30]See Mk 14.60–64; Mt 26.62–66; Lk 22.66–71.
[31]See Mk 15.1–15; Mt 27.11–26; Lk 23.1–25.
[32]See Mk 14.61, 15.5; Mt 26.63, 27.12–14.
[33]See Mk 14.65; 15.19; Mt 26.67; 27.30.
[34]Cf. Heb 11.35–38.
[35]Or, "deadly pretentiousness."

overbearing tone in your discussions. Instead, in everything get rid of pomposity. Be good to your friend, gentle to your servant, patient with the cocky, kind to the humbled. Console the afflicted, visit the distressed, disdain none. Be pleasant when addressing others, cheerful when replying to them, courteous, affable to all. Never sing your own praises, nor get other people to sing them. Never engage in uncivil conversation. Conceal as far as possible your own excellence.

Where sin is concerned, accuse yourself and do not wait for others to rebuke you. Then you will be like *the righteous man who accuses himself at the beginning of his speech* [Prov 18.17]. Then you will be like Job, who was *not deterred by the populous crowd* in the city *from declaring* his own fault *before them* [Job 31.34]. Do not be severe in rebuke. Do not be quick to make accusations nor be emotional when you do so, for this smacks of surliness. Do not condemn in matters of minor importance as if you were perfectly righteous. Receive those who have been caught in a trespass and restore them spiritually, as the Apostle exhorts, *considering yourself, lest you also be tempted* [Gal 6.1].

Make as much effort not to be glorified by others as some people make to be glorified, if you are really mindful of Christ who says that a reward from God is lost by voluntarily seeking renown from other people and doing good to be seen by other people. For he says: *they have received their reward* [Matt 6.2]. Therefore, do not deprive yourself by wanting to be noticed by others. Since God is a great witness, strive for honor with God. For he renders a splendid reward. But have you been deemed worthy of a privileged position? Do people treat you with respect and glorify you? Bring yourself down to the level of your subordinates, *not as lording it over those in your charge* [1 Pet 5.3], nor behaving like worldly rulers. For the Lord bade whoever wishes to be first to be the slave of all.[36]

---

[36]See Mk 10.44.

To sum things up, strive after humility in such a way that you come to love it. Love it and it will glorify you. In this way you will travel the good road leading to glory—that true glory which is found among the angels and with God. Christ will acknowledge you as his own disciple in the presence of his angels, and he will glorify you if you imitate his humility. For he says: *Learn from me, for I am meek and humble in heart, and you will find rest for your souls* [Mt 11.29]. *To him be glory and might for every and ever. Amen* [1 Pet 4.11].

Homily on Envy

INTRODUCTION

Envy can be distinguished from jealousy. Though the two are often used synonymously in English, philosophers, both classical and modern, distinguish them. Greco-Roman philosophers considered both envy and jealousy to be rivalrous or competitive emotions—that is, emotions generated because of some form of rivalry or competition with others.[1] Envy, jealousy, and the other rivalrous emotions were all seen as species of distress (*lypē*). Aristotle had understood envy (*phthonos*) as distress over the prosperity of one's equals in status.[2] The Stoics considered envy more broadly as distress over another's goods, emulation (*zēlos*) as distress over another's having what you desire, and jealousy (*zēlotypia*) as distress over another's desiring what you have.[3] These Stoic terminological distinctions, however, were not always respected: both *zēlos* and *zēlotypia* came to be used for jealousy, and both were also used more or less synonymously with *phthonos* as terms for envy.[4] Thus the semantic confusion between envy and jealousy in English has precedent in ancient Greek. Technically speaking, envy is distress over another having a good that you lack, whereas jealousy is distress

---

[1]See Paul M. Blowers, "Envy's Narrative Scripts. Cyprian, Basil, and the Monastic Sages on the Anatomy and Cure of the Invidious Emotions," *Modern Theology* 25 (2009): 21–43 at 23–5. Also see the essays in David Konstan and N. Keith Rutter, eds., *Envy, Spite and Jealousy: The Rivalrous Emotions in Ancient Greece* (Edinburgh: Edinburgh University Press, 2003).

[2]*Rhetoric* 2.10–11 (1387a–1388b); *Nicomachean Ethics* 2.6 (1107a).

[3]SVF 3.412–416.

[4]See Blowers, "Envy's Narrative Scripts," 25 and 40 nn. 20–21 (with references to further literature).

over the desire to prevent another from taking what you possess. Yet
it is linguistically permissible in English to use the word "jealousy" in
the sense of envy.[5] But it is not a perfect synonym, since "jealousy"
is also used in English in its technical sense, that is, defensiveness
about one's own good.[6]

The Christian concept of envy is twofold. It is the resentment
experienced by one person when another person is perceived to
have some good that he or she lacks, coupled with the strong desire
that the other person be deprived of it.[7] In Latin Christianity, envy
(*invidia*) has long been considered one of the seven deadly sins. This
list was first formulated by Pope St Gregory the Great (+604). But
Gregory himself was revising an earlier monastic list of the eight
principal thoughts or vices that was originally drawn up by Evagrius
of Pontus (+399) and then popularized John Cassian (+435).[8] Envy,
however, does not appear on this earlier list, though of course it
was not unknown to these monastic theologians.[9] Before Evagrius,
Origen had recognized envy as one of the chief sins.[10] Indeed, since
the days of the apostles envy has been seen as a hindrance to the

[5]For example, one can intelligibly say either, "I am envious of your new car," or,
"I am jealous of your new car." In both cases it is clear that the speaker lacks a new
car but desires one.

[6]For example, one can speak of a "jealous God," but not of an "envious God."
While the former is theologically sound, the latter is problematic. Another example:
if a man says, "I become jealous when other men flirt with my girlfriend," it is clear
that he is distressed over losing her to a rival for her affections. But the same man
would not say, "I become envious when other men flirt with my girlfriend," since the
meaning of this sentence is not equivalent to the first and in fact is not clear at all
without further context.

[7]On the Christian concept of envy, see W. Herbst, "Envy," in NCE 5:269; L. Des-
brus, "Envie," in DThC 5.1:131–134; Édouard Ranwez, "Envie," in DSpir 4.1:774–785;
and Karl-Heinz Nusser, "Neid," in TRE 24:246–254.

[8]Gregory, *Moralia* 31.45; Evagrius, *Praktikos* 6–14; Cassian, *Institutes*, Books
5–12.

[9]E.g., Evagrius, *To Eulogios* 17.18; *On the Vices opposed to the Virtues* 8. In the
latter, Evagrius adds jealousy as the ninth principal thought to the eight. See also
Cassian, *Conferences* 18.15–16.

[10]Irénée Hausherr, "L'origine de la théorie orientale des huit péchés capitaux,"
Orientalia Christiana Periodica 3 (1933): 164–75.

Christian life.[11] Nonetheless, while the evangelists present Jesus as aware of the envy of his opponents, they do not attribute to him any specific teaching on the vice.[12] In fact, nowhere in the Old and New Testaments is envy itself ever the focus of attention. Yet in spite of lack of a scriptural teaching on envy, it became a key concept in early Christianity. The Church Fathers often cite Scripture to lend authority to their teaching on envy, but its real basis is to be found in Greek literature and philosophy.[13]

That Basil would devote an entire homily to envy is perhaps the result of the specific audience for which Basil wrote. Vasiliki Limberis has suggested that the particular socio-economic situation of Caesarea fostered fierce rivalry for various honors which were in limited supply.[14] In Basil's world, much like our own, there was intense competition among the elites of society for prestige based on external achievements, for example, wealth and its trappings, political power, oratorical pre-eminence, and even physical vigor and good looks. It was a culture in which wealth was conspicuous and ostentatious, in which prosperity and renown were counted among the highest goods. This spirit of competition pervaded the whole of society from top to bottom. No matter how insignificant the stakes, any chance to elevate oneself above others was deemed worth the effort. The Christians of Cappadocia were not immune to this all-pervading spirit, regardless of whether they were financially blessed or deprived, politically powerful or voiceless, or socially prominent or obscure. And so, it is not surprising, given this environment, that some of the Christians for whom Basil exercised pastoral care had succumbed to envy, deeming enviable the good fortune of their

[11]See e.g., Rom 13.13; 1 Cor 3.3; 2 Cor 12.20; Gal 5.20–21, 5.26; 1 Tim 6.4; Titus 3.3; Jas 3.14, 3.16; 1 Pet 2.1; *Didache* 5.1.

[12]See Mt 27.18; Mk 15.10; see also Acts 5.17, 13.45, 17.5.

[13]Matthew W. Dickie, "Envy" in ABD 2:529–32. On Basil's indebtedness to Greco-Roman philosophy in his treatment of envy, see pp. 125–126 below.

[14]See Vasiliki Limberis, "The Eyes Infected by Evil: Basil of Caesarea's Homily, On Envy," *Harvard Theological Review* 84 (1991): 163–84 at 169–75. See also Blowers, "Envy's Narrative Scripts," 26.

neighbors, bitterly resenting their blessings, and maliciously hoping for a reversal of their luck.

In this homily Basil is concerned not only with the aetiology of envy but also its cure.[15] His diagnostic and therapeutic approach is reflected in his descriptors for envy, repeatedly calling it a "passion" (πάθος), an "evil" (κακός), and an "illness" (νόσος). Basil does not attack ambition or love of honor itself (φιλοτιμία), which may seem to be the root cause of envy, but rather "the insidious proliferation of envy" that destroys society.[16] For he sees envy as a corruption and perversion of human ambition. In fact, Basil identifies the devil as the root cause of envy. All human enviers are his disciples and agents. Hence to be envious is to succumb to demonic temptation and manipulation.[17] Scripture is filled with examples of human beings impelled to envy by the devil.

Envy, however, is not overcome through direct confrontation with the devil. Paul Blowers has argued that Basil's approach to the therapy of envy recognizes "the possibility for enhancing certain salutary emotional scripts over other, unhealthy ones, and for acquiring virtuosity in the discharge of morally appropriate competitive emotions in specific situations."[18] The key here is "refraining or replacing (not annihilating) the judgments that propel" envy.[19] In other words, Basil tries to alter the ground rules of the arena in which competition for honor takes place. He suggests that virtue alone is what truly confers honor. Transient earthly goods such as wealth are rather the instruments of virtue, insofar as they can be put to a good use or not. Thus Basil is proposing a radical "reorientation of the judgments that underlie the competitive passions."[20] Honor is redefined in terms of

[15]See Limberis, "The Eyes Infected by Evil," 180–4; Blowers, "Envy's Narrative Scripts," 31–2.

[16]Blowers, "Envy's Narrative Scripts," 27; see also Limberis, "The Eyes Infected by Evil," 175–80.

[17]Blowers, "Envy's Narrative Scripts," 27–31.

[18]Blowers, "Envy's Narrative Scripts," 26–7.

[19]Blowers, "Envy's Narrative Scripts," 27.

[20]Blowers, "Envy's Narrative Scripts," 32.

virtue which is within our power (ἐφ' ἡμῖν), not transitory earthly goods not within our power but the result of happenstance. Note that Basil is not advocating a good use of envy. Envy remains a passion, an evil, and an illness whose root cause is the devil. Rather, he seeks to redirect each person's competitive desire for honor—which Basil considers fundamentally good, or at least neutral thing that can be put to a good use—to a salutary and not a harmful end. And so, Basil exhorts his audience, as Vasiliki Limberis says, "to rid themselves of envy and acquire virtue, not through desire for the ascent to God, but through love of honor (φιλοτιμία)."[21] Within human nature itself lie the basic instinct and resources for virtue.

Basil's treatment of envy draws eclectically upon Greco-Roman philosophy. His own definition of envy is Stoic.[22] Basil's descriptions of the symptoms of envy may owe something to Plutarch's treatise *On Envy and Hatred*.[23] His understanding of the remedy for the illness of envy is rooted in Aristotelian and Stoic thought. While Aristotle had recognized that the competitive emotions could be salutary (i.e., when used to motivate the acquisition of noble or virtuous ends by love of honor), the Stoics rejected all rivalrous emotions as useless.[24] Since the Stoics considered what was truly good to be within our power (ἐφ' ἡμῖν) and what was not within our power to be indifferent, accordingly competition for what was not good was pointless.[25]

[21]Limberis, "The Eyes Infected by Evil," 184.

[22]See p. 133 n. 5 below.

[23]Matthew Dickie, "The Fathers of the Church on the Evil Eye," in Henry Maguire, ed., *Byzantine Magic* (Washington, DC: Dumbarton Oaks, 1995), 9–34 at 19 n. 30.

[24]Blowers, "Envy's Narrative Scripts," 23–4.

[25]See Epictetus, *Handbook* 19: "You can be invincible if you do not enter any contest in which victory is not within your power. See that you are not carried away by the appearance, in thinking that someone is happy when you see him honored ahead of you or very powerful or otherwise having a good reputation. For if the truly good things are within our power, neither envy nor jealousy has a place, and you yourself will want neither to be a general nor a magistrate nor a consul, but to be free. And there is one road to this: despising what is not within our power." This translation is taken in slightly modified form from Nicholas P. White, *Handbook of Epictetus* (Indianapolis: Hackett, 1983), 16.

And so, Basil has adopted the Aristotelian idea that love of honor (φιλοτιμία) can motivate and undergird a healthy competition, and combined it with the Stoic idea that virtue alone is good because it alone is within our power (ἐφ' ἡμῖν). Thus the healing of the illness of envy requires re-educating the mind as to what constitutes true good (i.e., virtue) and redirecting our fundamental, ambitious impulse away from the noxiousness of envy to this healthy end.

Basil opens the homily with an account of the destructiveness of the passion of envy (§1). While God is utterly free from envy, the devil seethes with it. Envious people are the devil's accomplices and thus liable to the same condemnation as he is. Envy is the most destructive passion because it harms the envier far more than the envied. In this connection Basil deploys two striking metaphors: envy destroys the souls as rust destroys iron, and envy consumes the soul as vipers gnaw through the wombs' of their mothers in order to be born.

Basil next offers a Stoic definition of envy as "distress caused by your neighbor's prosperity" (§1). He then turns to a description of the various ways in which the illness of envy presents itself. The envious person is then vividly depicted as in a state of continual anguish and despair over the external and internal goods of his neighbor. He is like a naked man easily injured by the blows and pricks of his neighbor's fertile fields, thriving household, happiness, bravery, fitness, good looks, prudence, oratorical eloquence, and the honor he receives for his munificence. What adds insult to injury is that the envious person is embarrassed to divulge the cause of his anguish and distress, as if he knows the irrationality of his envy.[26] Thus he is forced to keep his envy repressed within, where it slowly festers and consumes him. The envious person seeks relief from his illness in only one way, namely, seeing the person whom he envies deprived of his good fortune (§2).[27] With *schadenfreude* he gloats over the misfortune of his neighbor and does all that he can to heighten the pain of his neighbor's loss.

[26]Cf. Plutarch, *On Envy and Hatred* 5 (537e).
[27]Cf. Plutarch, *On Envy and Hatred* 6 (538b-c).

The next major section of the homily analyzes classic scriptural cases of envy. Returning to a theme mentioned in the opening paragraph, Basil sees the devil as the primordial source of envy (§3). He speculates that the devil envied God because of the divine generosity toward humanity. But since the devil was impotent to take vengeance on God, he took it instead upon human beings. It is for this reason that the devil wages such a furious war against human beings.[28] Cain is the first disciple of the devil, envying Abel for the honor bestowed upon him by God. Since Cain, like the devil himself, was incapable of attacking God, he got revenge on God by murdering Abel.[29] Other scriptural accounts of envy unmask its inherent irrationality. Basil interprets Saul's murderous rage against David as driven by envy of the very benefits he has received from him. Basil depicts David as virtuous in all his deeds, especially in his repeated sparing of Saul's life. But these incidents only add fuel to Saul's envy. In the end, Saul is illogically jealous of David's virtuous acts, from which he himself benefited.[30] Basil wryly notes that while fierce beasts are tamed when treated with kindness, the envious strangely become more savage.[31] The story of Joseph further demonstrates the absurdity of envy (§4). When his brothers heard that Joseph had a dream that others would pay homage to him, envious of this future honor they sought to forestall its fulfillment by selling him. But the logic here, notes Basil, is flawed. If Joseph's dream was true, nothing they could have done would have prevented its fulfillment. But if his dream was false, why be envious of him? In the end, the goal of the actions motivated by their envy was forestalled by the providence of God. But the greatest scriptural example is the Jewish envy of Jesus.

[28]For attempts to explain the devil's envy, see Blowers, "Envy's Narrative Scripts," 28; James Kugel, *Traditions of the Bible: A Guide to the Bible As It Was at the Beginning of the Common Era* (Cambridge, MA: Harvard University Press, 1998), 121–4; and Henry Ansgar Kelly, *Satan: A Biography* (Cambridge: Cambridge University Press, 2006), 70–9, 180–4, and 200–1.

[29]For attempts to interpret the story of Cain and Abel in terms of envy, see Blowers, "Envy's Narrative Scripts," 28–30 and 41 n. 51; Kelly, *Satan*, 77–8.

[30]See Limberis, "The Eyes Infected by Evil," 166.

[31]Cf. Plutarch, *On Envy and Hatred* 7 (538c-d).

Basil surmises that they were envious of his miracles and accordingly did all that they could to put an end to them, and finally put him to death. In all these examples, the malice of the devil is in evidence. With the single weapon of envy, "from the foundation of the world to the consummation of the age, the devil inflicts wounds upon all people and strikes them down, destroying our life and rejoicing in our destruction" (§4). Through the same passion by which he fell he causes the fall and destruction of others.

Attention is then shifted to four more aspects of envy. First, based on Proverbs 23.6 and Ecclesiastes 4.4, Basil explains how envy crops up among those who are most intimately connected with each other. "Envy," he says, "is the disease to which friendship is most liable" (§4). Yet, secondly, there is one thing about envy which is praiseworthy: it harms only the envier, not the envied. Merely coveting the goods of one's neighbor does not cause them to diminish. At this point Basil addresses the third topic, belief in evil eye (βάσκανος ὀφθαλμός), a belief which was widespread in ancient Mediterranean culture.[32] Envious persons were thought to possess an evil eye, which could send out some sort of deadly discharge and thereby inflict harm upon those whom they envied.[33] Basil dismisses this belief as superstition and an old wives' tale.[34] But he does admit that the demons can use the inclinations and even the eyes of the envious for their own purposes. Therefore, Basil rejects that the evil eye is controlled by random cosmic forces and connects it with the aetiology of envy explicated in this homily. Thus what seems to be the

[32]On Basil's discussion of the evil eye, see Limberis, "The Eyes Infected by Evil," 175–80; and Dickie, "The Fathers of the Church on the Evil Eye," 18–21.

[33]This belief is not as far-fetched as it sounds given ancient theories of vision. One ancient theory held that the eye sent out a ray from itself. Basil discusses this theory and others at *Eun.* 3.6 and *Sab* 7. See p. 302 n. 44 below, and Mark DelCogliano and Andrew Radde-Gallwitz, *St. Basil of Caesarea: Against Eunomius*, FOTC 122 (Washington, DC: Catholic University of America Press, 2011), 193 n. 20, for relevant ancient sources.

[34]Dickie, "The Fathers of the Church on the Evil Eye," 19–20, suggests that here Basil is expressing contempt of the theory he dismisses, not its adherents. In fact, it is Plutarch's theory that Basil is rejecting.

insidious work of the evil eye is really envious persons succumbing to manipulation by the devil.[35] Finally, Basil notes that the perception and judgment of envious persons is distorted (§5). They do not praise what is normally—and rightfully—esteemed by society, such as virtue and oratorical eloquence. Rather, like vultures and flies which gravitate toward stenches and festering sores, envious persons glory in the faults and failings of others, relishing the opportunity to broadcast such misdeeds to tarnish reputations. In this connection, Basil compares envious persons to painters "who indicate the identity of the figures they depict by a crooked nose, or by a scar, or by some deformity, whether natural or the result of illness" (§5). Jean Bernardi has suggested that this passage implies that Basil was against realism in art and in favor of the idealism that would later characterize Byzantine painting.[36] In any event, envious persons have distorted perception also insofar as they belittle praiseworthy virtue by calling it its neighboring or opposing vice. For example, courage they call rashness, justice severity, generosity profligacy, and thriftiness stinginess. Though the envious desire such goods, since they lack them they show no appreciation for them.

Basil next elaborates the cure for envy (§5). The first step is to realize that no human circumstance of prosperity, whether wealth, power, health, or oratorical excellence, is the highest good since all of these are fleeting. Rather, these are the instruments of virtue, not to be used for self-aggrandizement but to help others. It is here that Basil devotes some lines decrying envy of the person who possesses oratorical eloquence, the ability to interpret the Scriptures, the gifts of teaching, and who is honored because of them. One cannot help but see in this section Basil's response to those in his community who envied him. Envy is unfounded, he explains, because whatever

[35]Dickie, "The Fathers of the Church on the Evil Eye," 21, notes that Basil is somewhat inconsistent, or at least unclear, regarding his claim that the envious do not have the power to inflict harm through their eyes.

[36]Jean Bernardi, *La prédication des pères cappadociens* (Paris: Presses universitaires de France, 1968), 59–60. Interestingly Rufinus omitted this passage in his translation of *Inv*, perhaps indicating, suggests Bernardi, his approval of artistic realism.

good the orator possesses is shared with all who are willing to listen to him. All alike can benefit from his teaching. But instead the envious person is stung by the applause the orator receives and would spitefully prefer that no one be benefited by him. And so, anyone who possesses temporal goods, which are instruments of virtue, should use them "in the right way" and manage them "according to right reason" (§5). If he does so, he is rightly esteemed and honored. But if he does not do so, he is to be pitied for squandering his opportunities to be virtuous. Either way, there is no place for envy in this calculus. Whoever realizes that earthly goods never confer true honor will not be envious of them. In order to eradicate envy, one must redirect ambition, or love of honor (φιλοτιμία), to the acquisition of virtue, as if changing the course of a stream. For virtue alone is within our power (ἐφ' ἡμῖν). And it is not in limited supply; all who strive for it can attain it. Virtue is the true good that confers true honor and from it no one is excluded. Hence, envy is unwarranted. The homily concludes with Basil's pointing out that hypocrisy is the fruit of envy (§6). Since the envious person cannot reveal the hatred of his neighbors hidden in his heart, he puts on an outward show of love. The homily ends with a few lines of exhortation to get rid of envy, quoting the Pauline texts Galatians 5.26 and Ephesians 4.32.

In this homily, Basil, like many other Christians and non-Christians of his era, conflates the terms for the competitive emotions originally distinguished by Greco-Roman philosophers. He uses three terms synonymously for envy. Most frequent is the standard Greek term, *phthonos*, which is translated consistently as "envy."[37] Another term, used much less frequently, is *baskania*, which is always translated as "jealousy" and is meant to be understood in its non-technical sense as a synonym of envy.[38] Basil also uses the term *zēlos* a few times. It is never used in its technical Stoic sense

---

[37]The cognate adjective and verb are translated respectively as "envious" and "to envy."

[38]The cognate adjective is translated as "jealous," whereas the cognate verb is translated as "to be jealous of."

or as synonym of *zēlotypia*, but it is synonymous with *phthonos*. Various translations of *zēlos* and its cognate adjective and verb are employed.[39] These different translations will give the reader a sense of Basil's varied vocabulary when discussing envy. Note that in this homily Basil does not discuss jealousy in its technical sense; his exclusive focus is on envy.

Authenticity. The authenticity of this homily is certain and has never been doubted. It is one of the eight homilies of Basil translated into Latin by Rufinus of Aquileia in the early 400s.[40] It is also widely attested in the best manuscripts of Basil's homilies.[41] Nothing within the homily itself suggests that Basil is not its author.

Context and Date. There is nothing in this homily that is help-ful for determining its original context and date. On three separate occasions in this homily Basil critiques those who are envious of the successes of an orator. Based on these critiques Jean Bernardi situates this homily in the period of Basil's presbyteral ministry (362–370), viewing them as a largely subconscious response on the part of Basil to those who begrudged his rhetorical prowess.[42] In fact, Bernardi even suggests that it was this homily which precipi-tated Basil's rift with his bishop, Eusebius, and his departure from Caesarea. In other words, in this homily Bernardi thinks that Basil was offering a thinly-veiled, public critique of his bishop. If this is correct, then the homily would have to be dated to late 363.[43] None-theless, while Basil's critique of those envious of orators is insistent, particularly in §5, where autobiographical elements seem to abound, in the end Bernardi's suggestion is nothing more than speculation. Even if Basil was subconsciously (or even deliberately) defending

[39]The noun, which is used only twice, is translated as "jealousy." In each case, the word is footnoted to signal that it translates neither φθόνος nor βασκανία. The cog-nate adjective is translated as "enviable" since it is always used of the good or person envied, and the cognate verb as "to deem enviable."

[40]PG 31.1753–1761.

[41]See BBV ii.1091–5.

[42]Bernardi, *La prédication*, 58–60; Raymond Van Dam, *Families and Friends in Late Roman Cappadocia* (Philadelphia: University of Pennsylvania Press, 2003), 32–3.

[43]For this date, see p. 52 above.

himself against his detractors, there is no reason to place this homily earlier rather than later in his ecclesiastical career. Bernardi's suggestion has not been accepted by others.[44] Envy was surely a topic on which Basil frequently preached, and nothing precludes this homily in its present form from being a final version attained through years of revision.[45] Therefore, this homily cannot be dated more precisely than to the entire span of Basil's ecclesiastical ministry, 362–378.

Translation. The following translation is based on Julien Garnier's edition as reprinted in De Sinner ii.127–136 (=PG 31.372–385).[46] In crafting my translation, I benefited from the Latin translations of Rufinus and Garnier, as well as from Sister M. Monica Wagner's English translation of the homily in the Fathers of the Church series.[47]

TRANSLATION

1   God is good and the giver of goods to those who are worthy. The devil is evil and the author of every kind of vice. And just as freedom from envy belongs to the One who is good, so too does jealousy belong to the devil. So then, brothers, let us guard against the passion of envy, lest we become accomplices in the works of our adversary and so find ourselves condemned along with him by the same judgment. For if he who is puffed up with pride falls into the condemnation of the devil,[1] how will the envious person escape the

[44]Jean Gribomont, "Notes biographiques sur s. Basile le Grand," in Paul Jonathan Fedwick, ed., *Basil of Caesarea: Christian, Humanist, Ascetic. A Sixteen-Hundredth Anniversary Symposium* (Toronto: The Pontifical Institute of Mediaeval Studies, 1981), 21–48 at 30.

[45]See Paul Jonathan Fedwick, "A Chronology of the Life and Works of Basil of Caesarea," in idem, ed., *Basil of Caesarea: Christian, Humanist, Ascetic. A Sixteen-Hundredth Anniversary Symposium* (Toronto: The Pontifical Institute of Mediaeval Studies, 1981), 3–19 at 9 n. 31.

[46]CPG 2865.

[47]M. Monica Wagner, *Saint Basil: Ascetical Works*, FOTC 9 (New York: The Fathers of the Church, Inc., 1950), 463–474.

[1]See 1 Tim 3.6.

punishment that has been prepared for the devil? For no passion more destructive than envy is implanted in the souls of human beings. While having no adverse effects on those outside,[2] it is the primary and personal evil of the one who possesses it. For just as rust destroys iron, so too does envy destroy the soul that has it.[3] Or rather, just as vipers are said to be born by gnawing through the womb that conceived them, so too it is the nature of envy to consume the soul which brought it to birth.[4]

For envy is distress caused by your neighbor's prosperity.[5] Hence the jealous person is never free from anguish, never free from despair. Is your neighbor's field fertile? Is his household thriving with all that contributes to a good life? Is the man never unhappy? All these things feed the illness and increase the pain of the jealous person. Thus he is no different from a naked man who is injured by everything. Is someone brave? In good shape? These things strike the jealous person. Is someone else better looking? Another blow for the jealous person. Does so-and-so stand above the pack by reason of the superior talents of his soul? Is he admired and esteemed[6] for his prudence and ability to speak eloquently? Is another person rich, and greatly honored for his charitable donations and sharing with those in need, and highly praised by the recipients of his

[2] That is, those outside the envious soul, namely, those who are envied.

[3] This was a proverbial saying. It is attributed by Diogenes Laertius (*Lives of the Philosophers* 6.5) to Antisthenes, the pupil of Socrates who some ancients considered the founder of the Cynics. The same metaphor is found in Cyprian, *On Jealousy and Envy* 7 (CCSL 3A:78,119). Basil employs the same metaphor for envy in *Lak* 4.

[4] It was a widespread belief in the ancient world that vipers had to gnaw through their mothers' wombs in order to be born; see e.g., Herodotus 3.109; Aristotle, *History of Animals* 5.34. Basil employs the same viper metaphor for loans in *Ps14b* 3. He also mentions the idea in *Hex* 9.5.

[5] Envy was commonly defined as a kind of distress (λύπη) in ancient philosophy: "distress over either the present or past goods of your friends" (the Platonist definition at *Definitions* 416a); "distress over the prosperity of those who are like us or equal to us" (Aristotle, *Rhetoric* 2.9; see also *Topics* 2.2); and "distress over others' goods" (the Stoic definition of Chrysippus as reported in SVF 3.412–416; see also Plutarch, *On Curiosity* 518c, Epictetus, *Discourses* 2.12.8).

[6] Gk. φιλοτιμεῖται, which is cognate with φιλοτιμία.

benefactions? All these things are blows and wounds, striking the very center of jealous person's heart.

And what makes this illness unbearable is that the jealous person cannot divulge it. On the contrary, he hangs his head in shame, downcast, troubled, moaning, unnerved by this evil. But when asked about the cause of his suffering, he is embarrassed to disclose his affliction. "I am resentful and bitter. The goods of my friend aggravate me. I am depressed by the joy of my brother. I cannot bear the sight of others' goods. Instead I turn the good fortune of my neighbors into affliction." Now this is what he would say if he were willing to speak the truth. Since he chooses not to divulge any of this, in the depths of his heart he represses his illness, which slowly consumes his insides and eats him up.

2   So then, neither does he see a physician for his illness, nor is he able to find any sort of healing remedy for his passion, even though the Scriptures are filled with such cures.[7] Instead, he awaits relief from this evil in only one way: seeing one of those whom he envied fall upon hard times. This is the goal of his hatred: to see the person of whom he was jealous deprived of his happiness, to see the person whom he deemed enviable become an object of pity. When he sees him crying, when he observes his deep sorrow, only then does he make overtures of amity and become his friend. And he does not rejoice with one who is joyful but weeps with one who is sad.[8] And he bewails the reversal of his new friend's state in life, how he has fallen from such great prosperity into such dire straits, and he speaks of his new friend's former condition in glowing terms. He does not do this because he is humane and compassionate, but so that he may make his new friend's misfortune seem all the more terrible. He praises his child only after he has died and extols him with countless praises: "How beautiful he was to behold! How clever! How adept at

[7]The themes of the envier's inability to disclose his envy, what the envier would say if he could, and his resultant failure to seek healing for his envy are also mentioned in *Lak* 8.
[8]Cf. Rom 12.15.

everything!" While the child was alive he did not utter a kind word to him.[9] But if he sees that many others concur in this praise, he changes his course and becomes jealous of the dead child. Riches he admires only after they are lost. The body's elegance, vigor, and fitness he praises and extols only after they are ravaged by illness. And in sum, he is an enemy of good things when they are present but their friend when they are gone.

3   So then, what could be more destructive than this illness? It is the ruin of life, the corruption of nature, hatred of the gifts given by God to us, and opposition to God. What has driven that demon who is the source of all evil to wage war so furiously against human beings? Isn't it envy? Through envy he was exposed as one who fights openly against God. He was angry with God because of his generosity toward humanity, but it was upon humanity that he took his vengeance since he could not take it upon God.[10] By acting in the same way Cain showed that he was the first disciple of the devil,[11] having learned from him both envy and murder,[12] those kindred iniquities connected by Paul who said: *Full of envy, murder* [Rom 1.29]. So then, what did he do? He saw the honor bestowed [on Abel] by God, and he was inflamed with jealousy,[13] and he killed the recipient of the honor in order to attack the one who had bestowed the honor. Since he could not fight against God, he resorted to slaughtering his own brother.[14]

Let us flee this illness, brothers. It teaches us to fight against God. It is the mother of homicide, giving birth to violation of nature, ignorance of kinship, and disasters of the most irrational sort. Why are you distressed, my brother, when you have suffered nothing

[9]That is, to the child's father.

[10]The theme of the devil's envy is developed more fully in *Lak* 8–9; see also *Malo* 8.

[11]Cf. 1 Jn 3.12.

[12]Gk. *phthonos kai phonos*.

[13]Gk. ζῆλος.

[14]See Gen 4.1–16. Basil also interprets Cain's murder of Abel as rooted in envy in *Ep*. 260.3.

terrible? Why do you wage war against someone who enjoys his own goods but has not caused any of yours to diminish? Indeed, if you are indignant even when someone [whom you envy] is kind to you, isn't it blatantly obvious that you are jealous of the very benefits you have received? Saul acted in this way. He made the extraordinary kindnesses shown to him a cause for war against David. First, after Saul had been delivered from insanity by those melodious and divine songs [played by David on his lyre], he tried to run his benefactor through with a spear.[15] Next, it came to pass that after David saved his life and the lives of his soldiers from their enemies and delivered Saul from embarrassment before Goliath,[16] at the victory celebrations the dancers attributed to David ten times more responsibility for what had happened: *David killed his ten thousands, and Saul his thousands* [1 Sam 18.7]. Because of this one statement—and the fact that truth itself testified to its accuracy—Saul initially attempted to become his murderer and destroy him through treachery,[17] but then forced him to become a fugitive.[18] But not even then did he let go of his hatred, but in the end he marched out against him with three thousand picked men and scoured the deserts. And if he had been asked about the pretext for this war, he would have surely responded that it was the kindnesses shown to him by that man. Even though he was apprehended while asleep at the very time of the pursuit and could have been easily slaughtered as he lay before his enemy, once again his life was saved by that righteous man. For David kept his hands from injuring him.[19] Not even by this act of kindness was Saul

[15]See 1 Sam 16.23; 18.10–11; 19.9–10.

[16]See 1 Sam 17.1–58.

[17]See 1 Sam 18.20–19.7. Presumably the "treachery" mentioned by Basil refers to Saul's request that David, whom Saul had engaged to his daughter Michal, give him a hundred foreskins of the Philistines as a marriage present, hoping that David would be killed in the attempt. When David unexpectedly succeeded, the enraged Saul ordered his execution, but Jonathan persuaded his father to rescind the order. Thus, as Basil put it, Saul "attempted to become his murderer."

[18]See 1 Sam 19.11–18.

[19]See 1 Sam 24.1–22. According to source critics, David's sparing of Saul's life in this passage stems from the so-called Late Source and is a doublet of 1 Sam 26.1–25,

moved. But once again he gathered his soldiers, and once again he pursued him, until he was caught for a second time in a cave, by the same man.[20] Here David demonstrated the greater illustriousness of his virtue, while Saul only made his own wickedness more obvious.

Envy is the form of hatred that is the hardest to tame. For while acts of kindness make those who are otherwise our enemies more gentle, the experience of being shown kindness irritates the invidious and malicious person even more. And the more he is shown kindness, the more he grows indignant and displeased and disgusted. For he is more upset by the power of his benefactor than he is thankful for the kindness shown to him. What sort of wild beast surpasses him in ferocity? Which savage animals outstrip him in fierceness? Dogs become gentle when fed. Lions become tamed when treated with kindness. But when treated kindly jealous persons become all the more savage.[21]

4 What made the noble Joseph a slave? Wasn't is the envy of his brothers?[22] It is worth our while to marvel at the irrationality brought on by this illness in this story. Because they feared that his dreams would be fulfilled, they made their brother a slave, thinking that if he were a slave, no one would ever have to pay homage to him.[23] And yet if dreams are true, is there any scheme at all that can prevent the events they foretell from being fulfilled? But if the visions seen in dreams are false, why be jealous of someone who is self-deceived? In the present case, however, the cleverness of Joseph's brothers was foiled by the providence of God. For the stratagem by which they hoped to impede the event foretold proved to be the very

where the same incident is based on the Early Source. In contrast, Basil views the two stories as separate but similar events. Note that Basil confuses the details of the two accounts. It is in 1 Sam 26.1–25 that David caught Saul while he was asleep. Here in 1 Sam 24.1–22 David has a chance to kill Saul because Saul was relieving himself in the cave where David was hiding.

[20]See 1 Sam 26.1–25.
[21]The same metaphor for envy is employed in *Lak* 8.
[22]See Acts 7.9.
[23]See Gen 37.5–28.

means of preparing the way for its fulfillment. After all, if Joseph had not been sold, he would not have gone to Egypt. He would not have been snared by the plots of that licentious woman when he maintained his self-control. He would not have been thrown into prison. He would not have become acquainted with the servants of Pharaoh. Nor would he have interpreted those dreams whereby he obtained the rule of Egypt and was paid homage by his brothers when they came to him because of the famine.[24]

Let us turn our thoughts to that envy which is the greatest of all and connected with matters of the greatest importance: that envy which the madness of the Jews caused to break out against the Savior.[25] Why did they envy him? Because of his miracles. What were these miraculous works? The salvation of the needy. The hungry were fed, and the one who fed them was treated with hostility. The dead were raised, and the one who gave them life was resented. Demons were expelled, and the one who commanded them to depart was plotted against. Lepers were cleansed, and the lame walked, the deaf heard, and the blind saw, and the one who did all this good was put to flight. And finally they handed over to death the one who had granted them life, and scourged the liberator of human beings, and condemned the judge of the world. Envy is so evil that it led to all this. And with this one weapon, from the foundation of the world to the consummation of the age, the devil inflicts wounds upon all people and strikes them down, destroying our life and rejoicing in our destruction. He fell through envy and through the same passion brings about not only his own destruction but also ours.

Therefore, that wise man showed his wisdom when he did not allow us even to dine with a jealous man.[26] For he used sharing meals together to speak about every possible form of fellowship in life. Just as we are careful to place easily combustible items as far as possible from the fire, so too we must, insofar as it is possible,

[24]See Gen 39–44.
[25]See Mt 27.18; Mk 15.10; see also Acts 5.17, 13.45, 17.5.
[26]See Prov 23.6. Basil also discusses this verse in *Lak* 4 and 8.

avoid friendships which involve association with the jealous, that we may position ourselves out of the range of the darts of envy. For it is not possible to get entangled with envy in any other way than by approaching and establishing intimacy with it. Indeed, according to the saying of Solomon: *jealousy*[27] *comes to a man from his companion* [Eccl 4.4]. And so it is. A Scythian is not jealous of an Egyptian, but each one is jealous of the fellow members of his own nation. And among the fellow members of his own nation, he does not envy those whom he doesn't know but those with whom he is the most familiar. And among those with whom he is the most familiar, [he envies] his neighbors, his fellow workers, and those otherwise closely associated with him. And among these again, those who are the same age as he, his relatives, and his brothers. And in sum, just as red mildew is the sickness to which wheat is most prone, so too envy is the disease to which friendship is most liable.

Yet in fact one thing about this evil can be praised: the more intensely it has been stirred up, the more troublesome it is for the one who possesses it. For just as javelins launched with great force bounce back to the thrower when they strike something impervious and resistant, so too the emotions that arise from envy harm only the jealous person himself, since they do not trouble the one whom he envies. For who has ever caused the goods of his neighbor to diminish simply by agonizing over them? Yet when afflicted by such anguish the envious person consumes only himself.[28]

But at present those who suffer from jealousy are thought to be more deadly than poisonous animals. While such creatures bite or sting to inject poison, which then gradually causes the infected part of the body to putrefy, some think that envious persons can even cause harm with their eyes alone. And so it is thought that when envious persons resent the well-toned bodies of those in the prime of their life and the full vigor of their youth, they cause their bodies to waste away and suddenly lose all their bulk, as if some sort of

[27] Gk. ζῆλος.
[28] This single praiseworthy aspect of envy is also mentioned by Basil in *Lak* 4.

deadly discharge were flowing from their envious eyes, causing these bodies to dwindle and rot away.[29] But I think that this explanation should be dismissed as folklore and the kind of thing that old hags chatter about in the women's quarters. Yet I tell you this: the demons, who hate all that is good, when they find inclinations in line with their own, make as much use of them as they can to achieve their own objectives. And so, they can even use the eyes of the jealous to serve their own purposes. Why then aren't you horrified at making yourself a servant of this deadly demon? Why instead do you admit that evil whereby you will become not only the enemy of those who do no wrong but also the enemy of God who is good and altogether free from envy?

5   Let us flee this intolerable evil. It is what the serpent teaches, the demons concoct, the enemy sows. It is the down payment for punishment, the barrier to piety, the path to Gehenna. It is deprivation of the [heavenly] kingdom. You can tell that people are envious simply by looking at their faces. Their eyes are dry and dull, their cheeks sunken, their eyebrows furrowed. Their soul is troubled by the passion and lacks the critical ability to discern the truth of any matter. They praise neither the practice of virtue, nor the ability to speak eloquently (even if it is adorned with dignity and grace), nor anything else that is enviable and admired. Just as vultures gravitate toward a stench, flying past many meadows and many sweet-smelling and fragrant places; and just as flies go past healthy flesh and head straight for the sore; so too jealous persons pay no attention to the splendid way of life and the great accomplishments of the virtuous, but instead focus on their faults. And if it should come to pass that such people have made a mistake (there are many human circumstances in which this can happen), envious persons announce it to the world in the hope of making these men known only for their lapses. They are like those wicked painters who indicate the identity of the figures they depict by a crooked nose, or by a scar, or

[29]Here Basil speaks of the evil eye; see p. 128 above.

by some deformity, whether natural or the result of illness. Envious persons are experts at belittling what is praiseworthy by distorting it into something worse, and they are skilled at discrediting virtue on the basis of its nearby vice. The courageous person they call rash; the self-controlled person, unfeeling; the just person, severe; the prudent person, calculating. In addition, a person of refined tastes they discredit as fastidious; the generous person as profligate; in contrast, the thrifty person [they call] stingy. And in general, upon all forms of virtue they do not neglect to bestow a name borrowed from its opposing vice.[30]

What then? Shall we limit this discourse to denouncing this vice? But that would be a kind of half-cure. For it is not useless to help a sick person understand the seriousness of his illness in order to provoke in him the appropriate concern for his sickness, but to abandon him at this point without guiding him toward health is nothing other than to let the sick person remain stuck in poor health. What then? How can we avoid suffering this illness in the first place? Or if we have contracted it, how can we be free of it? The key is to judge no human circumstance as great or marvelous in itself: neither prosperity in human endeavors, nor renown which fades away, nor bodily health. For we do not define the [highest] good in terms of transitory things, but we have been called to share in everlasting and true goods. And so, by no means is the rich man enviable because of his riches, nor the powerful man because of the sublimity of his dignity, nor the strong man because of the vigor of his body, nor the wise man because of the great power of his eloquence. For these are instruments of virtue when used in the right way, containing within themselves no intrinsic means to happiness. So then, whoever uses them in the wrong way is pitiable, like a man who purposely wounds

---

[30]The account of virtue and vice here is Aristotelian: virtue is the mean between two extremes, one of excess, the other of deficiency, which are opposed not only to each other but also to the mean; see *Nicomachean Ethics* 2.6–8. Basil lists only one extreme for each virtue, either an extreme of excess (e.g., courageous and rash) or of deficiency (e.g., self-controlled and unfeeling). See *Sab* 1, where Basil lists the two extremes of courage, rashness and cowardice.

himself with the sword he received to defend himself against his enemies. But whoever manages what is under his control in the proper way and according to right reason, and is a [trustworthy] steward of the gifts he received from God,[31] and does not hoard them for his own personal enjoyment, such a one is rightly given praise and affection because of his love for the brothers and his generous character.

Again, someone stands out because of his prudence, and he is honored because he speaks eloquently about God, and he is an interpreter of the sacred oracles. Do not envy this person, nor ever wish that this expounder of the sacred utterances be reduced to silence, simply because he has obtained, by the Spirit's grace, some measure of approval and praise from his audience. For the good he possesses is also yours, and through your brother the gift of instruction has been sent to you—if you should choose to accept it. So then, no one blocks a gushing spring, and no one blindfolds his eyes when the sun is shining, nor is anyone jealous of those who have the benefit of the shining sun, but rather prays that he too may enjoy the light. But when spiritual teaching is gushing in the church and a pious heart is welling up with the gifts of the Spirit, why don't you give your attention with gladness? Why don't you accept this beneficial teaching with gratitude? On the contrary, the applause of the audience stings you, and you would prefer that no one be benefited or offer praise. What excuse will you make for this reaction when you stand before the Judge of our hearts?

So then, what is good for the soul must be regarded as good by nature. If anyone has a superabundance of riches and takes pride in his power and in the vigor of his body, and uses what he possesses in the right way, we should have affection for such a person and treat him with respect insofar as he possesses the ordinary instruments for living this life and manages them according to right reason. So when it comes to donating his resources, he will be ungrudging[32] to the needy and give material support to the infirm. He will regard

---

[31]See Lk 12.42.

[32]Gk. ἄφθονος, literally, "unenvying."

all his remaining wealth as belonging no more to himself than to anyone in need. Anyone who does not adopt this attitude in these matters is to be held as pitiable rather than looked upon with envy because his opportunities for being evil are greater. For this is nothing more than to be destroyed by a great deal of exertion and trouble. Now if riches are a gateway to wickedness, the rich man is pitiable. But if they are of service for virtue, jealousy is out of place since all alike benefit from the riches—unless anyone through extreme wickedness would even resent what is good for himself!

In sum, when you elevate your mind above human realities through your powers of reasoning and fix your attention on what is truly good and praiseworthy, you will be far beyond thinking that any corruptible and earthly good is a source of happiness or enviable. In anyone who has acquired this habit of mind, who is not obsessed with worldly goods as if they were of great value, it is impossible for envy ever to be present. If you are desirous of nothing but personal glory and want to outshine the crowd, and if for this reason you cannot bear to be in second place (for this too is an occasion for envy), then as if changing the course of a stream, redirect your ambition[33] to the acquisition of virtue. Free yourself entirely from the desire to get rich in any way that you can and to be renowned for your worldly accomplishments. For these are not within your power.[34] Instead, be righteous, and self-controlled, and prudent, and courageous, and patient in your sufferings for the sake of piety. In this way you will save yourself, and insofar as you possess these greater goods you will win greater distinction. For virtue is within our power,[35] and anyone willing to make the effort can acquire it. In contrast, a large fortune, and bodily vitality, and high ranking dignities are not within

[33]Gk. φιλοτιμία.

[34]Gk. ἐπὶ σοι, "within your power." This is a variation of the phrase described in the next note.

[35]Gk. ἐφ' ἡμῖν, "within our power." This is an originally Stoic expression that refers to those things for which humans are morally responsible (see LS 62). Like many other Christians, Basil follows the basic Stoic teaching that virtue and vice alone are within our power.

our power.[36] So if virtue is a greater and more lasting good and is universally acknowledged as preferable, we ought to pursue it. But virtue cannot be present in the soul unless the soul is purified of all the passions, especially jealousy.

6   Don't you see how great an evil hypocrisy is? And how it is the fruit of envy? For it is especially because of envy that duplicity crops up among human beings, when within the depths of their heart they repress their hatred but put on an outward show of love. Like those rocks hidden under the shallow waters of the sea, it is an evil that cannot be seen beforehand by those who let down their guard. So if death has flowed to us from that source,[37] as if from a spring, and also the loss of goods, and alienation from God, and the violation of the laws, and at the same time the ruin of all that is good and beautiful in our life, let us obey the Apostle. *Let us not become vainglorious, provoking one another, envying one another* [Gal 5.26], but instead *let us be kind, merciful, forgiving one another, even as God forgave you in Christ* Jesus our Lord [Eph 4.32]. With him, to the Father, and with the Holy Spirit, *be glory forever and ever. Amen* [1 Pet 4.11].

[36]Gk. οὐκ ἐφ' ἡμῖν. See the previous note.
[37]Cf. Wis 2.24.

Homily on Detachment from Worldly Things, and on the Fire that Occurred Outside the Church

Introduction

The theme of detachment from the fleeting goods of this world often recurs in the literary corpus of Basil.[1] Indeed, Basil considered it was the very purpose of the biblical book of Ecclesiastes to reveal the vanity of the transient realities of this world so that we would not greatly desire them.[2] Surely if he thought an entire book of Scripture was devoted to this theme, he must have judged it to be of supreme importance. According to Basil, the problem with the goods of this world, whether material resources such as wealth and property, or social capital such as reputation and political power, or physical endowments such health and good looks, or personal gifts such as intelligence and eloquence, is that we tend to identify them as the highest good. But in reality they are not, and our preoccupation with them is misplaced. At best, temporal blessings can be used as means to eternal goods; at worst, they impede the acquisition of ultimate blessings.

In this homily Basil attributes our confusion between transitory and everlasting goods to a basic misunderstanding. Our fundamental will and desire for good things is not the problem. Rather, we are mistaken about which goods are worthy of our desire, that is, those goods that bring us lasting benefit (i.e., salvation and eternal

[1]See *Ps14a* 1–2, *Hum* 1, and *Inv* 5 for examples in this volume.
[2]See *Prov* 1.

life), and which goods trick our desire into settling for something less than what truly would satisfy it, that is, those goods that do not merely distract us from the attainment of everlasting goods but also thereby cause us great harm. Accordingly, Basil conceives of the solution to this problem in intellectual rather than volitional terms. In other words, it is not a question of acquiring new desire, but rather of gaining knowledge of the true and lasting goods to which we should direct our desire. Basil believes that this knowledge is precisely what Scripture reveals (not only in Ecclesiastes but elsewhere too) and it is what he explicates in this homily.

Simply put, the goods we should seek in this life are not those fleeting goods of the world for which most people strive, but rather the virtues, which alone of all our acquisitions in this world stay with us in the next (§1–6). Emphasis is given in this homily to the virtuous use of money, of divesting oneself of wealth to help the poor and needy, another of Basil's favorite themes (§7–8).[3] In other words, Basil sees detachment from material goods as the prerequisite to virtue and Christian charity, as well as the means of practicing them. Perhaps why Basil chose to connect detachment and the care of the poor and needy owes something to the specific context in which this homily was preached. One of the remarkable features of *Mund* is that, as Basil is concluding, his audience insists that he continue to speak (§9). Basil obliges—apparently speaking from this point on extemporaneously—and increases the homily's length by a third. The audience wanted Basil to speak about the fire that had ravaged the area near the church on the previous day but spared the church itself. Basil reports their request as he is wrapping up the homily, and then describes the course of the fire, attributing it to the "fury of the devil." He relates that it was started "in the vicinity of the church" and then spread from there devouring all in its path, including a number

[3]See especially *Dest, Div, Fam,* and *Ps14b.* These four homilies are translated in C. Paul Schroeder, *St Basil the Great: On Social Justice,* PPS 38 (Crestwood, NY: St Vladimir's Seminary Press, 2009), and discussed at length in Susan R. Holman, *The Hungry are Dying: Beggars and Bishops in Roman Cappadocia* (Oxford: Oxford University Press, 2001).

of homes, until it threatened the church itself, before miraculously being extinguished. Perhaps because some members of the community had lost all they had in the fire Basil chose the theme of detachment as the most appropriate response to the crisis.[4]

Basil begins the homily by praising his audience, amazed that his repeated rebukes have not led them to think of him as a pain in the neck, but rather have roused them to goodwill and zeal (§1). He states that he seeks to help them avoid the nets of the devil whose daily war against us is intense. The devil, explains Basil, attacks us by twisting our desires so that we do not seek what is truly beneficial but what is harmful for us. And he does this using stealth and trickery, taking advantage of our lack of understanding. And so, in the opening paragraph Basil announces his subject: we do not understand what is truly beneficial to us, and what we think is good for us actually harms us. Basil spends the first part of the homily (§1–6) correcting this misunderstanding.

To clarify the methods of the devil, Basil picturesquely depicts the devil as a robber concealed alongside the road ready to ambush unsuspecting passersby. He "hides behind the shadows of worldly delight" (§1) to lure us into his traps. By using this comparison, Basil introduces one of the controlling metaphors of the homily, namely, that life is the road to salvation but a road lined with many dangers, the dangers of transitory worldly goods in which the devil hides. Therefore, we must travel the road of this life always on the lookout that we not be diverted by distractions such as wealth, fine food and drink, exquisite homes, sumptuous parties, beautiful people, and political power. Not only does Scripture admonish us against all these delights, but also the devil lurks beneath them, hoping to snare us and drag us to his lair, that is, to death. And so, rather than being advantageous to us, these transitory goods bring about our ultimate ruin.

Therefore, while walking the path of life, we must, like travelers or runners, strive to journey as lightly as possible, i.e., unburdened

[4]On this, see the more extensive comments below on pp. 161–162.

by preoccupation with transitory goods, in order to reach the end of salvation (§2). At this point Basil defends and qualifies his metaphor of life-as-road. He finds precedent for the metaphor in the Psalms (118.1, 118.29, and 17.32–33). He also justifies it by comparing life to walking, in which each foot exchanges place with the other in rapid succession. Just as walking takes place step by step, so too life progresses stage by stage, starting from birth and ending with death. But unlike roads which lead from city to city, one can never leave the road of life. We are swept along its path by the flow of time, propelled forward toward death. Thus we should not let life simply slip away in enjoyment of passing pleasures, but prepare for death and final judgment. For we do not know how much time has been allotted to us by the Lord. His tone here is nearly rhapsodic as he recounts our unstoppable journey along the path of life and the inevitability of death.

Having nuanced the road-as-life metaphor, Basil next turns to what is needed to make our journey along it as swift as possible (§3). We should take only what truly becomes our personal possession and get rid of all burdens that impede our forward progress, which can never be our personal possession. This, however, is difficult to do, since we tend to burden ourselves with what can never truly be ours (i.e., transitory material and earthly goods) and to disdain what is truly natural to us (i.e., virtue). We expend all our energy in the acquisition of the former, though even a child can understand that we never truly possess these things. Basil then describes how the pleasures of riches, food and drink, and sex can never be truly ours (§3–4). We do not take money with us when we die. Sometimes we lose all that we have even before death. Over-indulgence in food and drink brings such satiety and disgust that we prefer to get rid of it rather than for it to remain within us. And as for illicit sex, when frenzy leads to intercourse, as soon as the sting of the flesh has faded, says Basil, regret for lack of sexual restraint enters in. Even athletic trainers know that loss of sexual control leads to laughter, not winning the contest. Here Basil displays his rhetorical skill in capturing the poignant regret experienced after succumbing to ill-advised sexual desires. And so, since all such pleasures are alien to our nature and can never become our constant personal possession, it is best to pass them by on the road of life as impediments.

So then, what is truly ours? Next Basil turns to those pursuits which can become our personal possessions and thus truly benefit us (§5). First of all, we possess a soul and its vehicle, the body, each of which must be cared for in a salutary way. We have been given these principally to practice virtue, "to bring about upon the earth a reflection of the good order in heaven" (§5). We are judged and recompensed by God according to our conduct in this life. Virtues are acquired through diligent practice but lost through a willing turn to vice. Unlike earthly goods, virtues remain with us in the next life and rank us with the angels. As for the flesh, it must be disciplined, never indulged (§6). Here Basil cites a number of Pauline texts to support his teaching about the care of the body (2 Cor 4.16; 2 Cor 5.1; 1 Tim 6.7–8). We must attend to it as much as is needed for it to serve the soul. For an over-indulged body makes a poor vehicle for traveling the road of life. In fact, it will bring any forward progress to a halt.

Having corrected the misunderstanding about what truly harms and benefits us, about what impedes and fosters progress along the road of life, Basil turns to the virtuous actions that should ensue (§7). While there is still time, we should cast off the burdens of preoccupation with transitory worldly goods, like sailors who jettison their heavy cargo during storms to save their lives. But unlike sailors we do not become impoverished when we jettison our burdens. Rather, we gain even better riches for the soul—virtue. Furthermore, when we jettison our riches by charitable donations to the poor and needy, it is not lost at sea but transferred to safer ships, namely, the stomachs of the poor. At this point Basil shifts into a more insistent exhortatory tone, beseeching his audience to turn their burdensome wealth into something that benefits them by distributing it to the poor and needy (§8). He encourages them not to be like the rich man who refused to help Lazarus. If they fail to help the many Lazaruses still lying before them, they too will be sent to hell along with the rich man. And when they cry for help along with him, they will be rebuked for seeking the kindness which they failed to show during life.

Basil then drives home his point about assisting the poor and needy by suggesting that he and his audience "outshine that rich man when it comes to acting wickedly" (§8). It is not even for seemingly good reasons that we do not help the poor and needy, namely, out of a sense of thrift or to save money for our children to inherit.[5] Rather, we prefer to spend our money on wasteful expenditures, like huge feasts at which our behavior incites our guests to wickedness and does not teach them virtue. Then Basil vividly depicts how uncomfortable and merciless the rich can be when approached by the poor and needy, picturesquely describing the body-language of both parties. Their reactions range from loathing and disgust to indignation and suspicion. Such people, says Basil, will be submitted to a hellfire more severe than that rich man's.

Then Basil starts to wrap up the homily, saying that he would have liked "to explain ... everything that the bible teaches about that rich man" (§8) but time is up. Nonetheless, he is confident that his audience will make up for any deficiency in his presentation. But instead of finishing, Basil reports that some people in the audience are urging him not to stop, but to continue and speak about the "miracle" worked on the previous day (§9). We soon learn from Basil's dramatic narrative of the incident that on the previous day a fire had broken out near the church and threatened to engulf the church itself in its flames, but was suddenly extinguished when calamity seemed imminent. Basil attributes the fire to the "fury of the devil" and no doubt is describing an act of attempted arson.[6] The preservation of the church was apparently interpreted by Basil and his audience as a miracle of the Savior, who thwarted the devil's plan.

[5] In *Div* 7–8 and *Lak* 6–7 Basil dismisses the idea that either of these reasons can be used to justify not helping the poor and needy.

[6] See below pp. 160–161.

Basil seems less interested in describing the incident than in outlining the proper Christian response to it. He encourages his audience to make the wound that the devil received on the previous day all the more grievous (§9). How? Those who were untouched by the fire should help those who escaped from it with only body and soul intact, having lost all else. Those still with material resources should console those who sustained losses with food, clothing, and shelter. These acts of charity will add insult to the devil's injury. Apparently some of the community were distraught over the fire, questioning divine providence, God's judgment, and his administration of the universe (§10). Basil exhorts such people to prove their faith by virtuous actions toward the needy and not being saddened. For to succumb to sadness and doubting God would be to give a modicum of victory to the devil.

At this point Basil presents Job as the paradigm of patience in the midst of temptation and calamity. When Job said: *The Lord gave; the Lord has taken away. As it seemed good to the Lord, so too has it come to pass* [Job 1.21], he realized that God was in control. Basil notes that while the devil attacked Job in so many ways trying to get him to curse God, he never landed a lethal blow. Thus Job was never overcome by the devil, and so neither should any of those affected by the fire give in to despair. Basil runs through the various calamities experienced by Job. First is the loss of his flocks, and then the deaths of his children. Job responded to these disasters with Job 1.21, for which Basil provides an interpretative paraphrase in which Job speaks in the first person singular (this is a rhetorical technique called prosopopoeia). Here Job expresses his confidence in God's decisions and thus does not succumb to the devil's temptation to curse God. Basil next recounts the devil's assaults upon Job's flesh and how the devil manipulated Job's wife into berating her husband to get him to curse God (§11). Basil elaborates the scriptural words of Job's wife using prosopopoeia. In response to both the attacks upon his flesh and the abuse of his wife Job remained steadfast in piety. Once again employing prosopopoeia, Basil puts an extended speech on the lips of Job in response to his wife, which is a kind of commentary on Job 2.10, *If we received good things from the Lord's hand, shall we not bear the bad?* Here Basil reminds his audience that everyone's life has times of good and bad. We should comfort ourselves in present difficulties by remembering past prosperity. Life is like a river, whose waters are not always pure but sometimes muddy. It is wrong to ask the Lord for only good things in life. In his providence all things will work for our benefit. Hence we should not seek to understand the mysterious ways of God, but only to accept what he gives, even in painful situations (§12).

It was by speaking these words (presumably Job 1.21 and 2.10, understood according to Basil's interpretive paraphrases of them) that Job warded off the attacks the devil. Soon thereafter, Job's trials were recompensed with renewed prosperity. In this connection Basil devotes a few lines to resolving an exegetical problem: why did Job receive back double the amount of riches but the same number of children? Basil surmises that since the dead children's souls are immortal, at the final resurrection Job will gather around himself both his deceased children and their replacements, thus amounting to double the original number. Hence as a recompense in this life, Job only needed the same number of children as had been killed in the storm. Basil concludes the homily with an exhortation to bear with the calamity of the fire started by the devil with the same patient endurance with which Job bore his sufferings caused by the devil.

Basil's treatment of Job in §10–11 should be considered a pioneering effort in the history of interpretation.[7] The Book of Job was occasionally cited and alluded by the authors of the New Testament

[7]On the patristic interpretation of Job, see Charles Kannengiesser, "Job chez les Pères" in DSpir 8:1218–25; C.A. Newsom and S.E. Schreiner, "Job, Book of," in John H. Hayes, ed., *Dictionary of Biblical Interpretation* (Nashville: Abingdon Press, 1999), 587–99 at 587–9; Manlio Simonetti and Marco Conti, *Job*, Ancient Christian Commentary on Scripture. Old Testament 6 (Downers Grove: InterVarsity Press, 2006), xvii–xxvi; and David L. Balás and D. Jeffrey Bingham, "Patristic Exegesis of the Books of the Bible. VI. Wisdom and Poetry: Job," in Charles Kannengiesser, *Handbook of Patristic Exegesis: The Bible in Ancient Christianity* (Leiden: Brill, 2006), 296–7 and 306–7. Basil's contribution is overlooked or minimized in these surveys.

books and second-century Christian writers.[8] The book became increasingly prominent in third-century authors such as Clement of Alexandria, Tertullian, and Cyprian of Carthage, who are the first to comment on the figure of Job, not merely to cite verses from the biblical book. Origen supposedly preached twenty-two homilies on Job, which were translated into Latin by Hilary of Poitiers, but these are now lost.[9] Nonetheless, a number of his comments on Job survive in the catenae.[10] Following a Jewish perspective on Job (see Ezek 14.14; 14.20), these early Christians upheld Job as a model of the virtues of justice, righteousness, humility, kindness, fear of God, detachment, wisdom, and above all patient endurance (ὑπομονή) in the midst of suffering that was seen as beneficial, medicinal, and pedagogical (see Jas 5.11).[11] Nonetheless, it is only in the last half of the fourth century and the first half of the fifth century that the Book of Job becomes the object of sustained exegetical attention. In this period the first commentaries on Job are written by Evagrius of Pontus, Didymus of Alexandria, John Chrysostom, Ambrose of Milan, Augustine of Hippo, Julian of Eclanum, as well as the commentary on Job attributed to Julian the Arian and the *Anonymus in Job*.[12] In this era, in addition to attention to Job's status as an exemplar of virtue, certain passages of Job become a resource for discussing sin, justice, and human freedom. But from the period separating Origen from these late fourth- and early fifth-century theologians and exegetes, the only authors who comment on Job in any significant way are Athanasius of Alexandria, Hilary of Poitiers, and Basil. Only a few

---

[8]See Mt 19.26 (Job 42.2); Mk 10.27 (Job 42.2); Lk 1.52 (Job 12.19; 5.11); 1 Cor 3.19 (Job 5.13); Phil 1.19 (Job 13.16); 1 Thess 5.22 (Job 1.1; 1.8; 2.3); 2 Thess 2.8 (Job 4.9); Jas 5.11; Rev 9.6 (Job 3.21); 1 Clement 17.3–4 (Job 1.1; 14:4–5); 20.7 (Job 38.11); 26.3 (Job 19.26); 30.4–5 (Job 11.2–3a); 39.3–9 (Job 4.16–18; 15.15; 4.19–5.5); Justin, *Dialog with Trypho* 46.3; 79.4 (Job 1.6; 2.1); 103.5.

[9]See B.F. Westcott, "Origenes" in DCB 4:96–142 at 108.

[10]PG 12.1031–1050.

[11]See 1 Clement 17.3–4; Justin, *Dialogue with Trypho* 46.3; Clement, *Stromata* 4.17 (citing 1 Clement 17.3–4); 4.25; 4.26; 7.12; Tertullian, *On Patience* 14; Cyprian, *On Work and Almsgiving* 18; *On Mortality* 10; *To Quirinus* 3.1; 3.6; 3.14.

[12]For discussion of these, see the studies cited in n. 7 above.

of the comments of Athanasius on Job are extant in the catenae.[13] Hilary wrote a *Tractatus in Job* (it is perhaps to be identified with his translation of Origen's homilies), but only two fragments of it survive.[14] Therefore, Basil's treatment of Job in §10–11 very probably constitutes the most extensive extant discussion of the exemplary biblical figure before the last quarter of the fourth century.[15]

Authenticity. The authenticity of this homily is certain and has never been doubted. It is widely attested in the best manuscripts of Basil's homilies.[16] Nothing within the homily itself suggests that Basil is not its author.

Context and Date. In the opening lines of this homily Basil acknowledges to his audience that he is a *xenos*—a guest, a stranger, a foreigner. This seems to indicate that he delivered this homily outside Cappadocia in a place beyond his jurisdiction. Since Basil made few trips outside Cappadocia as a bishop, this limits the possibilities for the original context and date of this homily. Based on this statement, in the late seventeenth century Louis-Sébastien Le Nain de Tillemont plausibly suggested that *Mund* was delivered in Satala in the Roman province of Armenia Minor in the course of Basil's mission there in the early 370s, a suggestion repeated ever since.[17] This has an

[13]PG 27.1344–1348.

[14]PL 10.723–724.

[15]It is possible that the commentary on Job attributed to Julian the Arian is earlier than *Mund*. Dieter Hagedorn, ed., *Der Hiobkommentar des Arianers Julian*, Patristische Texte und Studien 14 (Berlin: De Gruyter, 1973), lvi, dates the work to 357–365 based on the fact that it reflects the Heteroousian theology of Eunomius. But Julian need not be an exact contemporary of Eunomius in order subscribe to Heteroousian theology since the movement lasted until the 390s. Richard Paul Vaggione, *Eunomius of Cyzicus and the Nicene Revolution* (Oxford: Oxford University Press, 2000), 278 n. 106 and 319 n. 44, plausibly suggests that "Julian the Arian" may in fact be Julian of Cilicia, a known follower of Aetius and Eunomius (Philostorgius, *h.e.* 8.2). Hagedorn, *Der Hiobkommentar*, lvii, denies the identification.

[16]See BBV ii.1115–8.

[17]Louis-Sébastien Le Nain de Tillemont, *Mémoires pour servir à l'histoire ecclésiastique des six premiers siècles* (Venice: Pitteri, 1732), ix.300–1; Prudentius Maran, *Vita S. Basilii* 43.5 (PG 29.clxxiii); Jean Gribomont, *In Tomum 31 Patrologiae graecae ad editionem operum rhetoricorum, asceticorum, liturgicorum Sancti Basili Magni Introductio* (Turnhout: Brepols, 1961), 6; Jean Bernardi, *La prédication des pères cappado-*

immediate plausibility. In early 372 Emperor Valens entrusted Basil with the task of appointing pro-Roman bishops in both the Roman province of Armenia Minor and the independent kingdom of Greater Armenia.[18] But when Basil went to Armenia Minor, his mission was compromised when his orthodoxy came under suspicion because of his associations with Eustathius of Sebasteia. Most of what we know about the mission comes from Basil's account of it in *Ep.* 99, which he wrote in Satala and sent to Terentius, the Roman *dux Armeniae*. In this same letter Basil recounts his experiences and activities in Gerasa, Nicopolis, and Satala. There was surely enough time for Basil to have preached this homily while he was in Satala. Most scholars hold that Basil went to Armenia Minor in the summer of 372, but the trip may not have occurred until the summer of 373.[19]

ciens (Paris: Presses universitaires de France, 1968), 76–7; Paul Jonathan Fedwick, "A Chronology of the Life and Works of Basil of Caesarea," in idem, ed., *Basil of Caesarea: Christian, Humanist, Ascetic. A Sixteen-Hundredth Anniversary Symposium* (Toronto: The Pontifical Institute of Mediaeval Studies, 1981), 3–19 at 10 n. 49.

[18]On this Armenian commission and its broader significance, see Paul Jonathan Fedwick, *The Church and the Charisma of Leadership in Basil of Caesarea* (Toronto: Pontifical Institute of Mediaeval Studies, 1979), 104 and 144; Philip Rousseau, *Basil of Caesarea* (Berkeley: University of California Press, 1994), 278–87; Raymond Van Dam, *Kingdom of Snow: Roman Rule and Greek Culture in Cappadocia* (Philadelphia: University of Pennsylvania Press, 2002), 118–35; Noel Lenski, *Failure of Empire: Valens and the Roman State in the Fourth Century A.D.* (Berkeley: University of California Press, 2002), 177–8; and Susan R. Holman, "Rich City Burning: Social Welfare and Ecclesial Insecurity in Basil's Mission to Armenia," *Journal of Early Christian Studies* 12 (2004): 195–215 at 197–202.

[19]The following date the mission to 372: Tillemont, *Mémoires*, ix.300–1; Maran, *Vita S. Basilii* 43.5 (PG 29.clxxiii); Gribomont, *In Tomum 31*, 6; Bernardi, *La prédication*, 76–7; Van Dam, *Kingdom of Snow*, 128 and 233 n. 18. The following date it to 373: Fedwick, *The Church and the Charisma*, 146; idem, "A Chronology," 10; Rousseau, *Basil of Caesarea*, 284. *Ep.* 99 is dated to the summer 372 by Tillemont, *Mémoires*, ix.190; Maran, *Vita S. Basilii* 24.8 (De Sinner iii.clvi); Friedrich Loofs, *Eustathius von Sebaste und Chronologie der Basilius-Briefe: eine patristische Studie* (Halle: Max Niemeyer, 1898), 27; Roy J. Deferrari, *Basil. Letters 59–185*, Loeb Classical Library 215 (Cambridge, MA: Harvard University Press, 1928), 171; Yves Courtonne, *Saint Basile: Lettres I* (Paris: Société d'édition 'Les Belles Lettres', 1957), 214; and Fedwick, *The Church and the Charisma*, 145. The same letter is dated to 373 by Wolf-Dieter Hauschild, *Basilus von Caesarea: Briefe Teil II* (Stuttgart: Anton Hiersmann, 1973), 156; Fedwick, "A Chronology," 16; Rousseau, *Basil of Caesarea*, 240–1 and 284–5. Note

But Basil's status as a *xenos* is evident from more than his statement of the fact. Throughout the homily he ingratiates himself to his listeners, expressing his high admiration for them (see especially §1) and affirming their insightfulness by repeatedly interjecting, "as you know." He is confident that his audience can find the scriptural remedies for their faults which time did not permit Basil to elaborate (§8). This tactic of trying to win over his audience by flattery and persuasion was probably the rhetorical strategy he thought best suited to his status as an outsider. But other aspects of Basil's rhetoric also suggest that he was a guest in a foreign land. In the most extensive investigation of this homily to date, Susan Holman explores how Basil's rhetoric of social welfare in *Mund* fits the context of fourth-century Armenia Minor. After comparing Basil's rhetoric of philanthropy in *Mund* with that found in his other homilies on the same subject (preached in Cappadocia), she demonstrates that, while there are many common themes, one is conspicuously absent from *Mund*: the appeal to civic identity.[20] She attributes this to Basil's status as an outsider whose civic loyalties to the Roman Empire were not shared by his Armenian audience. "The audience loyalty he found at Satala," writes Holman, "depended on friendships, not on his identity as a Roman. Encouraging images of 'patriotism' in this marginal countryside might not help" the imperial agenda in Armenia Minor.[21] Holman notes that Basil's letters to the people of Satala exhibit this same silence on civic identity. Therefore, the rhetorical strategy employed by Basil in *Mund* seems to point to a location outside the Roman Empire, such as Armenia.

Most of those scholars who situate *Mund* in Satala, however, provide no more evidence than the fact that it was preached outside Cappadocia. To be fair, scholars like Tillemont, Gribomont, Bernardi, and Fedwick are clear that Satala is no more than a probable location (some also mention Samosata as a possibility, a Roman city

that in *The Church and the Charisma*, 145–6, Fedwick places *Mund* in 372 but the first Armenian trip in 373.

[20]"Rich City Burning," 207–11.
[21]"Rich City Burning," 211.

which Basil visited in 372, but Holman's work would appear to rule out this possibility). Though Satala is even said to be the most likely place, no reasons are given for this preference when there are other possible candidates. On the same mission we know that Basil also visited Getasa and Nicopolis. Perhaps he visited other cities as well. Only Prudentius Maran, in the *Vita S. Basilii* included in the Maurist edition of Basil's works, offers a reason for his position, albeit one that is vague. He says that when Basil was in Satala he "tried to correct many things which were customarily not done properly. This [homily] is sufficiently suitable for those to whom he spoke."[22] So Maran seems to be claiming that what we know about Basil's activities in Satala from *Ep.* 99 is echoed in *Mund.* This is surely a good approach. Yet when he summarizes the content of *Mund*, Maran does not discuss any possible connections with the events that we know took place in Satala.

We may ask, nonetheless, whether there is any justification for Maran's claim. Unfortunately, the evidence is meager. The only possible allusions in *Mund* to the events recounted in *Ep.* 99 stem from the opening lines of the homily. First, Basil's favorable reception in Satala reported in *Ep.* 99 seems to be echoed in the delight with his audience that he expresses here.[23] In addition, the opening line of the homily makes it clear that Basil was not speaking to them for the first time: "I would have thought, dearly beloved, since I prod you insistently on every occasion (*hekastote*) with the goad of my words . . . " A good deal hinges upon the word *hekastote*. By translating it *frequenter* Garnier seems to have interpreted it as meaning that Basil regularly or frequently spoke to this audience. If so, this would seem to preclude situating *Mund* during the Armenian mission, when he preached in places he never had before. But *hekastote* more properly means "on each occasion."[24] From *Ep.* 99 we learn of the extensive

[22]*Vita S. Basilii* 43.5 (De Sinner iii.ccl; PG 29.clxxiii): . . . *multa non belle fieri solita emendare conatus est. Id satis convenit iis quos alloquitur.*

[23]Also suggested by Holman, "Rich City Burning," 203.

[24]Cf. the translation of M. Monica Wagner, *Saint Basil: Ascetical Works*, FOTC 9 (New York: The Fathers of the Church, Inc., 1950), 487: "on every and all occasions."

discussions that Basil had with the people of Satala: providing disciplinary rules to correct customary transgressions, getting the people of Satala to request a bishop for their city, and reconciling them with the bishop Cyril (the *catholicos* of Armenia). Thus Basil spoke to the people of Satala on a number of occasions during his visit. From what we know of them, all the discussions would seem to have been of a prodding and exhortatory kind, and they square with Basil's comment a few lines further on that "on this present occasion too" he came "to give the same kind of exhortation." *Mund* could be but one exhortation in a series of them that were delivered while Basil was visiting Satala.

Yet at the same time the situation that obtained in Satala was undoubtedly similar to those in the other cities that Basil visited during the Armenian mission. As traveling to these cities used up a great deal of time, expense, and energy, and seeing that Basil had not visited them before, it seems unlikely that he would have been limited to only one speaking engagement in each city that he visited, whatever form it took. His hosts in each city would have wanted to take full advantage of Basil's visit, as best they could, and Basil himself most likely would have wanted to get as much done as he could in each city after so arduous a journey. And so, while the opening lines of *Mund* could be interpreted as echoing the details of the visit to Satala recorded in *Ep.* 99, they are not so specific as to eliminate the possibility that Basil was referring to a series of public conversations in another city.

A final possible connection between these opening lines and *Ep.* 99 is Basil's acknowledgement that he is "a man against whom similar charges have been made." It is unclear what sort of charges are meant. One possible interpretation is that here Basil is alluding to the fact that he arrived in Satala under a cloud of suspicion since his orthodoxy had become suspect earlier in the Armenian mission because of his association with Eustathius.[25] Note too that the charges of which he admits he has been accused are "similar" to

<hr>

[25] Also suggested by Holman, "Rich City Burning," 206.

those made against his audience and about which he spoke to them on an unspecified number of previous occasions and will speak about on this occasion too. Could it be that the Christians of Satala were favorable to Eustathius or at least also suspected of holding similar Pneumatological views? But in *Mund* there is no mention of the doctrinal issues that precipitated the charges against Basil. Nor are these doctrinal issues mentioned in *Ep*. 99 in connection with Basil's visit to Satala. So instead perhaps in the opening lines of this homily Basil is admitting that he is susceptible to the same moral faults and failings as his audience is, discussed on previous occasions and also to be discussed on the present one.[26] This sentiment would be in harmony with his overall strategy of endearing himself to his audience. But if Basil is attempting to lessen the gap between himself and his audience, and not referring to his Eustathian troubles, then the possibility of Satala as the specific location for *Mund* is reduced. Once again, any of the cities he visited during the Armenian mission is possible.

And so, while one could interpret these three features of the opening lines of *Mund* as echoes of *Ep*. 99 and thus indicative of its original delivery in Satala, the details are too vague to function as evidentiary proof that *Mund* was preached there. Nothing precludes these same details from being pertinent to the other cities that Basil visited during the Armenian mission. So it appears that the suggestion first proposed by Tillemont and repeated ever since, that *Mund* might have been preached in Satala, remains a conjecture for which there is no compelling evidence. The most the evidence allows us to say is that *Mund* was preached somewhere in Armenia Minor.

Two-thirds through the homily, at the urging of his audience, Basil begins to speak about a fire kindled by the "fury of the devil," which had destroyed the area near the church on the previous day (§9). Unfortunately, Basil's surviving correspondence from the Armenian mission says nothing about a fire; if it did, dating *Mund* might be easier. Most scholars who have tried to reconstruct the

[26]Throughout the homily Basil includes himself in his exhortations; see, e.g., §8.

original context and date of *Mund* have more or less ignored this fire. But since this fire was surely on the minds of both preacher and audience alike, our insight into the context of *Mund* might be enhanced if the genesis of this fire can be better understood.

Susan Holman correctly noted the significance of the fire for understanding the context of this homily.[27] She writes that Basil "is clearly describing a literal act of attempted arson that was explicitly directed at the physical church structures."[28] She suggests that this incident was a symptom of the social unrest and political turmoil of the region in this period, and provocatively asks, "Might it be, therefore, that the fire . . . was deliberately timed for Basil's visit? Why else might he try to avoid mentioning it . . . ? . . . Could the incident . . . be an early example of literal fire as a theological weapon by one's opponents?"[29] It is true that fire was a potent weapon in antiquity. So *Mund* seems to have been preached in a context of social or political violence and perhaps should be interpreted as Basil's response to it.

It is not likely that Basil's reference to the "enemy" active in the fire refers to a purely spiritual opponent, identified as the ultimate cause for a fire that was in reality simply accidental. In other words, Basil is not attributing a fire started accidentally to the malevolence of the devil. Rather, Basil appears to be attributing responsibility for the fire to a collection of antagonistic human agents. He seems to be employing a kind of metonymy whereby Basil emphasizes the supreme cause of the arson—the devil—instead of his human agents. He does this elsewhere. Basil begins another homily urging his audience to ignore an uproar outside the church—surely caused by people—and attributes the disturbance to "the enemy."[30]

The recounting of the fire further problematizes the thesis that *Mund* was preached in Satala. Given Basil's claims to success in Satala, it is not clear whether he would have had enough enemies there to precipitate the violence of arson. If he had encountered such

[27]"Rich City Burning," 203.
[28]"Rich City Burning," 204.
[29]"Rich City Burning," 206.
[30]*Lak* 1.

steep resistance that his opponents openly attempted to burn down the church, would not Basil probably have reported it to Terentius? So it is possible that this fire could have occurred in another of the cites which Basil visited during his Armenian mission.

Wherever Basil was when he preached *Mund*, he was preaching to members of a community which had just suffered a terrible ordeal. While sustaining significant losses, they still seem to have been thankful that the damage was not more extensive, as they wanted to rejoice over the miraculous victory. Oddly, Basil does not explicitly mention the fire before his audience insists that he do so. Nor is there anything stated before this that could plausibly be construed a veiled reference or allusion to the fire. It could be that Basil was deliberately trying to avoid mentioning it, perhaps unwilling to be derailed from his original homiletic plans by an act of arson that sought to disrupt his visit.[31]

But it stretches the limits of the imagination to think that Basil would have failed to respond in some way to the disaster just experienced by the community. Though detachment was one of Basil's most common homiletic themes regardless of context, it could well be the case that it was the fire itself which inspired him to preach on detachment from worldly goods in this specific situation. Basil and his audience had just been confronted with a concrete example of the instability and transitory nature of worldly goods. Perhaps Basil decided to generalize the spiritual lesson that could be drawn from the calamity rather than to focus specifically upon how those who had suffered loss should cope and how those who had been spared should respond. Since each group would have needed to hear a different exhortation, Basil may have thought it better to preach on a theme that was applicable to both. Indeed, in the addition to the homily, Basil alternates between addressing these two groups (§9–12). In the initial section, the various exhortations to detachment (§1–7) lead up to concluding exhortations about the care of the poor and needy (§ 8). It seems possible that Basil elaborated the

[31]Holman, "Rich City Burning," 206–7.

general theme of detachment in order to provoke the appropriate response from those who were unscathed by the fire, namely, to help those in need because of it, while at the same time to offer a spiritual perspective to those who had suffered losses. Note too that when he was asked to speak directly about the fire, Basil does devote several lines to it (§9), but then in the remainder of the sermon he quickly returns to the themes of helping the needy (§9) and detachment (§10–12), this time pointing to Job as an example.[32] Therefore, it is possible that the theme of detachment, though frequently found in Basil's homilies, was specifically chosen in this case because of the fire, even if it is not explicitly mentioned.

If this was how Basil chose to respond to the fire, it may have gone over the heads of his audience. For as Basil was concluding his homily, members of the audience made it clear that they wanted him to continue in order to speak specifically about the fire. Admittedly, the incomprehension of the audience seems to weaken the likelihood of the suggestion that the theme of detachment was deliberately chosen as a response to the fire. Yet this could also be attributed to the audience's misunderstanding Basil's subtle approach. Or perhaps they grasped his point about how to respond to the fire, but wanted him to speak explicitly about the fire so they could relive the drama and remember the miracle. As noted above, Basil obliged, but then quickly returned to the themes in the initial part of the homily, detachment and helping the needy. Basil seems to have been less interested in telling the story of the fire than in articulating the proper Christian response to it.

Therefore, it would seem that *Mund* was delivered at some location in Armenia Minor on the day after a fire had destroyed much property in the neighborhood of the church. This could have happened in any of the cities that Basil visited during his Armenian mission in the summer of 372 or 373 (or even during his later visit

[32]Cf. Holman, "Rich City Burning," 205: "Describing Job's similarly sudden catastrophes, Basil links together the key themes of the sermon: an inner transformed attitude of detachment as essential for right use of wealth and right practice of charity."

to Armenia in 375). Several comments made by Basil in the opening lines of the homily might be interpreted as allusions to his reception and activities in Satala, given what we know of his time there from *Ep.* 99. But the content of the homily itself does not necessarily require the events to take place in that city. And so, while Basil may have delivered *Mund* in Satala in the summer of 372 or 373, the available evidence suggests only a location somewhere in Armenia Minor during one of Basil's visits there, either in 372 or 373, or in 375.

It also seems that the homily is Basil's response to the violence of arson. It is possible that Basil chose to preach on one of his favorite themes, detachment, specifically because of the damage caused by the fire, as he deemed it the message most appropriate for both those who had suffered losses and those who had not. Therefore, Basil's exhortation to detachment in *Mund* may represent his pastoral response to a specific human misfortune, though presented in general enough terms to have wider application.[33]

Translation. The following translation is based on Julien Garnier's edition as reprinted in De Sinner ii.229–243 (=PG 31.540–564).[34] In crafting my translation, I benefited from Garnier's Latin translation and Sister M. Monica Wagner's English translation in the Fathers of the Church series,[35] as well as from the excerpts translated into English by Susan Holman in her article.

---

[33]My presentation of the context and date of *Mund* was greatly benefited from a series of e-mail exchanges with Susan Holman. I thank her for her gracious critiques and suggestions. The views expressed here, however, are my own.

[34]CPG 2866.

[35]M. Monica Wagner, *Saint Basil: Ascetical Works*, FOTC 9 (New York: The Fathers of the Church, Inc., 1950), 487–505.

Translation

1 I would have thought, dearly beloved, since I prod you insistently on every occasion with the goad of my words, that you would think of me as an annoying pain because I display an overconfidence that is appropriate neither for a guest nor for a man against whom similar charges have been made. Yet by my rebukes you have been roused to goodwill, and the blows from my tongue you have made into fuel for greater zeal. And none of this is unexpected. For you are wise in spiritual matters. *Rebuke a wise man, and he will love you* [Prov 9.8], says Solomon somewhere in his books. Thus on this present occasion too, brothers, I have come to give the same kind of exhortation, wishing, in whatever way I can, to help you avoid the nets of the devil. For the enemy of truth, dearly beloved, wages against us each day a war that is intense and takes many forms. Now he attacks us, as you know, by turning our desires into arrows against ourselves and continually drawing from us the means to do us harm. Since the Master limited most of his power by indissoluble laws and did not permit him, when he did attack, to wipe out our race from the earth once and for all, the envious one now wins victories over us through stealth by taking advantage of our lack of understanding.

Indeed, he acts like those wicked and greedy people whose business and purpose it is to get rich at others' expense, but who lack the power to use open violence. Such people are accustomed to lie in wait on the highways, and if they see a spot nearby, either split by deep gulleys or thickly shaded with dense foliage, they hide in it. In their hiding-places they are concealed from the farseeing eyes of travelers, and they leap upon their prey in surprise. And thus no one can see these snares of danger before falling into them. He who has been our enemy and hostile to us from the beginning acts in a similar manner.[1] He hides behind the shadows of worldly delights, which are usually well-adapted for concealing the robber and rendering the ambusher unseen on the road of this life. And thus it is

[1] Cf. Jn 8.44; 1 Jn 3.8.

that he secretly sows in us the traps for our destruction without our even realizing it.

So therefore, if we really wish to run the road of this life in safety to the end, and to present to Christ both soul and body alike free from shameful wounds, and to receive the crowns of victory, we must keep the eyes of our soul always on the lookout in every direction. We must be suspicious of everything insofar as it brings delight, immediately run past such things, and not fix our mind on any of them—not even if gold appears before us in heaps, ready to come to the hands of any who want it, for *if riches abound*, he says, *set not your heart upon them* [Ps 61.11]; not even if the earth sprouts every kind of delicacy and offers us gorgeous places to live, for *our citizenship is in heaven, from which we also await a Savior, Christ* [Phil 3.20]; not even if there is dancing, and revelry, and drinking, and feasting accompanied by the flute, for *vanity of vanities*, he says, *all is vanity!* [Eccl 1.2]; not even if you are presented with beautiful bodies in which wicked souls dwell, for *from the face of a woman flee as if from the face of a serpent*, says Wisdom [Sir 21.2 altered]; not even if you are offered the authority to rule and absolute power, together with a throng of attendants and flatterers; not even if you are presented with a lofty and splendid throne to which nations and cities are subjected in voluntary servitude, for *all flesh is as grass, and all glory of man as the flower of grass; the grass is withered, and the flower is fallen* [Is 40.6–7]. For beneath all these fabulous delights lurks our common enemy, waiting to see if we will ever, enticed by what we see, turn from the path of uprightness and fall into his trap. And we ought especially to be wary, if we do run heedlessly after these delights and regard the pleasure of enjoying them as not harmful, that we do not swallow the fishhook of deceit hidden in the first taste; and then through this first taste grow attached, partly willingly, partly unwillingly, to these pleasures, and are dragged by them, without our realizing it, to the dreadful lair of the robber, that is to say, to death.

2   Thus it is necessary and advantageous for all of us, brothers, to
ready ourselves like travelers or runners, and once we have figured
out how to make this journey as light as possible for our souls, to
push on straight to the end of the path. And no one should consider
me a coiner of new names because I just called human life a "path."
For David the prophet also spoke of life using this term. On one
occasion he says somewhere: *Happy are the blameless on the path,
who walk in the law of the Lord* [Ps 118.1]. On another occasion he
cries out to his Master: *The path of injustice put far away from me,
and by your law have mercy on me* [Ps 118.29]. Then, when he sang
the praises of God's swift help against his abusers as he accompanied
himself on the sweet lyre, he said: *And who is god but our God? The
God who girded me with power and made my path blameless* [Ps
17.32–33].

He had a good reason for thinking that this term was always
appropriate for the life of human beings upon the earth, whether
marvelous or dismal. For just as those who are hastening to complete
a strenuous journey easily reach the end of their path by taking alternating steps forward, their feet vying with each other to complete
the course, and continually relegate the foot in the front, once it has
been planted on the ground, to second place in a rapid exchange
with the other; so too those brought to life by the Creator arrive
at the end of their life by embarking right at the beginning upon
the particular parts of time, continually leaving behind the past for
the future. Doesn't the present life seem to you like an endless path
spread before you and a journey divided into periods like stages?
For each traveler it begins with the travails of our mothers, but the
course ends with the lodgings of our tombs. It leads all people to
these, some quickly, some more slowly, and some advancing through
all the intervals of time, others not even making it through the first
stages of life.

So then, as for those other roads which lead from city to city, it
is possible to get off them and not travel on them, if one so wishes.
But as for this path, even if we wish to slow down its course, it seizes

us against our will and draws those upon it to the end appointed by
the Master. And it is impossible, dearly beloved, for anyone, once he
has bolted through the gate which leads to this life and embarked
upon this path, not to come to its end. Each of us, after leaving the
wombs of our mothers, is at once seized and swept along by the flow
of time, continually letting go of the day already lived and never able
to return to yesterday, even if we want to do so. Yet we take pleasure
in being borne forwards, and find joy in exchanging one period of
life for the next, as if we were acquiring something great, and judge
it a happy day when a boy becomes a man or when a man becomes
a respected elder. We fail to recognize, then, that the time used up at
each stage of life adds up to the time that we have already lived. And
we do not realize that our life is being spent, even if we always measure it according to what has passed by and flowed away. Therefore,
we do not grasp how indeterminate is the time which the One who
has sent us on this journey wants to give us to complete our course.
Neither do we know when he will open the entrance gate for each
runner, nor do we realize that we should be prepared each day for
our departure there and wait for the decision of the Master with our
eyes fixed upon him. For he says: *Let your loins be girt and your lamps
burning, and you should be like men who are waiting for their lord to
come home from the marriage feast, so they may open to him at once
when he comes and knocks* [Lk 12.35–36].

3　We are not willing even to give careful consideration to what
sort of loads will make our journey light, those which can improve
us when we have gathered them and make our life hereafter exceed-
ingly joyful, since they become the personal possessions of those
who have them. Nor do we consider what sort of loads are heavy
and cumbersome and drag us to the ground, those which by nature
are utterly unsuited for human beings, not even allowing the ones
who have them to enter through that narrow gate.[2] On the contrary,
those which we should have gathered we ignore, but those which we

[2]See Mt 7.13–14.

should disdain we gather. And those which can be united with us and truly become an adornment natural to soul and body alike, to these we are not attentive at all; but those which will never belong to us but only mark us with shame, these we attempt to gather, laboring without purpose and toiling in great toils, like a self-deceived man who wants "to draw water in a leaky jar."[3] For surely it is obvious, I think, even to every child, that none of the things which bring joy in this life, the things over which most people go crazy, is truly ours or can become ours by nature. Rather, it is clear that they do not belong to anyone at all, neither to those who appear to enjoy them, nor to those who never come near them.

For if some were to amass gold in boundless measure in this life, not even then does it remain their personal possession in perpetuity. Despite all their efforts to secure it, either it deserts them while they are still alive by passing over to those more powerful, or it abandons them at the point of death, not being accustomed to depart along with those who owned it. Those dragged to that inescapable road by the One who forcibly separates our souls from this miserable flesh, turn back time and again to their riches and bewail the sweat expended upon them from their youth. But their wealth has eyes only for the hands of others, after inflicting upon them nothing but the toil of gathering and the crime of avarice. If someone were to possess upon the earth thousands of acres,[4] and magnificent homes, and herds of every kind of animal, and to exercise absolute authority among men, not even then would he enjoy them forever. Instead, although renowned for these things for a brief span of time, he will in his turn leave behind his abundance to others when he has been placed under a little bit of dirt. And what is more, in many cases even before he comes to the tomb, even before he departs from here, he will see his goods passing over to others, perhaps even to his enemies. Are we not aware that so many fields, so many homes,

[3]A common proverb for laboring in vain derived from the punishment assigned to the Danaids in Hades; see Xenophon, *Oeconomicus* 7.40; Plato, *Gorgias* 493b; Aristotle, *Politics* 1320a32. Basil cites it elsewhere: *Ieiı* 10 and *Litt.* 9.

[4]Literally, "thousands of plethra." A *plethron* was 100 Greek feet.

so many nations and cities, even when possessed by those who were still living, gave renown to other masters? Indeed, how those once slaves ascended to the throne of sovereign rule? How those once called lords and masters were pleased to stand with their subjects, and bowed down to their own slaves, when, as if by a roll of the dice, their fortunes suffered a sudden reversal?

4   But as for the foods and drinks we have developed, and all that outrageous wealth has concocted, beyond what is needed, to gratify the insatiable stomach that refuses nothing, could such things ever be ours, even if they were poured into us continually? As a matter of fact, there are some treats which produce only a little pleasure when tasted in passing, but when they are eaten to excess they become troublesome and immediately we feel disgust for them and are eager to get rid of them, thinking that our life would be seriously endangered if they were to remain in our bowels for any length of time. Indeed, over-indulgence has brought death to many or made it so that they no longer enjoy anything.

And as for lascivious intercourse, and impure copulation, and all such deeds of a soul carried away by sexual frenzy, is it not clear that these acts are altogether damaging and blatantly harmful to nature? That instead they bring about both the loss and diminution of what truly belongs to each? For by acts of sexual commerce the body is weakened and deprived of the nutriment that is best suited and most essential for its members. And so, everyone who has wallowed in these beds of lasciviousness, as soon as the deed is done, when the sting of the flesh has faded away and the mind, having reached the loathsome limit of its activities and returned to itself as if from a bout of drunkenness or some such turbulence, takes the opportunity to consider where it is—it is at this point that overwhelming regret for his lack of sexual restraint enters into him. For he notices that his body has become quite enfeebled, and slow to do what he needs to do, and weak in every way. In fact, this is understood even by physical trainers. A rule of sexual abstinence has been laid down in the wrestling schools to protect the bodies of the youths from such pleasures. It does not even allow the contestants themselves so much as to look upon splendid physiques, if indeed they want to have their heads crowned. For a loss of sexual control as one trains to wrestle leads to laughter, not a crown.

5   Since these pleasures are altogether alien to us and excessive, and cannot become the personal possession of anyone, it is best to run past them with our eyes closed. Yet it is fitting to expend great care on those things which are truly ours. But what is truly ours? The soul by which we live, which is light and intelligent, and needs none of things that weigh us down. And the body too, which the Creator gives to the soul as a vehicle for living this life. And so, this is a human being: a mind united to a suitable and fitting body. This is what the all-wise Artisan of the universe forms in the wombs of mothers. This is what the time of travail brings to light from those dark inner chambers. This is what has been appointed to rule over the earth. It was for this that creation was spread out as a place to practice virtue. It was for this that a law was laid down, to imitate the Artificer in his power and to bring about upon the earth a reflection of the good order in heaven. This is what departs when it is summoned from here. This is what stands at the tribunal of the God who sent it. This is what is judged. This is what receives the recompense for its conduct here.

In addition, anyone can discover that the virtues become our possession when they are woven into our nature through diligent practice. Nor is it their custom to abandon us while we toil upon the earth, unless we drive them away willingly and forcibly by giving entrance to vices. As we hasten to the next life, they speed us forward. They rank the one who possesses them with the angels. They shine forever under the eyes of the Creator. But as for riches, political power, worldly distinction, self-indulgence, and the whole throng of such things that increase daily through our lack of understanding, they neither enter into life with us nor accompany anyone departing from this world. Rather, that saying uttered by that just man of old remains true and valid for every human being: *Naked I came from my mother's womb, and naked I shall return* [Job 1.21].

6 So then, whoever is resolved to act in his own best interests will be especially concerned for his soul and will make every effort to keep it pure and noble. If the flesh is either consumed by hunger, or struggling with cold and heat, or afflicted by illnesses, or suffering something violent from anyone, he will consider it of little consequence, in the case of each of these adversities saying and uttering what Paul said: *Even though our outward man is wasting away, nonetheless our inward man is being renewed day by day* [2 Cor 4.16]. And when he sees mortal dangers approaching, not even then will he show fear. Instead he will take courage, saying to himself: *For we know that if the earthly tent we live in is destroyed, we have a building from God, a house not made with hands, eternal in the heavens* [2 Cor 5.1]. Now if anyone wishes to have regard for his body too, as it is the soul's only necessary possession and its co-worker for living upon the earth, he will give his bodily needs minimal attention, only just enough to keep it together and maintain its health through moderate care so that it can serve the soul. In addition, he will do all he can to avoid over-indulgence lest the body become unruly. But if he ever sees his body inflamed by desires for more, even beyond what is advantageous, he will cry out and prescribe to it what Paul said: *We brought nothing into this world; it is clear that we cannot take anything out of it. If we have food and clothing, with these we shall be content* [1 Tim 6.7–8]. For by continually reciting these words to his body and crying out to it, he will render it ever docile and agile for its journey to heaven and will possess a co-worker for the tasks that lie ahead. But if he allows his body to be given over to unbridled self-indulgence and to be stuffed with as much food as possible every day, he will in the end, like some wild beast, be dragged down to the earth by the violent counter-reactions he experiences, and there he will lie, groaning to no avail. And when he is led to the Master and asked for the fruit of the journey on earth entrusted to him, then he will loudly wail since he has nothing to give. And he will dwell in perpetual darkness, fiercely blaming self-indulgence and its deceit, by which he was robbed of the opportunity for salvation. He gains nothing from his tears. For David says: *In Hades who shall give you praise?* [Ps 6.6].

7   So then, let us flee [self-indulgence] as quickly as possible, lest we voluntarily choke ourselves to death. And so, if anyone baited in the past has either amassed a dust heap of riches for himself through acts of injustice and imprisoned his mind by worrying over them, or defiled his nature with the indelible filth of lasciviousness, or surfeited himself with other offenses, let him, while there is still time, before he comes the final destruction, cast off the greater part of his burdens. Before his ship sinks, let him jettison the cargo he ought not have accumulated. Let him imitate those who work on the sea. For these men, even if they are transporting necessities on the ship, when a raging tempest arises from the sea and threatens to engulf the ship that is loaded down with cargo, as quickly as they can, they jettison most of what weighs them down and are unsparing in casting their merchandise into the sea. They do this to raise the ship above the waves and possibly give only their souls and the bodies a chance to escape from the danger. Now it is surely far more appropriate for us rather than for them to think and act in this way. For they lose in an instant whatever they jettison and eventually fall into poverty by force of circumstance. But as for us, the more we jettison our wicked burdens, the more we shall accumulate even better riches for the soul. For fornication and all such things are utterly destroyed when they are jettisoned and are brought to non-existence when washed away by our tears. And then holiness and justice take their place, and being light things, they are not likely to be engulfed by any waves. And yet, when money is jettisoned in the good way, it is in fact not lost to those who have jettisoned it and flung it overboard. Rather, as if transported to other, safer ships—the stomachs of the poor—it is saved, and its arrival in the

safe harbor is anticipated, and it is kept for those who jettisoned it as an ornament, not a source of danger.

8 Therefore, dearly beloved, let us resolve to do the humane thing for ourselves: if we really want to turn our burdensome wealth into something that benefits us, let us distribute it to many people. They will bear it in abundant joy and deposit it in the lap of the Master, as in a safe storeroom, *where neither moth consumes nor thieves break in and steal* [Mt 6.20]. Let us give permission for our riches, which are intended for this purpose, to be poured upon the needy. Let us not ignore the Lazaruses who even now still lie before our eyes, nor begrudge them the crumbs from our table, which would be enough to satisfy them.[5] Let us not emulate that savage rich man, lest we go with him to the same fires of hell, where with importunate cries we will beg not only Abraham, but also anyone who has lived a virtuous life; yet our beseeching will not benefit us at all. For *a brother does not ransom; shall anyone ransom?* [Ps 48.8]. Each person whom we beg will shout at us, saying: "Do not seek the kind and humane treatment which you yourself neglected to show others! How can you desire to be the recipients such great acts of kindness when you refrained from those of lesser sort? Enjoy what you have gathered during your lifetime. Weep now, for in the past you showed no mercy when you saw your brother weeping." Such is what they will say to you—and rightly so.

I am afraid, however, that they will attack us with words even more pointed than these: as you know, we outshine that rich man when it comes to acting wickedly. For it is absolutely not in the interests of thrift that we pass by our brothers when they lie prostrate on the ground. Nor is it to safeguard our wealth for our children or other family members that we close our ears to the needy. On the contrary, we do such things to redirect our expenditures to inferior pursuits, thereby making our wasteful spending a whetstone of wickedness for those who would cater to us. For how many men

[5]See Lk 16.19–31.

and women gather around the tables of the rich? Some of them amuse the host with obscene jokes; others enkindle the fires of lust by indecent glances and gestures. Some aim to provoke laughter in the host by witty banter; others deceive him with false praise. And not only are the attendees rewarded with feasting so sumptuously, but also they go home with their hands full of costly gifts. And they learn from us that the pursuit and practice of such things is more advantageous than virtue.

But if a poor man who is so hungry that he can barely speak presents himself to us, we turn away him, even though his nature is the same as ours. We feel loathing for him and get away from him as quickly as we can, as if we are afraid that walking slowly would cause us to share in his misfortune. And if he bows down to the ground because he is ashamed of his circumstances, we say that he is putting on a pretense. But if he boldly looks us in the eye on account of his oppressive pangs of hunger, instead we call him a shameless lout. And if he happens to be wearing clothes given to him by someone else, and they are in good shape, we drive him away as greedy swindler and swear that he is feigning poverty. But if he is covered with rags that are falling to pieces, instead we drive him away as a smelly dirtbag. And neither by appealing to the name of the Creator in the midst of his supplications, nor by continually praying for us that we too may not fall into similar sufferings, can he bend our merciless decision. For these reasons I suspect that the fires of hell will be more severe for us than they were for that rich man.

So then, if time permitted and there were enough energy for it, I would explain to you everything that the Bible teaches about that rich man and elaborate upon these passages. But you are weary, and now it is time to dismiss you. If we ourselves have omitted anything through deficiency of mind and tongue, formulate it for yourselves and apply it like a kind of medicine to the wounds of your soul. For the Scripture says: *give a wise man an opportunity, and he will become wiser* [Prov 9.9]. *God is able to make every blessing abound in you,*

so that always having enough of everything in every respect you may
provide in abundance for every good work [2 Cor 9.8].

9   As you can see, our homily has already been brought into port.
Yet now some brothers want me to launch out again on this journey
of advice and counsel. They urge me not to pass over the miracles
wrought yesterday by the Master, nor to be silent about the trophy
which the Savior erected against the fury of the devil, but rather to
provide you with an opportunity for hymns of joyful exultation.

Once again, as you know, the devil has shown his fury against
us: having armed himself with the flames of fire, he marched against
the precincts of the church.[6] But once again, our common mother[7]
won the victory and turned the engines of war back upon the enemy.
He has accomplished nothing, save to publicize his hatred. Grace
blew a wind that countered the forward momentum of the enemy;
the sanctuary[8] remained unharmed. The tempest stirred up by the
enemy lacked the power to shake the rock on which Christ built the
sheepfold for his own flock.[9] He who long ago in Babylon extinguished the fiery furnace was stationed at our side in the present.[10]
Can you imagine how the devil groans today because he failed to
reap what he had planned to gain from this attempt? For the enemy
started a fire in the vicinity of the church to destroy our prosperity.
And the flames were fanned in every direction by his violent blasts,
spreading over all that lay in their path and feeding upon the sur-
rounding air. They were being driven into contact with the holy
places[11] and brought us to the brink of calamity. But then the Savior
turned the flames back upon the one who had kindled them and

---

[6]Gk. τοῖς τῆς ἐκκλησίας σηκοῖς. See n. 11 below.

[7]That is, the church.

[8]Gk. ὁ νεώς. See n. 11 below.

[9]See Mt 16.18.

[10]See Dan 3.49.

[11]Gk. τῶν ἀνακτόρων. Though Basil mentions "the precincts of the church," "the
sanctuary," and "the holy places," it is not clear if he is referring to distinct architec-
tural elements of the church complex or merely employing synonyms for the church
building.

bade his madness to fall on him. Indeed, the enemy readied the bow of treachery, but he was forbidden to let an arrow fly. Or rather, he let it fly, but it was turned back upon his own head. He has reaped those bitter tears which he prepared for us.

But now, brothers, let us make the enemy's wound more grievous. Let us intensify his sorrow. I will tell you how, but you will have to do it. There are some who were rescued from the dominions of the fire by the Creator and have nothing to live on in the future. For only with their soul and body did they escape the dangers. So let those of us who remain untouched by these difficult experiences make our own resources available to them. Let us embrace those brothers who barely escaped with their lives. Let each of us say to each of them: *He was dead, and is alive again; he was lost, and is found* [Lk 15.24]. And let us clothe each of their bodies, which are just like ours. Let us oppose these insults of the enemy by providing consolation. And so, even though he has caused harm, it will not seem that he has caused any great harm; even though he started a war, he will display no conquest; and even though he robbed the brothers of their resources, he will be openly defeated by our charitable donations.

10   And as for you, brothers, you who have escaped this danger: do not fall into a deep funk over the evils which have occurred, nor be troubled in your mind. Instead, clear away the mist of sadness, revive your souls by thinking more courageous thoughts, and turn what happened into an opportunity for winning crowns. For if you remain untroubled, you will be seen as proven in your faith, shining like gold proved genuine by fire.[12] And you will increase the enemy's shame even more since he could not get you to shed even a single tear by his plots!

Remember the patience of Job. Tell yourselves what he told himself: *The Lord gave; the Lord has taken away. As it seemed good to the Lord, so too has it come to pass* [Job 1.21]. Now do not let your sufferings mislead any of you into thinking and claiming that there

[12]Cf. 1 Pet 1.7; Prov 17.3.

is no providence arranging our affairs. Nor let anyone find fault with the Master's administration and judgment.[13] Gaze rather upon that athlete and make him your adviser for the better course. Review all Job's contests, one after the other, in which he bested his opponent. Though the devil launched so many missiles at Job, he did not land a lethal blow. For he snatched away the prosperity of Job's family and plotted to overwhelm him with a rapid succession of reports about terrible events. In fact, while the first messenger was still announcing a terrible misfortune, another messenger came with the sorrowful news of worse incidents. And the dreadful episodes piled up one atop the other, and the catastrophes were like onrushing waves: before the first bout of tears had abated, a reason for another was already upon him.[14]

But that just man stood like a bulwark, withstanding the blasts of the tempest and reducing the violent waves to foam. And he let out this gracious cry to the Master: *The Lord gave; the Lord has taken away. As it seemed good to the Lord, so too has it come to pass* [Job 1.21]. Indeed, he did not consider anything that befell him worthy of tears. But when someone came and announced that a violent wind toppled the place where his sons and daughters were feasting and celebrating, only then did he rend his garments, showing his natural sympathy and testifying by his actions that he was a loving father.[15] Yet even at that moment he set a limit and a measure for his sadness and made the best of what happened by saying the following pious words: *The Lord gave; the Lord has taken away. As it seemed good to the Lord, so too has it come to pass* [Job 1.21]. He all but uttered the following: "I was called a father for as long as he who made me one wished it. He decided, in turn, to take away my crown of offspring. I do not fight with him over what belongs to him. Let what seems good to the Master prevail. He is the Artificer of my progeny; I am his instrument. Why should I, his servant, be annoyed without due

[13]Basil's homily *Malo* is directed against those who doubted divine providence.
[14]See Job 1.13–17.
[15]See Job 1.18–20.

cause and complain about a decree which I cannot repeal?" By firing
such words that just man shot down the devil.

11   When in turn the enemy saw that Job was victorious and could
not be shaken by any of these assaults, he brought up another engine
of war: trials for his very flesh. Thrashing his body with unspeakable
blows, he made it ooze streams of worms. Knocking the man off a
kingly throne, he set him upon a dunghill.[16] And yet, even though he
was afflicted with these horrible sufferings, he remained unmoved;
even though his body was being mangled, he kept the treasury of
piety untouched in the hidden recesses of his soul.

So when the enemy realized that there was nothing else that
he could do, he happened to remember that ancient treachery.[17]
Accordingly, he tricked the mind of Job's wife into holding an impious and blasphemous opinion and attempted to use her to make the
athlete waver. After restraining herself for a long time, she stood
before that just man, stooping over him, clapping her hands at what
she saw, and berating him for the rewards his piety had brought.
She told him the story of the longstanding prosperity of their family and contrasted this with their present tribulations. She made it
plain what kind of life he had obtained from these misfortunes and
what kind of recompense he had received from the Master for his
many sacrifices.[18] On and on she spoke, uttering words worthy of
womanly faint-heartedness but yet capable of disturbing any man
and demoralizing even a noble mind: "*I go about as a wanderer and a
hired servant* [Job 2.9d LXX]. Though a queen I serve and have been
compelled to look at the hands of my household servants.[19] Though
I once fed many, now I am glad to be fed at the expense of strangers." And [she added that] it would be better and more beneficial if
he were to cut himself from the earth by uttering impious words,

[16]See Job 2.7–8 and 7.5.
[17]See Gen 3.1–20.
[18]Here Basil paraphrases Job 2.9a–e LXX, which constitutes a major expansion
of Job 2.9 MT.
[19]Cf. Ps 122.2.

thereby sharpening the sword of the Creator's wrath, rather than to prolong the hardship of these struggles for himself and his wife by obstinately enduring in the face of these dreadful events.[20]

Grieved by these words of hers as by none of the previous evils, his face was filled with rage and he turned to his wife as if to an enemy. And what did he say? "Why have you spoken *like one of the foolish women* [Job 2.10]? Forgo this counsel, woman! How long," he said, "are you going to heap insults upon our life together by saying such things? You have told lies about my behavior—I wish you hadn't!—and have cast aspersions on my way of life by saying such things. It seems to me now that half of me has acted impiously, seeing that marriage made the two of us one body[21] and you have fallen into blasphemy. *If we received good things from the Lord's hand, shall we not bear the bad?* [Job 2.10]. Remind yourself of the good things from the past. Balance out the bad with the good. No person's life is altogether blessed. Continual prosperity belongs to God alone. So if you are upset by these present circumstances, comfort yourself by remembering the past. Now you weep, but you laughed in the past. Now you are poor, but you were rich in the past. You used to drink the limpid stream of life; be patient now as you drink these muddy waters. The waters of a river are not always pure. As you know, our life is a river, ever flowing and filled with waves one after the other. One has already flowed by, another is still passing, another has just emerged from its sources, another is about to do so, and all of us hasten to the common sea of death. *If we received good things from the Lord's hand, shall we not bear the bad?* [Job 2.10]. Are we compelling the Judge to supply us forever with the same things? Are we teaching the Master how he should arrange our life? He holds the authority over his own decisions. He directs our affairs in whatever way he wishes. He is wise, and he measures out to his servants only what will profit them.   **12** Do not engage in futile investigations of the Master's judgment; only love the ways in which he has

[20]See Job 2.9.
[21]Cf. Mt 19.5–6; Mk 10.7–8; Eph 5.31.

dispensed his wisdom. With pleasure receive whatever he gives to you. In painful situations show that you are worthy of that joy that used to be yours."

By speaking these words Job repulsed the devil's attack and brought upon him the disgrace of total defeat. What happened next? His affliction fled from him, as if it had marched upon him without a plan and could accomplish nothing further. His flesh recaptured a youthful glow. His life flourished again with all good things. Double the amount of riches flowed into his house from all places.[22] Hence one half of the riches he now possessed made it seem as if he had lost nothing and the other half was given to that just man as the recompense for his patience. But why did he receive double the amount of horses, mules, camels, sheep, fields, and all that contributes to luxurious living, yet the number of the children born to him was equal to the number of those who died? Because when irrational beasts and all riches pass away, they are brought to complete destruction. But in contrast, children, even when they are dead, continue to live in the best part of their nature.[23] So then, honored again with other sons and daughters by the Creator, even this possession he held in double measure. For while those children of his who were present with him brought joy to their parents in this life, the others who predeceased him awaited their father. At some point in the future, all of them will stand around Job, when the Judge of human life gathers the universal church together, when the trumpet that signals the coming of the king blasts into the tombs and demands back the bodies deposited in them.[24] At that time too those who now appear to be dead will come into the presence of the Architect of the universe more quickly than the living. This is the reason, I think, why he measured out to Job double the amount of his other riches and judged that Job would be satisfied with an equal number of children.

[22]See Job 42.10–13.
[23]That is, their souls are eternal.
[24]Cf. Job 19.25–26.

Do you see how many good things the just Job gathered to himself through patient endurance? And as for you, if any difficulty has come upon you from the fire started yesterday by the treachery of the demons, patiently bear it and calm the distress from your suffering by thinking better thoughts. Indeed, as it is written, *entrust your cares to the Lord, and he will support you* [Ps 54.23]. To him *glory* is fitting *forever and ever. Amen* [1 Pet 4.11].

Homily Delivered in Lakizois

INTRODUCTION

Not only is this homily one of Basil's least known and least studied sermons, it is also his least thematically unified homily.[1] It is more or less a hodgepodge of discussions about various vices—in particular, partiality, anger, envy, and greed—according to a structure that is not immediately apparent. This homily is similar to *Prov* and most of his homilies on the Psalms (such as *Ps14a* and *Ps115* in this volume), in that a number of topics are addressed in its course. But the structure of those homilies is clear, as they are line-by-line commentaries on discrete sections of Scripture and Basil attempts to draw out a cohesive teaching. Not so here. From the opening paragraph of this homily we learn that Basil intends to comment on particular verses of Scripture taken from passages publicly read earlier that day (§1). Apparently there were readings from the Psalms, Proverbs, the historical books of the Old Testament, the New Testament letters, and the gospels. It is not clear in what context this great variety of scriptural texts was read. It could have been in a liturgical service. But it is also possible that they were read in connection with the annual synod that Basil was attending (§5). At any rate, the homily deals only with verses from Proverbs: 11.25, 12.13a, 22.24, 23.6, and 23.10. Perhaps the story of the Good Samaritan (Lk 10.29–37) was read earlier in the day too since Basil gives an interpretation of Luke 10.30 (§9).

The theme which Basil attempts to use to connect the various sections of the homily is that the wily devil employs different tactics

---

[1] L. Ellies Du Pin, *Nouvelle bibliothèque des auteurs ecclésiastiques* (Utrecht: Jean Broedelet, 1731), ii.194, called it "plus composé" than Basil's other homilies.

to seduce different people (§1). The devil determines that vice to which a person is already prone and then offers his own temptations to it. But at the same time Scripture offers remedies for each vice to which the devil might tempt a person. Therefore, the scriptural verses discussed by Basil provide either remedies for vices or furnish an opportunity to speak about their remedies. At the beginning of the homily Basil intimates that he will speak about envy, anger, greed, and pride (§2). The topic of pride, however, never comes up.[2] The first vice with which Basil deals is partiality, or respecting persons, which was not mentioned earlier. After this he turns to anger (§3), then briefly to envy (§4), then more extensively to greed (§5–7), and then Basil returns to envy (§8–9). The homily then ends abruptly.

It is hard to make sense of this structure, and it raises many questions. What determined the order in which Basil discussed the vices and interpreted verses from Proverbs? Why did Basil treat envy twice (§4 and 8), both times in the context of interpreting the same verse, Proverbs 23.6? What does the abrupt end to the homily indicate? Did the homily originally include a discussion of pride, which is now lost? Or did Basil abort his planned discussion of pride? All these questions and others like them cannot be adequately addressed here. Nonetheless, an attempt at solving one of these puzzles will be made below.[3]

A good portion of Basil's teaching on the vices of partiality, anger, greed, and envy is paralleled elsewhere in his corpus.[4] Though it is not explicitly stated in this homily, the virtues opposite to the vice of partiality are charity and justice, which were frequent topics for Basil.[5] He dedicated entire homilies to anger (*Ira*) and envy (*Inv*), and there are numerous similarities between them and *Lak*.[6]

---

[2]For Basil's teaching on pride, see *Hum*, translated in this volume on pp. 108–119.

[3]See pp. 189–190.

[4]See the cross-references in the footnotes to the homily for precise details.

[5]For example, see *Prov* 8–9 and *Ps14a* 6 in this volume.

[6]*Inv* is translated in this volume on pp. 132–144. See the translation of *Ira* by Nonna Verna Harrison, *St Basil the Great: On the Human Condition*, PPS 30 (Crest-

His teaching on greed echoes his remarks found especially in his so-called homilies on social justice (*Div, Dest, Fam*, and *Ps14b*).[7] But Basil does not merely repeat himself in this homily. For example, while Basil mentioned the devil's envy in *Inv*, he did not elaborate on this theme there. But the bulk of the discussion of envy in *Lak* is concerned with this theme. Thus *Lak* complements *Inv* nicely. While there is some overlap, in many cases in this homily Basil nuances, expands upon, or adds to his teaching on the same topics found elsewhere.

The homily delivered in Lakizois opens with a reference to uproar outside the building where Basil was preaching, which he attributes to the "enemy," the devil (§1). He exhorts his audience not to be distracted by the tumult by calling to mind the scriptural passages read earlier that day in the morning. As mentioned above, apparently there were readings from the Psalms, Proverbs, the historical books of the Old Testament, the New Testament letters, and the gospels. Basil encourages each member of his audience to find a teaching in the scriptural passages heard that will be spiritually beneficial in resisting that vice to which he or she is already inclined. For the devil seduces people by determining that vice to which a person is liable and then offering enticements to it. Basil assures his audience that Scripture provides remedies for every vice, mentioning in particular envy, anger, greed, and pride (§2). All of these are discussed in what follows, except pride, by interpreting select verses from Proverbs.

Basil first deals with Proverbs 12.13a, *The one who looks upon smooth things shall obtain mercy* (§2). As mercy is obtained as a result of a praiseworthy action, Basil wonders in what sense simply looking upon smooth things, which is involuntary, can be praiseworthy. Observing that most of what we see upon the earth is rough

wood, NY: St Vladimir's Seminary Press, 2005), 81–92. An older translation can be found in M. Monica Wagner, *Saint Basil: Ascetical Works*, FOTC 9 (New York: Fathers of the Church, Inc., 1950), 447–461.

[7]All these homilies are translated in C. Paul Schroeder, *St Basil the Great: On Social Justice*, PPS 38 (Crestwood, NY: St Vladimir's Seminary Press, 2009).

(like fields of crops), he questions whether this verse means that we will be condemned for looking upon rough things. No doubt Basil is being somewhat playful here, in order to point out that Proverbs 12.13a must be interpreted "according to the higher sense," that is, figuratively.

According to Basil, "looking upon smooth things" means treating people equitably regardless of their social rank, economic status, or outward appearance. Partiality has no place in the Christian life. The poor should be treated no differently from the rich, strangers no differently from family members. Basil justifies this practice by appealing to our common humanity and shared basic needs. "Give to your brother and to the stranger," says Basil. "Do not turn your brother away, and make the stranger your very own brother" (§2). It is wrong to care for our relatives but to spurn strangers because in fact both spiritually and biologically we share a common descent: our common father is God our Father in heaven; our common mother is the earth from which we have been formed. We are all siblings: anyone who asks for our help is a descendant of Adam just as we are and has received the same grace from the Lord as we have. Yet treating some people with more honor is not in itself wrong. It is only wrong when this is done based on social rank, economic status, or outward appearance. Rather, people should be honored not based on such externals, but based on their virtues hidden within. Virtue alone confers distinction and honor. Hence Basil is not advocating the eradication of social distinctions within the Christian community, but arguing for new criteria on which to base distinctions.

Basil then switches topics, turning to anger (§3). He begins by engaging in an imaginary dialogue with his audience to get them to acknowledge that they are afflicted by irascibility. He exhorts them to find the remedy for this affliction in the Scriptures because, as is indicated by Proverbs 11.25 (*an irascible man does not command respect*), anger is a great sin. Basil explains that an irascible man loses respect because when a person is angry he takes on a beastlike appearance. This boarish form of the irate man is vividly described in a physiognomic manner, with Basil depicting the biological, emotional, and mental changes brought on by rage. This brings Basil to Proverbs 22.24, *And do not associate with an irascible man.* Just as the barking of one dog tends to provoke another dog to bark, so too the irascible man tends to engage even those who are calm and peaceful in escalating angry exchanges. And so, it is better to avoid contact with the irascible altogether.

Next Basil deals briefly with envy, citing but not yet interpreting Proverbs 23.6, *Do not dine with a jealous man* (§4). All that he says at this point is that envy consumes human hearts more than rust consumes iron, and that the sole advantage of envy is that it afflicts only the envier, not those envied. Then what follows is a detailed account of greed given in the course of interpreting Proverbs 23.10, *Do not remove ancient borders, nor enter the possession of orphans* (§5). Taking what is not rightfully yours out of greed is not only a sin, but it is irrational. For what you acquire in this life does not remain your possession forever, but is passed on to your heirs. Greed must be checked as quickly as possible because like fire it consumes everything in its path insatiably. Strangely, the greedy person takes no delight in his possessions, but is distressed over what he still lacks. His life is filled with sleeplessness, worry, and anxiety over being dragged into court for despoiling orphans, over imagined thieves, over his grown sons whom he suspects want to push him aside and take control of his holdings, and over storing up enough money for uncertainties in the future. At this point, Basil interrupts his discussion on greed to justify why he is preaching on the vices in the first place and explains the purpose of the synod currently in session. An annual synod is convoked, he explains, for the purpose of providing instruction that is otherwise hard to come by because of a lack of teachers.[8] Once the meeting ends, the attendees should remember what they learned and put it into practice, looking forward to the next gathering.

---

[8]Cf. the purpose of synods stated in *Trin* 2.

Then Basil resumes his treatment of greed, again interpreting Proverbs 23.10 (§6). One should not use their children as an excuse for greedily accumulating money and possessions. A better inheritance to bequeath to them is the example of the charitable use of money. For if you despoiled orphans in this life, when you die others will despoil the children you have left behind as orphans. But if you cared for orphans in this life, when you die others will care for your orphaned children as their own. Furthermore, you did not pray for children so that you could use them as an excuse for the sin of greed (§7). Once again Basil emphasizes that it is better to leave to your children an example of the pious use of money than money and possessions greedily and unethically acquired.

The remainder of the homily is about envy. Basil begins by discussing how envy is the quintessential passion of the devil (§8). Originally created with the authority of an angel, the devil was roused to envy when he realized that God honored human beings above all other creatures. While all other creatures were created for the sake of human beings, human beings were made for the sake of God, to give glory to him. Envious of human beings and noticing that the woman was naturally inclined to tenderness, the devil ensnared her by making her inclination to virtue into an inclination to vice. Basil's description of the natural tenderness of mothers, who routinely neglect their own needs to care for their children, is a rare appreciative view of women in his corpus.

Before continuing his discussion of the devil's envy, Basil recounts the ways in which envy manifests itself, echoing *Inv* 1–2: the envier is unable to disclose his envy and refuses to seek healing for his envy (§8). Adopting an exhortatory tone, Basil then urges his listeners not to fall into the snare of devil, remembering that humanity now lives exiled from paradise because of him. In fact, the devil has wronged humanity twice: not only is he responsible for our exile from paradise, but he also thwarts our return through countless schemes.

Next Basil resumes the topic of the devil's envy (§9). He came to hate God because God honored human beings above all other creatures by making them in his image and likeness. Since he could not attack God directly, the devil attacked God indirectly by attacking his image, human beings. In this context Basil uses two metaphors to drive home his point. First, the devil is like an angry Roman citizen who throws rocks at an effigy of the emperor since he cannot attack the emperor himself. Second, the devil is like a leopard in the arena who attacks the depiction of a man on placard, which was apparently used to taunt the beast. These metaphors provide the reader with picturesque glimpses into fourth-century life in Cappadocia.

The homily concludes with an admittedly odd exegesis of the story of the Good Samaritan from the Gospel of Luke (§9). Basil notes that Jerusalem is located in a mountainous region, whereas Jericho is in low country.[9] So in traveling from Jerusalem to Jericho, the man went from the heights to the depths, that is, from incorruptibility to sin. Basil focuses on the fact that the robbers first beat the man then stripped him. The beating is interpreted as the act of committing sin, whereas the stripping as the loss of incorruptibility. Basil justifies this figurative interpretation by the fact that in actual beatings, robbers strip their prey first, then beat the person in order to preserve his clothes. So clearly the unusual sequence of the events in the scriptural account contains an insight into the deleterious effects of sin. And then the homily concludes rather abruptly, though it does have Basil's signature quotation of 1 Peter 4.11 tacked on.

As mentioned above, the structure of this homily is quite mystifying, but the homily itself may provide two clues that contribute to explaining it. First, in the last paragraph of §5, as mentioned above, Basil interrupts his interpretations of verses from Proverbs and discussions of vices to justify why he is talking about these topics and explains the purpose of the synod. It was perhaps with these lines, even if they are not quite exhortatory, that Basil intended to conclude the homily. By this point in the homily he had interpreted all five verses from Proverbs (11.25, 12.13a, 22.24, 23.6, and 23.10) in the course of discussing all four vices: partiality (§2), anger (§3), envy

[9]Basil geography is actually a bit off here; see pp. 191–192 below.

(§4), and greed (§5). The remainder of the homily simply expands upon or continues previous interpretations and discussions: Proverbs 23.10 and greed in §6–7, and Proverbs 23.6 and envy in §8–9. It is unclear what might have prompted him to resume his discussions of greed and envy, and interpretations of Proverbs 23.10 and 23.6, if indeed the last paragraph of §5 was intended to be the conclusion.[10] But there is another clue that suggests a different way of understanding the structure of the homily. In §4 Basil had quoted but did actually interpret Proverbs 23.6, and he devotes only a few lines to the topic of envy. Perhaps realizing this omission he sought to rectify it in §8–9. In this case, the interruption in the last paragraph of §5 would just be a digression in the course of his treatment of greed and interpretation of Proverbs 23.10 in §5–7.

Authenticity. Julien Garnier was the first to raise doubts about this homily's authenticity.[11] His main objection was made on stylistic grounds, judging that Basil could not possibly be responsible for the poor style that the homily occasionally exhibits.[12] Garnier was not saying that the style of this homily is wholly inconsistent with those items of Basil's homiletic corpus of undisputed authenticity. Indeed, he admitted that the homily is thoroughly Basilian.[13] Rather, Garnier's objection is based on the assumption that Basil was always a master stylist; hence, instances of poor style preclude Basil's authorship. Of course this is a woefully inadequate criterion for determining the homily's authenticity.[14] Note too that, while

[10]Cf. *Mund* 9, where Basil notes that, as he was wrapping up the homily, his audience urged him to continue speaking.

[11]"Praefatio," §IV, 12–15 (De Sinner ii.x–xiv; PG 31.23–30).

[12]As an example, here is Garnier's view of Basil's description of the relative locations of Jericho and Jerusalem in *Lak* 9: "These are the words of a man who says vain things in a serious way, not of a most dignified Father, who everywhere teaches things that are most appropriate and useful" ("Praefatio," §IV, 14 [De Sinner ii.xiii; PG 31.28]).

[13]"The author, whoever he is, either wanted to appear to be Basil himself or was certainly eager to be Basilian" ("Praefatio," §IV, 15 [De Sinner ii.xiii; PG 31.28]). Garnier surmises that the many echoes of Basil's other homilies in this one misled previous editors to think that it was Basil's.

[14]For further comments on Garnier's dubious "stylistic" criteria, see pp. 89–90, 216, and 267.

Prudentius Maran retained Garnier's classification of this homily, he signaled that he did not always agree with Garnier's stylistic assessments by adding bracketed comments of dissent to Garnier's discussion. Even still, it cannot be denied that this homily contains several stylistic infelicities.

Garnier offered two further objections, both related to the Scriptures. First, he was hesitant to ascribe this homily to Basil because its author claimed that the verse, *The one who looks upon smooth things shall obtain mercy*, was from Proverbs (§2). In other words, Basil, as a Father of the Church, could not possibly have been mistaken about the contents of the Bible—another dubious assumption on the part of Garnier. But here Garnier betrays a certain ignorance. While not found in Hebrew Masoretic Text or the Latin Vulgate, this verse does appear in the Greek Septuagint, as Proverbs 12.13a. Basil has simply quoted the version of the Old Testament used in his era. Second, Garnier found Basil's interpretation of Luke 10.30 perverse, as it was used to show the devil's hatred of God and human beings rather than love of neighbor (§9). Here Garnier's assessment appears to be guided more by prejudice about what he thinks the biblical text should mean than by a willingness to accept a creative, and perhaps odd, figurative exegesis on the part of Basil. Therefore, Garnier's objections to the authenticity of this homily are without merit. Nonetheless, his opinion continues to have influence since it has been frequently repeated in widely-used resources and the reprint of his edition in J.-P. Migne's *Patrologia Graeca* remains the most readily available version.[15]

One aspect of this homily that bears upon its authenticity concerns the author's inaccurate account of the geography of Palestine in

[15]E.g., Blomfield Jackson, "Prolegomena: Sketch of the Life and Works of Saint Basil," NPNF ii.8, xiii–lxxvii at lxxii; Otto Bardenhewer, *Patrology: The Lives and Works of the Fathers of the Church* (St Louis: Herder, 1908), 279; J. Tixeront, *A Handbook of Patrology* (St Louis / London: Herder, 1920), 171. Maurice Geerard, *Clavis Patrum Graecorum. Volumen II. Ab Athanasio ad Chrysostomum* (Turnhout: Brepols, 1974), p. 167 still ranked it among the Basilian *dubia*, though the 1998 *CPG Supplementum* (ed. M. Geerard and J. Noret) drops this classification. It is also ignored in Bernardi's study of Cappadocian homilies.

§9. Garnier saw this as an indication that Basil was not the author.[16] But this need not be the case. In §9 the author notes that Jerusalem is "in a mountainous region" and Jericho is down near the Dead Sea. Of course this is mistaken: Jericho is ten miles north of the Dead Sea in the valley of the Jordan River. This inaccuracy could be attributed to the author's unfamiliarity with the region, but the author speaks as if he has first-hand knowledge of the area: "If any of you were to see the place, you would know the truth of what I am saying . . . " So the homily seems to have been preached by someone who had visited Palestine but was not very familiar with its geography. Basil fits this description perfectly. It is very likely that Basil visited Palestine in the late 350s during a journey which took him throughout the east in search of Eustathius of Sebasteia and during which he learned about the burgeoning monastic movements in many places.[17] Hence these lines about the geography of Palestine do not preclude Basil's authorship, though of course they do not prove it since surely many other people who had visited Palestine remain uncertain about its exact geography.

More recently, the noted Basilian scholars Jean Gribomont and Paul Jonathan Fedwick have affirmed the authenticity of this homily. In his preface to the Brepols reprint of PG 31, Gribomont noted that this homily is found in all the best manuscripts of Basil's homilies and thus that there seemed to be no compelling reasons to reject it as inauthentic.[18] Fedwick confirmed this assessment.[19] The many parallels between this homily and others of Basil (see the footnotes

[16]See n. 12 above.

[17]*Ep.* 223.3. For a discussion of the historicity of Basil's trip to Palestine, see Brouria Bitton-Ashkelony, *Encountering the Sacred: The Debate on Christian Pilgrimage in Late Antiquity*, The Transformation of the Classical Heritage 28 (Berkeley: University of California Press, 2005), 44–8.

[18]*In Tomum 31 Patrologiae Graecae ad editionem operum rhetoricorum, asceticorum, liturgicorum Sancti Basilii Magni Introductio* (Turnhout: Brepols, 1961), 6.

[19]Paul Jonathan Fedwick, "A Chronology of the Life and Works of Basil of Caesarea," in idem, ed., *Basil of Caesarea: Christian, Humanist, Ascetic. A Sixteen-Hundredth Anniversary Symposium* (Toronto: The Pontifical Institute of Mediaeval Studies, 1981), 3–19 at 10; BBV i.xviii; ii.viii and ii.1103–1105.

to the translation) also seem to point to Basil's authorship. To my knowledge no further objections have been raised against its authenticity. Thus we can view this homily as genuine.

Context and Date. If the phrase *en Lakizois* refers to a place, then this is the only sermon of Basil whose title names where it was preached.[20] But locating Lakizois has proved elusive. Louis-Sébastien Le Nain de Tillemont suggested that it was situated within the diocese of Caesarea, though he offered no evidence for this.[21] Julien Garnier declined to speculate: "At what corner of the earth was located the place where this homily is said to have been delivered we are not even able to offer a conjecture."[22] Paul Jonathan Fedwick tentatively suggested that "Lakizois" was a corruption of "Lazikē."[23] This was the Greek name for Egrisi, a Georgian region on the eastern shore of the Black Sea, and was derived from the name of the tribe of the ruling elites, the Laz. If Fedwick's conjecture is correct, then the title would mean something like "delivered in Lazikē," or perhaps "among the Laz." In fact, the Coptic tradition attributes to Basil two homilies on St Michael the Archangel preached in Lazikē, although they are certainly spurious.[24] But in the end Fedwick's suggestion that the word is a corruption remains conjecture, and besides, there is no other evidence that Basil ever traveled so far northeast.

Taking *en Lakizois* as denoting a time rather than a place, Susan Holman suggested that *Lakizois* is somehow related to the rare verb λακίζω, meaning "to tear" (and related to *lakis*, "a rent, rendering"). If so, then the title would mean something like "delivered in a time of disruption," or "during a split or schism," either in a theological or political sense. But she considered this conjecture "a bit of a stretch,"

[20]One possible reason for this exception is the homily's lack of thematic unity, which might have made giving it a title challenging.

[21]Louis-Sébastien Le Nain de Tillemont, *Mémoires pour servir à l'histoire ecclésiastique des six premiers siècles* (Venice: Pitteri, 1732), ix.300.

[22]"Praefatio," §IV, 12 (De Sinner ii.x; PG 31.23).

[23]Fedwick, "A Chronology," 10 n. 45.

[24]BBV ii.1223–1224; Tito Orlandi, "Basilio di Cesarea nella letteratura copta," *Rivista degli studi orientali* 49 (1979): 49–58 at 56–58.

given lack of evidence for the use of this verb.[25] So returning to the
traditional view that "Lakizois" is a place, she suggested another
possibility, that it was a Hellenization of the Armenian word *łakiš*,
meaning "fortified camp." If so, the title would incorporate what
local Armenians called the place where Basil preached.[26] Since Basil
preached at least one other homily (*Mund*) in a Roman outpost in
Armenian-speaking territory (possibly Satala), Holman's suggestion
is attractive.[27] But her conjecture raises the question why the name
used by the locals was used in the title when the common Greek
name could have been used. So in the end there is no compelling
interpretation of "Lakizois." While it probably does refer to a place,
the identity of that place remains obscure.

But there is further evidence for Holman's suggestion of an
Armenian context, even if the precise meaning of *en Lakizois*
remains unclear. Basil begins the homily by adverting to an uproar
outside the building in which he was preaching (§1). The external
disturbance seems to have been deliberately generated to interfere
with whatever was taking place inside the building. This incident
calls to mind the fire started outside the church where Basil preached
Mund, an example of the social unrest gripping the region during
his Armenian mission.[28] Later on in the sermon, Basil reveals that
he is preaching at an annual synod, most likely away from Caesarea
since he alludes to the fact that he is providing the attendees with
moral instruction they usually do not receive due to a local lack of
teachers (§5). Finally, much of the homily focuses on social justice
amidst economic and class disparities. Basil exhorts his listeners
to treat all with fairness and equity, neither favoring those who are
rich or personally connected with you, nor despising those who are
poor or strangers. As in *Mund* no appeal is made to civic identity

[25]Susan R. Holman, "Rich City Burning: Social Welfare and Ecclesial Insecurity
in Basil's Mission to Armenia," *Journal of Early Christian Studies* 12 (2004): 195–215
at 214.

[26]Holman, "Rich City Burning," 214.

[27]See pp. 154–159 above.

[28]See pp. 159–162 above.

in his philanthropic rhetoric. Based on this evidence, Holman has suggested that this homily is closely connected with *Mund*, meaning that *Lak* quite possibly could also have been preached during Basil's mission to Armenia in the summer of 372 or 373.[29]

Translation. The following translation is based on Julien Garnier's edition as reprinted in De Sinner ii.836–848 (=PG 31.1437–1457).[30] In crafting my translation, I benefited from Garnier's Latin translation, as well as from the excerpts translated into English by Susan Holman in her article.

TRANSLATION

1   The enemy opposes us, out of sheer contentiousness trying to drown out our words with the uproar outside. But we are not ignorant of his designs. Let us direct our ears and minds to the words said here and have pity on those excluded from hearing them, not letting our mind wander to those outside. Instead, let your heart be where your body is. Please recollect the oracles of the Spirit read to you early this morning, the teachings that profit the soul, the cures that heal the soul. Remember the lessons learned from the Psalms. Please gather the counsels from the Proverbs. Investigate the beauty of the historical narratives. Add to these the exhortations of the Apostles. Set on all these as their crown the memory of the sayings of the Gospels. In this way you can return home with some advantage gained from them all, each receiving something beneficial from the Spirit against that to which he is readily inclined. Generally speaking, in a church in which there are many persons, there are as many different inclinations as there are persons. There are as many different ages as there are sins. Now the artifices of the devil are diverse and wily. He seduces different people in different

---

[29]Holman, "Rich City Burning," 212–3 and 215. On the context of *Mund*, see pp. 154–163.

[30]CPG 2912.

ways: he notices that to which a person is already inclined and offers his own enticements to it.

2   Who stands here with a soul afflicted by envy?[1] I hope that no one does! And this is a fitting prayer for me to make. But since it is only with great difficulty that a human nature does not have any of the passions, whether small or great, let each one pick something beneficial from the passages read earlier. Are you jealous? Receive healing. Are you irascible? The remedy is available. For all these have been discussed. And if possible, we will speak briefly, culling what is best from each of the passages read earlier. Are you greedy? The remedy is here. Are you proud? Here you will tame your pride. Here you will curb the haughtiness of your soul—if you want to! Return home only after you have drunk all the goods from the spiritual sayings as if from a gushing spring and fully slaked your thirst in this way.

The first saying in Proverbs is said in the manner of proverbs, in that obscurity is employed to train our intellect: *The one who looks upon smooth things shall obtain mercy* [Prov 12.13a LXX]. Have you grasped the meaning of this passage on your own? Or, being a diligent pupil, do you seek to learn in what sense *the one who looks upon smooth things* shall merit praise?[2] For it is things which depend on choice that merit praise. Now we human beings do not see whatever qualities we wish, but the qualities of natures as they are seen. And so, if something is rough on the surface, it is seen exactly as it exists by nature. But if we cast our eyes upon smooth things, on what basis does the *one who looks upon smooth things* merit praise? Things are smooth when they have an even surface, whereas something is rough when at first glance it is uneven in its formation. So since

[1]As in *Inv*, in this homily Basil uses φθόνος ("envy") and βασκανία ("jealousy") as synonyms. Unlike in *Inv*, however, in this homily βασκανία and its cognates occur more frequently than φθόνος. On Basil's understanding of envy and jealousy, see pp. 130–131 above.

[2]Gk. ἐπαινεθήσεται, "shall merit praise." Other mss support the ἐλεηθήσεται, "shall obtain mercy." Garnier was probably correct to prefer the former to the latter, which is most likely a scribal correction to Basil's alteration of the scriptural text of Prov 12.13a.

visible natures are uneven, how can the Scripture praise *the one who looks upon smooth things* instead of the one who looks upon rough things? Indeed, does it condemn the one who looks upon mountains, and peaks, and chasms, and dense woods, and the continuous fields of crops which make earth's surface rough? Or the sea frequently made rough by the winds? Or the land split by the plow and cut into rough sections, its smoothness taken away? So then, will the one who looks upon these things be condemned? Indeed, where is the just judgment of God, if we are condemned for what we experience involuntarily? If I were to behold the earth's uneven nature (for it is seen exactly as it is created), would I be condemned for this?

Instead, please interpret *the one who looks upon smooth things* according to the higher sense.[3] The differences that exist among the brothers are obvious to you: one is poor, another rich, one is a stranger, another a family member. Either they are judged by you when you sit on a jury, or they need you to share your goods with them. If you sit in judgment, do not look upon uneven things, do not look upon the rich person as lofty, nor the pauper as lowly. If the person who seeks to have his needs met is standing at your door, not even in this situation should you look upon uneven things. Don't say: this one is my friend, this one is my relative, this one is my benefactor, but that one is a stranger, a foreigner, an unknown. When you look upon uneven things, you will not obtain mercy. Look upon smooth things. They have one and the same nature: they—both this one and that one—are human beings. They have one and the same

[3]Basil's interpretation of Prov 12.13a "according to the higher sense," i.e., figuratively, is not easy to follow. He regards "looking upon smooth things" as treating all people with equity regardless of social rank, economic status, or external appearance. This manner of dealing with others is the opposite of "looking upon rough, uneven things," in which people are not judged with equal fairness precisely because of such differences. The Greek words translated as "smooth things" (λεῖα) and "uneven things" (ἀνώμαλα) could also be construed as adverbs, i.e., "smoothly" and "unevenly, inconsistently." This may be playing a role in Basil's exegesis. Hence, he encourages his audience to "look upon smooth things," that is, to look upon people smoothly, i.e., in a consistent manner, on an equal basis, as equals, and not unevenly, i.e., in an inconsistent manner, on an unequal basis, not as equals.

need: both have the same poverty. Give to your brother and to the stranger. Do not turn your brother away, and make the stranger your very own brother.[4]

So then, we must *look upon smooth things*. Do not prefer the friend who can meet his own needs to the foreigner. He[5] wants you to be the comforter of those in need, not a respecter of persons,[6] not someone who gives to his relative but spurns the stranger. All are our relatives, all our brothers, all descendants of one father. If you seek our spiritual father, it is he who is in heaven.[7] If you seek our earthly parent, it is mother earth, for all of us have been formed from the same clay.[8] Hence we are siblings in terms of our fleshly nature, siblings in terms of our spiritual generation. The blood he[9] has from the first man is the same as yours; the grace he received from the Lord is the same as yours.

So then, *look upon smooth things*, that you may *obtain mercy*. Don't say: "This one is rich and worthy of honor; that one is poor, and I despise the poor." Do not allocate honors unevenly in these situations of economic disparity. For the rich person is a liar, the rich person is rapacious, the rich person is immoral, the poor person is just. So do not pay attention to external appearances, but enter into what is hidden within, and allocate the different honors based on what you find there. Honor the one who possesses honors. What is more honorable, virtue or riches? Why do you judge on the basis of externals, not investigating what is hidden within? Note that Bel was bronze outside, but inside clay was kept hidden under the gleaming bronze.[10] If you see those who are illustrious in this life, realize that bronze gleams all around their outsides, but inside they are clay, the bronze covering their inner corruption. Yet many have gold inside,

[4]Cf. Mt 25.34–46.
[5]That is, God.
[6]Cf. Jas 2.1, 2.9.
[7]See Mt 5.16, 5.45, 6.1, 6.9, 7.11, 7.21, 10.32, 10.33, 12.50, 16.17, 18.10, 18.14, 18.19, 23.9; Mk 11.25.
[8]See Job 33.6; cf. *Eun.* 2.4.
[9]That is, the supplicant, whether rich or poor.
[10]See Dan 14.7.

but wear a earthen covering outside. This is the treasure hidden in the earthen vessel.[11] This person exercises self-control, and that person is a prostitute. Who is richer? The one with self-control? Or the one with money gained wickedly? The memory of the former will never fade away; the riches of the latter are temporary. For the one, a thief does not break in;[12] for the other, today riches abound but tomorrow they dwindle away. And so, *look upon smooth things*, with equal fairness and in the same way. Yet do not eliminate the distinctions among those who are honored, that you may obtain mercy.

3 *And do not associate with an irascible man* [Prov 22.24]. Now tell me: is there anyone among us who thirsts for glory but is not irascible? Do you thirst for glory? You do not *look upon smooth things*. Are you irascible? *And do not associate with an irascible man*. Do you see how only a few words are needed for the correction of sins? Therefore, unless we can knock on your ears with our voice, we will not instill in your heart an understanding of what was said. So ask me instead: "What was read that pertains to me?" O you irascible dunce, know that what pertains to irascible people is what pertains to you! Say: "This passion afflicts me, I recognize my infirmity." Accept the cure. If you go to a physician and see the expensive medicines stored in the various containers, consider which one is best suited for your affliction. A man who has hurt his foot does not seek healing for his eye. But a man who has injured his eye seeks the remedy suitable for this affliction.

Therefore, let each take from the Scripture what relates to the passion which afflicts him. Are you irascible? Hold your anger in check. For he says *an irascible man does not command respect* [Prov 11.25]. Learn from the Scripture. Let the Scripture be a mirror for your face. Learn there. Since your impious reasoning has clouded your mind, not allowing you to realize how great a sin anger is, the Scripture tells you: *An irascible man does not command respect.* How

[11] See 2 Cor 4.7.
[12] See Mt 6.20–21.

does the irascible man lose respect? He loses his human appearance and assumes the appearance of a beast. Consider the irate man: he seethes with anger and his eyes are changed. They are not the same eyes. He sees red.[13] Blood rises up in him, boils around his heart, surrounds the membranes of his eyes. He becomes suffused with blood when he succumbs to this passion. He alters his eyes. *An irascible man does not command respect.* If you see the irate man sharpening his teeth, know that such a man is like a wild boar, revealing his anger within by gnashing his teeth. If you see the irate man foaming at the mouth; if you see him uttering unintelligible nonsense in his heart; if you see the irate man unable to remember his father, unable to recognize the body of his child, conducting himself disgracefully in everything in order to satisfy his impulses, then you are seeing the loss of respect brought on by irascibility. Use another's evil to cure yourself, lest you also lose respect as he did. *An irascible man does not command respect.*[14]

And do not associate with an irascible man. It's a bad thing to be chained to a dog and to have to endure his endless barking. *An irascible man does not command respect.* Flee interaction with him. For it is inevitable that you will learn some of his ways. He utters an insult, and stirs up the anger in you. Just as one dog's barking provokes another's barking, so too[15] is the anger in you, which hitherto was calm and silent, aroused by what another says. You start barking at one another, and then locked in a battle against one another, you hurl disgraceful words like bullets launched from a sling. He utters an insult, and you top what he said, imitating the initial insult. Upon receiving the insult made in response to his, he does not check his impulses, but turns and brings his sin to new heights. He wants to best you by uttering an even harsher insult. But when you are insulted again, you are roused even more. And that's how a competition in evils unfolds. But whoever emerges victorious in contests

[13]Literally, "he sees fire."

[14]A similar interpretation of Prov 11.25 with reference to the altered, beast-like appearance of the irate man brought on by his irrationality is also found in *Ira* 1–2.

[15]Here I add οὕτω before the καί.

over evils is more wretched. *An irascible man does not command respect. And do not associate with an irascible man.*[16]

4 *Do not dine with a jealous man* [Prov 23.6].[17] Another passion takes up residence in the life of human beings, continually clinging to our souls and consuming our heart more than rust consumes iron: jealousy.[18] There are many evils in it, but there is one advantage: it is an evil for the very one who possesses it. For the jealous person inflicts little harm on the one of whom he is jealous, but is consumed by distress and groaning over the good fortune of his neighbor. And he does not infringe upon the lands of his neighbor, but is consumed by jealousy.[19]

5 *Do not remove ancient borders, nor enter the possession of orphans* [Prov 23.10].[20] Do not enter the possession of orphans, so that you may enter your own possession. Now the possession which is yours is the kingdom of heaven prepared [for you].[21] Do not move the borders of your fathers.[22] Do not covet your neighbor's field.[23] Do not add furrow to furrow to increase your holdings little by little. The more you enlarge your land by adding another's fields to it, the more deeply you establish sin in yourself. And the land, which you gained little by little and acquired through greed, remains here, no longer yours but belonging to your heirs, and you leave a livelihood unjustly obtained to the one to whom you are handing things over. While *the land remains forever* [Eccl 1.4], the sin follows you, like a dark shadow accompanying the soul. For just as a shadow follows the body, so too does sin stick close to the soul.[24]

[16]A discussion of how anger tends to escalate is also found in *Ira* 3.

[17]Basil also discusses this verse in *Inv* 4 and *Lak* 8.

[18]The same metaphor for envy is employed in *Inv* 1.

[19]This single advantage of envy is also mentioned in *Inv* 4.

[20]See Prov 22.28.

[21]See Mt 25.34.

[22]See Prov 22.28.

[23]See Deut 5.21.

[24]The greedy person's accumulation of land is also mentioned in *Div* 5.

Do not compound your sin. For the illness of greed is never stable but like the nature of fire. For as soon as fire is kindled by a fanning wind, it rushes to feed upon all the wood that it can, and no one can stop it until the wood is gone. What can hold the greedy man in check? He is more cruel than fire, consuming everything, never ceasing. He takes what belongs to his neighbor. Then another neighbor appears, and he appropriates what belongs to him too. He pays no attention to what he already has (for he has much), but to what he still lacks (for he has neighbors). He does not take delight in his possessions, but is distressed over what he still lacks. He is not interested in enjoying what he has already amassed, but is consumed with the desire to possess more.

This then gives birth to sleeplessness, worry, anxiety. The more his riches increase, the more worries about his possessions he has to endure. A judge awaits, and the greedy man looks this way and that, lest he be dragged into court, lest an orphan make his grievances[25] known in court. At night he plots which of the orphan's embittered advocates to groom, so that he can pay him for false testimony; he schemes how he will get the bereaved party to capitulate and how he will oppress him, even by hiding the truth in court; he plans how he will destroy both, the judge by misinformation and the child by despoliation. The very worries of the greedy man consume his soul. A dog barks, and the rich man thinks there is a thief. A sound of a mouse, and the heart of the rich man starts to pound. He is suspicious of his servant; he holds everyone in suspicion. He regards his grown sons as plotters, because their adulthood suggests that it's time to hand things over to them.

Another illness also afflicts the greedy. He counts his money on his fingers, some he publicizes, some he buries in the earth, storing it away for uncertain hopes. But these sorts of hopes are not true hopes. For if he were storing something away for true hopes, he would be preparing for everlasting hope. As it is, however, he hides uncertain riches in his bed, thinking that he can avert their sudden

[25]Literally, "tears."

loss in the future. But it is not clear whether there will ever be any need for them. Yet the time will come when he will regret not dispensing his riches. This is quite certain, I myself assure you.[26]

Now I must admonish you and discuss all the passions, and you must be attentive and gain some benefit from my words. And so, stripped of your sin like a serpent's skin, each of you may return home thus naked and yet clothed with justice, the one coming as the result of other. For this is a synod. Our fathers established these meetings so that when we gather together each year in a common assembly, we may receive what we cannot learn on a daily basis because of the dearth of teachers and admonishers. And after the meeting ends we should safeguard the exhortations and instructions[27] received there for the next time, and keeping each of them fresh in our memory, flee sin and pursue the work of justice.

6 *Do not remove ancient borders, nor enter the possession of orphans* [Prov 23.10]. Do not turn your children into excuses, O you greedy man. Are they children? Store up for them an everlasting treasure. Now this treasure is the pious use of money.[28] Bequeath to your children good memories instead of great riches. Do good to make all men fathers of your child. It is inevitable that at some point you will depart from this life, leaving behind your child in his minority and in need of guardians. Now if you were virtuous and good, each will raise your child as his own. For they will remember that you were also a father of orphans. But if you lived a wicked life, and caused distress for many people, and were meaner than every beast

[26]A discussion of how the greedy hide away money is also found in *Div* 3.

[27]Gk. ἐφοδία, literally, "supplies for traveling, provisions," but frequently used for the instructions and practices pertinent for the Christian life.

[28]Gk. θησαυρὸς δέ ἐστιν ἡ εὐσέβεια χρημάτων. Garnier notes that Combefis recommended adding προτιμότερος to the end of this sentence, so that it would read: "Piety is more precious than a treasure full of money" (see De Sinner ii.xi and ii.843 note g; PG 31.1449 n. 13). Garnier was favorable to this emendation, but rejected it on the grounds that not even a single ms supported this reading. He suggested that εὐσέβεια could be taken as the "pious use of money," which is the interpretation followed here.

to everyone whom you met, then when you depart from this life, you will leave behind your child as the common enemy of the living. For just as anyone who sees the offspring of a scorpion is afraid of its reaching adulthood and imitating its father, so too if your children are the heirs of their father's wickedness, all will plot against them before they reach adulthood.

So then, why do you amass so many plotters and enemies for your own children? And yet, even if you were to live for all time, it would be even more necessary for you to have the help and goodwill of many others. But since your riches are uncertain, do good so that you may leave behind many guardians [for your children]. If you do not, when you depart from this life and then the riches which you accumulated cannot be passed on and enjoyed [by your heirs], each will shake his head and say: "How is it possible that this man's ill-gotten possessions were not handed on to his descendents and children?" These things I say to you on the basis of human wisdom. But as for what the Lord says, which is what the gospel tells you, this you already know.

7   Do not turn your children into excuses. Why do you give a specious pretext for sinning? He who made the child also made you. He who supplies you with resources also will supply your child with a livelihood. Each will have to give an account of his own life to the Lord. Do you know for whom you lay up treasures? *He lays up treasures and does not know for whom he accumulates them* [Ps 38.7]. Often a child is used as an excuse for laying up treasures. But what you have accumulated may be either the plunder of a robber, or the wasteful expenditures of a sycophant, or the spoils taken from enemies in war, or the loot acquired when plague struck. For a person can be deprived of property in many ways. Tell me: when you asked God for children, when you wanted to become the father of sons and daughters, what did you add to your prayer? "Give me children, that I may become greedy and be handed over to Gehenna on account of my children." "Give me children, that I may ignore the commandments."

"Give me children, that I may despise the gospel." This is not what you said at that time, but you sought children who would be your helpers in earning a living. You have received helpers and partners.[29] By offering good advice and giving a good example teach them what sort of riches are suitable for God, the sort of riches you have often seen. For these riches are more valuable than a great amount of money. This inheritance is good, handed down from a father to his children. *Do not enter the possession of orphans* [Prov 23.10].[30]

8   And *do not dine with a jealous man* [Prov 23.6].[31] This too is said about jealousy. One must guard against this evil as much as is possible, because jealousy is the very passion that afflicts the devil himself.[32] For the devil was not created devilish at the outset; rather, he received the authority of an angel, but turned himself into a demonic being. And he became a wicked demon when he displayed all the characteristics of this wickedness and alienated himself from affinity with God, apostatizing because he saw that the man,[33] who was such a small living being, was nonetheless more honored than every other creature. Being older than the man, he saw that all swimming things had been produced by a word. For God said: *Let the waters bring forth creeping things with living souls* [Gen 1.20]. By a word he made the whales that live in the Atlantic Ocean.[34] By a word he made the animals that walk on land. By God's command they were brought into being.[35] By a command came into existence the huge elephants and camels. Horses, and oxen, and all huge and strong

[29]Here I omit τοῦ βίου since Garnier (De Sinner ii.844 note d; PG 31.1147 n. 9) notes that it is not found in any mss.

[30]An exhortation not to use your children as an excuse for greed is also found in *Div* 7–8.

[31]Basil also discusses this verse in *Inv* 4 and *Lak* 4.

[32]The theme of the devil's envy is mentioned but not elaborated in *Inv* 3 and *Malo* 8.

[33]Gk. ἄνθρωπος, literally, "human being." Here Basil speaks of the human race in the person of Adam.

[34]See Gen 1.21.

[35]Garnier suspects that this sentence was a marginal note that was later mistakenly inserted into the text (De Sinner ii.845 note b; PG 31.1452 n. 21).

animals were created in herds by one command. And what is even more amazing, by a command the sky was created, by a command the sun, by a command vegetation, by a command the waters, both those spread above the sky and earth and those poured into empty places: all were created by a command.

But the man was formed by his hands. The devil saw the honor given to the man, and he became jealous. He saw that the man was more honored than the sun. For the one was brought into being by a command, whereas the other was fashioned by the hands of God. The one was created for the sake of the man, whereas the man for the sake of God: the man, so that God could be glorified; the sun, so that it could serve human beings. The devil reflected upon the honor given to the man. He saw that all else was created first and the man last, that God provided the man with a fully furnished house, as if he were the head of household. For he did not make the man first, such that he would be created in a state of poverty.[36] Instead, he made the sky to create a natural shelter for the man. He spread the land underneath to give the feet of the man solid ground to walk on. He caused the land to bloom with all sorts of plants that bear vegetables and fruits. Everything was given to the man. Beasts of burden were given in herds. The entire created order was created. So many animals were provided: those that flock together, the wild beasts for exercising the body, those owned for hard work which they would grow to love, those willingly at his side who would serve the created man without delay. The devil saw that the earth spontaneously produced fruit for them. All creation waited for those who would enjoy it, and the man was brought to feast on it. The devil saw that God, the lover of humanity, was not content with having the man enjoy the earth, but wanting the man, his very own ornament, to have a special dwelling-place, he established him in paradise.[37]

[36]Gk. ἵνα πτωχός. Garnier, following the Paris edition, added a μή, "so that he would not be created in a state of poverty," despite the fact that there was no ms support for this word (see De Sinner ii.845 note c; PG 31.1452–1453 n. 22). However, as sense can be made of the Greek without this emendation, it seems best not to add it.

[37]Gk. ἀλλ' ἐξαίρετον ἐνδιαίτημα, τὸ ἴδιον ἐγκαλλώπισμα, τὸν ἄνθρωπον ἑαυτοῦ

The devil saw the many goods bestowed upon the man for his enjoyment; he saw guardian angels attending him; he saw God speaking the same language as human beings, using his very own voice to converse with them, in every way teaching the small child that he could attain to likeness to God. After the devil reflected upon the man, after he realized that the Lord called this small living being to honor equal to the angels, that he would guide him through virtue and self-control in matters of this life to the perfection of the soul, the devil did something wicked.[38] Indeed, for as long as the man was alone, the devil had no way to ensnare him. But [he found a way] when the woman was created, a living being who is tender. For the Creator needed to produce a being who was naturally tender, so that she might nourish her little children readily through loving kindness. For if the woman were severe, she would not take the wailing infant in her arms to embrace it in her bosom, nor would she neglect her own nourishment and instead offer her breast to feed[39] the nursing child. On the contrary, even now a mother's heartfelt compassion not infrequently chases away the sleep from her eyelids[40] when the small infant starts to fuss. Therefore, so that the infant could be nourished, the female was created with a tender nature, a being full of tenderness and loving kindness. So then, the devil turned his attention to the tender woman who was soft and weak, and made her inclination to virtue into an inclination to vice.

So then, this is the very evil that afflicts the devil himself, envy. Envy cannot be divulged, cannot be healed. Someone whose head

βουλόμενος ἐχεῖν, κατέστησεν ἐν τῷ παραδείσῳ. There are textual problems with this clause in the mss, which the early editions tried to correct through emendations (see De Sinner ii.845 note d; PG 31.1453–1454 n. 23). Garnier preferred the reading of Codex Regius, which reads ἐκεῖ instead of ἐχεῖν and placed the comma after βουλόμενος: which translated would read "but wishing the man, his very own ornament, to be his special dwelling-place, there he established him in paradise." I have emended the ἐκεῖ to ἐχεῖν, on the grounds that the former is a corruption of the latter, and thus avoiding the addition of words as in the early editions.

[38]Gk. ἐπονηρεύσατο ὁ διάβολος. Here I follow Garnier's construal of this independent clause (see De Sinner ii.846 note a; PG 31.1454 n. 25).

[39]Literally, "to benefit."

[40]See Ps 131.4.

hurts tells the physician about his headache. What does someone who is ill with envy say? "The goods of my brother cause me distress." This is the truth, but everyone is ashamed at such words.[41] What are you complaining about? Your own evil or another's good? Now we tame dogs by feeding them, but we make the jealous man even meaner by being his benefactor.[42] For he does not rejoice over the good things he has experienced, but is distressed over your abundance because you have the means of satisfying his need.

So do not fall into the snare of the devil. He became jealous of you. He became jealous. He banished you from paradise. Because of him you have thorns.[43] Because of him you have sweat.[44] Because of him you live in the place of banishment to which you fell. Do not forget your ancient homeland. Remember your nobility. Remember the homeland from which you were banished. Remember the one who inflicted such great losses upon you. Do not make peace with him, nor ever enter into association with him. For he has done you wrong twice: in the beginning he drove you out and now he disrupts your return. He acted on his jealousy of your first goods through a woman, and again by using the artifices of women he prevents their restoration. He invented fornication to keep you from entering into paradise. He was not satisfied with the first loss he inflicted upon you. He concocts other ploys to hinder your return. He robs you [of paradise] by getting you to lie, since lying is a wall that blocks those journeying to paradise.

9   His schemes are countless. His offspring are cruelty, harshness, greed, abusiveness. All that the word of truth[45] hates belongs to the devil. He hates humanity because he is the enemy of God. He hated

[41]The themes of the envier's inability to disclose his envy, what the envier would say if he could, and his resultant failure to seek healing for his envy are also mentioned in *Inv* 1–2.

[42]The same metaphor for envy is employed in *Inv* 3.

[43]See Gen 3.18.

[44]See Gen 3.19.

[45]See Eph 1.3, Col 1.5, 2 Tim 2.15, Jas 1.18.

God first. He stiffened his neck against God almighty.[46] He despised the Master. He alienated himself from God. Not being able to defeat God, when he saw that the man was in the image and likeness of God,[47] he unloaded his own wickedness on the image of God. He acted like an angry man who throws rocks at the emperor's image because he cannot throw them at the emperor himself, striking the wood that bears the effigy. In the arena I myself have often seen those animals who have the greatest hatred for human beings; indeed I have both seen and heard them.[48] Now I don't want to say anything that might scandalize you, only that leopards have a kind of natural anger for human beings and it is their nature to attack the eyes in particular. So those who taunt the furious beasts show them an image of a man on piece of papyrus. And the leopard, who misjudges the situation on account of its raging impulses, tears the papyrus to pieces as if it were a man, thereby showing its hatred for human beings. In the same way too the devil showed his hatred for God by attacking his image since he was not able to touch God. And so, the war being waged against us demonstrates that the wicked one is the enemy of God and first waged war against the Master.

He brought the man down from Jerusalem to Jericho, from the heights to the depths.[49] Jerusalem is located in a mountainous region, whereas Jericho is down by the Salt Sea.[50] If any of you were to see the place, you would know the truth of what I am saying, that Jericho is located in the low districts of Palestine, whereas Jerusalem is set upon a summit, occupying the top of the mountain which rises up through all the land. So from the heights to the depths the man came, and as a result *he fell among robbers* [Lk 10.30]. He departed from the safety of Jerusalem, and as a result he was easily caught

[46]See Job 15.25.

[47]See Gen 1.26.

[48]Gk. καὶ εἶδον καὶ ἤκουσα. Here I follow the emendation of Maran (see De Sinner ii.xiii). Garnier had ἢ εἶδον ἢ ἤκουσα.

[49]See Lk 10.30.

[50]That is, the Dead Sea. Basil's geography is somewhat inaccurate. Jericho is ten miles north of the Dead Sea in valley of the Jordan River.

by the robbers in the wilderness, who rained blows upon him and stripped him. First they rained blows upon him and then they stripped him naked. The blow rained upon the soul is sin; the soul is stripped naked when its robe of incorruptibility is removed. Now sin deprives us of the grace given to us through *the washing of regeneration* [Titus 3.5]. Fornication is a blow; adultery, another blow; envy, also a blow. Each of these is a blow, a blow that wounds us where it matters most, a blow rained upon us by robbers, by demons who facilitate our slide toward sin. After receiving blows, the wounded man is stripped. If what we are talking about were a physical attack, first they would strip the man to spare the clothing, and then rain blows upon him. Or once they stripped him, they would rain blows upon him, so that the clothing could be saved and the wounded man beaten. Yet in the present case the blows come before the stripping, to teach you that sin precedes the loss of the gift given to you through the Lord's love for humanity. To him *be glory for ever and ever. Amen* [1 Pet 4.11].

Homily on Psalm 115
(Ps 116.11–19 MT)

[1]*I believed; therefore I spoke.*
But I was greatly humbled.
[2]*I said in my bewilderment:*
"Every human being speaks falsely."
[3]*What shall I return to the Lord*
for all that he returned to me?
[4]*The cup of salvation I will take,*
and upon the name of the Lord I will call.
[5]*My vows I will pay to the Lord*
in the sight of all his people,
[6]*Precious in the sight of the Lord*
is the death of his devout ones.
[7]*O Lord, I am your slave;*
I am your slave and the son of your maidservant.
You broke through my bonds.
[8]*To you I will sacrifice a sacrifice of praise.*
[9]*My vows I will pay to the Lord*
in the sight of all his people,
[10]*in the courts of the Lord's house,*
in your midst, O Jerusalem.

INTRODUCTION

As in all his homilies on the Psalms, Basil's main goal in his homily on Psalm 115 is to make it relevant for Christians.[1] Broadly speaking, the theme of this homily is faith, though much else is discussed. The

[1]On the early Christian approach to the Psalms, see pp. 79–81 above.

first half of the homily is devoted to Psalm 115.1–2, which, according to Basil, teaches us about the necessity of faith. In the remainder of the homily he interprets Psalm 115.3–10 and discusses various aspects of a life of faith: suffering, martyrdom, death, the veneration of relics, praise, and so forth. In the second half of the homily he makes extensive use of the rhetorical and exegetical technique of paraphrase; in other words, Basil creatively summarizes and expands upon the words of the Psalmist in order to make their meaning clear and vivid. While he uses this technique elsewhere,[2] the extent to which it is employed here makes *Ps115* noteworthy.

Since the first verse of the Psalm opens with *I believed; therefore I spoke*, Basil begins the homily with a discussion of the role of faith in what we would today call "theological methodology" (§1). Any discourse on God must be rooted in faith, which is engendered in the soul not by deductive proofs and logical demonstration but by the work of the Spirit. A polemical tone can be detected in his opening words as he emphasizes simple belief in God over philosophical argumentation in the face of a current preference for the latter over the former. He does not name his opponents, but the rhetoric here and elsewhere in this homily indicates that Basil has in mind Eunomius and the Heteroousians.[3] In spite of his insistence on the necessity of faith and his denigration of logical demonstration, Basil then proceeds to suggest that theology is a deductive science, much as St Thomas Aquinas would do centuries later.[4] Aristotle had described deductive science in his *Analytica Posteriora* but the same basic concept is also found elsewhere, such as in Euclid's treatises. In short, in a deductive science a body of knowledge is rationally and logically constructed by repeatedly drawing conclusions from

[2] See for example *Mund* 10–11.

[3] See Mark DelCogliano, "Basil of Caesarea on Psalm 115 (LXX): Origen and Anti-Eunomian Rhetoric" [forthcoming]. On Basil's anti-Eunomian rhetoric in *Against Eunomius*, see Mark DelCogliano and Andrew Radde-Gallwitz, *St. Basil of Caesarea: Against Eunomius*, FOTC 122 (Washington, DC: Catholic University of America Press, 2011), 38–46. See also pp. 45–46 above.

[4] *Summa theologiae* 1a.1.2.

premises. Once drawn from premises, conclusions can then be used as premises from which to draw further conclusions, which themselves can be used as premises, and so forth. In this way, a systematic body of knowledge can be produced through deductive reasoning. As Basil puts it, every discipline or branch of knowledge proceeds "in a methodical and orderly fashion to its full realization" (§1). However, each deductive science is ultimately founded on certain first principles (or axioms) whose truth is self-evident and indemonstrable. Perhaps mathematical axioms are most familiar, such as "all right angles are equal to one another" and "things that equal the same thing also equal one another" (or if $a = b$ and $b = c$, then $a = c$). Based on axioms such as these the mathematical science of geometry was constructed. But virtually all fields of knowledge were conceptualized as deductive sciences in the ancient world. And so, Basil proposes that just as geometers, arithmeticians, and physicians give unquestioning assent to the first principles of geometry, arithmetic, and medicine, so too should theologians give unquestioning assent to the principles of the faith revealed in Scripture. One should simply assent to these principles of the faith, not futilely investigate what cannot be rationally understood, let alone quarrel about it.

Then, switching the focus of his attention, Basil attempts to understand the context in which the Psalmist uttered the words: *I believed; therefore I spoke* (§2). As these words are in the first line of the current Psalm, he detects a connection with the last line of the previous Psalm: *I shall be pleasing to the Lord in the land of the living* (Ps 114.9).[5] In other words, because the Psalmist *believed* that there was a land of the living he *spoke* the words of Psalm 114.9. After this Basil resumes his polemics, summing up his thoughts on the necessity of faith in theological discussions.

[5] In the Hebrew Ps 114 and Ps 115 are a single psalm (Ps 116). Greek versions of the Psalter separate the two, and so Ps 114.9 immediately precedes Ps 115.1. Basil's connection of Ps 115.1 with Ps 114.9 probably betrays his awareness that these two verses are part of the same psalm in Hebrew.

Moving to the next clause in Psalm 115.1, *But I was greatly humbled*, Basil explains that humility perfects faith (§2). Those who engage in theology without the requisite humility "measure" God by the standards of their own powers of reasoning. Relying solely on their own abilities, they lack the insight that comes from faith and refuse to stand in awe in the presence of the mysteriousness and incomprehensibility of God. In fact, the Psalmist reports in Psalm 115.2 that *every human being speaks falsely*, meaning that without faith and trusting on human reason alone human beings fail to comprehend the truth.

Then Basil tries to understand the historical context in which the Psalmist said *every human being speaks falsely*, for the same verse reports that he spoke *in bewilderment* (§3). Two possibilities are suggested. Either David, whom the church fathers understood to be the Psalmist, was bewildered because he realized that the truth could not be found without the help of God, or the bewilderment refers to the madness David feigned in the presence of Achish.[6] Then, changing subjects again, Basil denies the claim of some unnamed sophists that *every human being speaks falsely* is susceptible to the Liar paradox. In ancient philosophy, the Liar paradox used a particular kind of self-referential statement to demonstrate that contradiction results when it is analyzed on the principle of bivalence.[7] In its typical form the Liar statement is, "I am lying," or even better, "This sentence is false." If such a statement is true, then it turns out to be actually false. But if such a statement is false, then it must be true. And so forth. The truth-value of the Liar statement cannot be determined if bivalence is assumed. In this homily Basil is keen to deny that Psalm 115.2 is self-contradictory. He formulates the Liar paradox based on Psalm 115.2 to make the claims of the sophists clear. His refutation of their claim depends upon knowing the moral status of the speaker of the seemingly contradictory statement, as disclosed by other verses

[6]See 1 Sam 21.12–15.

[7]That is, the assumption that all statements have only one of two truth-values (true or false) and cannot have both or neither.

of Scripture. He claims that David, the speaker of Ps 115.2, is a god, thereby eliminating the possibility of self-reference in the verse and thus self-contradiction.[8]

The remainder of the homily sticks more closely to a line-by-line exegesis of Psalm 115 without the polemics and frequent changes of subject that characterized the first half. According to Basil, in Psalm 115.3–4 the Psalmist has become aware of God's innumerable gifts and realizes that the only way he can worthily repay the Lord is by giving him his very own life (§4). This interpretation is corroborated by his words: *The cup of salvation I will take* (Ps 115.4). Just as Christ spoke of his suffering as a cup (see Mt 20.22 and 26.39), so too the faithful Christian realizes that the only way in which he can truly repay the Lord is by offering his very own life in martyrdom. Those who are faithful, continues Basil, should not be terrified of death because *Precious in the sight of the Lord is the death of his devout ones* (Ps 115.6). Death is not the end, but the passage to eternal life, yet only for those who live a devout and just life. So we should not mourn the dead; rather, we should mourn when people are born because birth is inseparable from filth and ignominy, as Paul taught (see 1 Cor 15.42–43). The honor conferred by death is also proven by Christian customs. Unlike Jews who considered corpses defiling, Christians revere the relics of martyrs, whose bones confer "some share of the holiness that comes from the grace inherent in the body" (§4).[9]

The last section rapidly deals with Psalm 115.7–10 and employs the technique of paraphrase almost exclusively (§5). A number of themes are touched upon but not discussed in any detail: every creature's enslavement to the Creator by choice and by nature; the devil's seduction of humanity through Eve from enslavement to the Creator to enslavement to sin; and humanity's release from enslavement to sin through Christ's harrowing of hell. The sacrifice given to God by

[8]For a more detailed discussion of Basil's formulation the Liar paradox and his refutation of the claim that Ps 115.2 is susceptible it, see Mark DelCogliano, "Origen and Basil of Caesarea on the Liar Paradox," *Augustinianum* 51 (2011): 349–66..

[9]On this passage, see Mario Girardi, *Basilio di Cesarea interprete della Scrittura. Lessico, principi ermeneutici, prassi* (Bari: Epipuglia, 1998), 193–5.

the faithful Christian is neither animals nor other earthly products, but *a sacrifice of praise* (Ps 115.8) made on the altar of the mind. For God is self-sufficient and has no need of material goods; rather, God demands a good disposition and a true heart. Basil concludes the homily with the idea that the sacrifice of praise should be made *in the sight of all his people* (Ps 115.9) and in the midst of Jerusalem (see Ps 115.10), that is, publicly with the community, not privately apart from others. Bringing his paraphrasing to an end and resuming the polemical tone found at the beginning of the homily, he condemns those who "have abandoned the church and gather in profane houses" (§5), presumably the Eunomians who have separated themselves from the churches with which Basil was in communion. He ends the homily with an exhortation to avoid association with such people and to persevere in faith.

Authenticity. In the Maurist edition of Basil's works Julien Garnier placed *Ps115* among the works falsely ascribed to him.[10] He offered two main reasons for this opinion. First, in the catenae that he examined fragments from this homily were not attributed to Basil. Second, the poor style that this homily occasionally exhibits precluded its Basilian authorship—another instance of Garnier's dubious "stylistic" criteria.[11] As mentioned above, while Prudentius Maran agreed with Garnier that the poor style precluded Basilian authorship, he affirmed that the content of the homilies on the Psalms deemed spurious by Garnier was Basilian.[12] Specifically regarding *Ps115*, Maran noted a number of parallels with Basil's genuine works.[13] The reprint of the Maurist edition by J.-P. Migne and the ubiquity of his *Patrologia Graeca* ensured the dominance of Garnier's opinion about *Ps115* through the twentieth century.[14]

[10]"Praefatio," §VI, 39 (De Sinner i.xxxv–xxxvi; PG 29.cciii–cciv).

[11]On his "stylistic" arguments, see pp. 89–90, 190–191, and 267.

[12]See p. 89 above.

[13]*Vita. S. Basilii* 41.4–5 (De Sinner iii. ccxxxix–ccxl; PG 29.clxiv–clxv).

[14]E.g., Blomfield Jackson, "Prolegomena: Sketch of the Life and Works of Saint Basil," NPNF ii.8, xiii–lxxvii at xxxii; J. Tixeront, *A Handbook of Patrology* (St Louis/ London: Herder, 1920), 171; Berthold Altaner, *Patrology* (Freiburg: Herder, 1960), 339; Johannes Quasten, *Patrology, Vol. 3* (Westminster, MD: Newman Press, 1960), 218.

More recently, noted Basilian scholars have maintained the authenticity of *Ps115*. In his preface to the Brepols reprint of PG 30 Jean Gribomont suggested that it should be seen as an authentic work of Basil because of its wide attestation in best manuscripts of Basil's homilies.[15] Jean Bernardi, Paul Jonathan Fedwick, and Mario Girardi have agreed with Gribomont's assessment.[16] Furthermore, Fedwick has confirmed that the homily is widely attested in the best manuscripts of Basil's homilies.[17] And so, if we add this evidence for authenticity based on the manuscript tradition to Maran's observation that in terms of content *Ps115* is Basilian, then today, based on both external and internal evidence, nothing suggests that Basil is not its author.

Context and Date. The homily itself does not contain any details that would allow us to reconstruct its original context and date with any certainty. Basil does mention that he is preaching in a "great church" (§1), and surely his audience consisted of a variety of Christians, baptized and unbaptized alike,[18] but no other details are forthcoming. Even Bernardi could not detect in this homily any allusion to some current event or situation that would help date it.[19] Furthermore, the anti-Eunomian rhetoric of the homily does not help in dating it, as this is found in homilies from early[20] and late

Maurice Geerard, *Clavis Patrum Graecorum. Volumen II. Ab Athanasio ad Chrysostomum* (Turnhout: Brepols, 1974), 166, ranked it among the Basilian *dubia*, though the 1998 *CPG Supplementum* (ed. M. Geerard and J. Noret) drops this classification. Finally, *Ps115* was omitted in the only English translation of the homilies on the Psalms: Agnes Clare Way, *Saint Basil: Exegetic Homilies*, FOTC 46 (Washington, DC: The Catholic University of America Press, 1963).

[15] *In Tomum 30 Patrologiae graecae ad opera Sancti Basilii Magni Adnotationes* (Turnhout: Brepols, 1960), 3.

[16] Jean Bernardi, *La prédication des pères cappadociens* (Paris: Presses universitaires de France, 1968), 22–3; Paul Jonathan Fedwick, "A Chronology of the Life and Works of Basil of Caesarea," in idem, ed., *Basil of Caesarea: Christian, Humanist, Ascetic. A Sixteen-Hundredth Anniversary Symposium* (Toronto: The Pontifical Institute of Mediaeval Studies, 1981), 3–19 at 10; Girardi, *Basilio di Cesarea interprete*, 193.

[17] See BBV ii.1039–41.

[18] Bernardi, *La prédication*, 33.

[19] Bernardi, *La prédication*, 28.

[20] See *Prov 7* and pp. 45–46 above.

in his career.[21] Perhaps the homily was preached on the feast of a martyr, as the topics of martyrdom and relics occur (§4). Paul Jonathan Fedwick cautiously dates this homily broadly to 363–378.[22] This seems to be the most prudent course. Hence all that can be said with confidence is that *Ps115* was delivered at some point during Basil's ecclesiastical ministry, either as a presbyter or as a bishop.

Translation. The following translation is based on Julien Garnier's edition as reprinted in De Sinner i.525–532 (=PG 30.104–116).[23] In crafting my translation, I benefited from Garnier's Latin translation.

Translation

1   *I believed; therefore I spoke. But I was greatly humbled. I said in my bewilderment: "Every human being speaks falsely"* [Ps 115.1–2]. Let faith be the prerequisite for discussing God: faith, not logical demonstration. Faith is superior to rational methodologies when it comes to drawing the soul to assent. It is not the logical necessity of deductive proofs that engenders faith, but the activity of the Spirit. *In the name of Jesus Christ of Nazareth, arise and walk!* [Acts 3:6]. What followed this command was the work of the Spirit, and those who witnessed this miracle were compelled to admit the divinity of the Only-Begotten. Tell me, what is more compelling for assent, a complicated set of syllogistic premises entailing the logical conclusion, or a clearly seen miracle so great that it surpasses all that is humanly possible? Yet currently such things are not held in high regard. Indeed, what now inspires confidence when discussing God is not the works of the Spirit, but rather elaborate demonstrations which place their hope in the plausibility of the wisdom of the world, not in the powerful and clear revelation of the Spirit. It was through those who believed God in simplicity of heart without engaging in

[21]See *Fide, Verb, Sab,* and *Trin.*
[22]"A Chronology," 10.
[23]CPG 2910.

futile investigations that the Spirit gave this revelation for the salvation of the many. Would that it be granted even to me to believe in so worthy a manner, so that now *in* this great *church* of God *I may speak five words with my mind* [1 Cor 14.19]!

And let no one scoff at these words because we urge our audience to give unquestioning assent to the things about which we are speaking. For the principles of each discipline need to remain unexamined when imparted to students, since it is impossible for those who quarrel about first principles to proceed in a methodical and orderly fashion to their full realization. And this you would learn from those outside.[1] For if you were to disagree with the first principles of geometry, it would be impossible to draw conclusions about what they entail. And anyone who opposes the first principles and elements of arithmetic closes off the way to what logically follows from them. Likewise, the principles of medicine remain unproven to practitioners of medicine. And in sum, in any discipline that proceeds in a methodical and orderly fashion to its full realization, one cannot require demonstrations of the initial premises. Rather, whoever has received the unexamined first principles of the rational arts must look for the consequence of the premises in what logically follows from them. So then, in this way too the mystery of theology requires assent based on unquestioning faith. For he says: *one must believe that God exists* [Heb 11.6], not "one must investigate what he is," nor "one must quarrel about what he is." And in sum, if *faith is the assurance of things hoped for, the conviction of things not seen* [Heb 11.1], then do not strive at present to see what is laid up for the distant future, do not make what is hoped for doubtful. For it is still impossible to attain knowledge of these things.

2 So then, we say these things about faith in a general way because of those who quarrel about words and place their hope in empty expressions. Now it seems to me that the present Psalm has a logical connection with the thought expressed in the previous Psalm.

[1]That is, non-Christians outside the church.

For there he says: *I shall be pleasing to the Lord in the land of the living* [Ps 114.9].[2] So then, after talking about the land he has not seen as if he knew it well, he provides the reason for his declaration about these obscure matters when he says: *I believed* (that is, he believed that there is a land of the living); *therefore I spoke* (that is, he spoke, saying: *I shall be pleasing to the Lord* in it). In sum, the soul that enters into discussion without faith will utter vapid nonsense because the words it utters do not refer to anything real. Therefore, the basis of prudent discussion is faith firmly settled in the heart of the speaker.

Then he adds how we can achieve the perfection of faith: *But I was greatly humbled* [Ps 115.1]. He who has not humbled his own mind does not say in imitation of the Apostle: *Brothers, I do not yet consider myself to have comprehended* [Phil 3.13]. Rather, he contrives to comprehend the substance of God, measuring what is incomprehensible by the standard of his own reasoning and thinking that God is such as he himself has grasped with his reasoning. And in sum, if anyone makes his own mind the measure of what really exists, he does not realize that it is easier to measure the entire ocean with a tiny cup[3] than to understand the ineffable majesty of God with the human mind. *Puffed up without reason* [Col 2.18] and putting on airs through the vanity of his intellect, he is not able to say: *I believed; therefore I spoke.* For he cannot add what follows: *But I was greatly humbled.* Indeed, he passes his life in self-conceit and arrogance, and he glories in empty words, bereft of the strength that comes from faith.

Then he[4] humbles not only himself, but also in one fell swoop every member of the human race, each of whom is related to him and shares a common nature. For he says: *I said in my bewilderment: "Every human being speaks falsely"* [Ps 115.2]. Hence he who is not

[2]In the Hebrew Ps 114 and Ps 115 are a single psalm (Ps 116). Greek versions of the Psalter separate the two, and so Ps 114.9 immediately precedes Ps 115.1.

[3]Gk. *cotyla*.

[4]That is, the Psalmist.

helped by faith but enters into discussion according to his own lights, who trusts in human preparations when it comes to comprehending the truth, speaks falsely, seeing that he has fallen very far from the truth.

3 He said that he said these words *in bewilderment*. What does he mean by bewilderment? Either: "When I gazed upon human nature and investigated whether some truth was to be found anywhere among human beings, nowhere could I find truth without the help of God. This incredible fact astounded me and I cried out: *Every human being speaks falsely*."[5] Or: "In that bewilderment which I simulated in the presence of Achish, when I feigned madness and derangement because I realized that I needed to misrepresent myself and falsify the true situation in order to escape the danger of my enemies, at that time I said: *Every human being speaks falsely*. I had recourse to speaking falsely not by choice, nor in order to do evil to my neighbors, but entirely because I was in a precarious situation."[6]

By no means does the prophet contradict himself when he speaks, as some sophists try to argue, claiming that the prophet is guilty of self-refutation. For if *every human being speaks falsely*, and David is a human being, then clearly David also speaks falsely. But if he speaks falsely, then no one should believe what he claims. And if what he said is not true, and not every human being speaks falsely, then David should also be exonerated of speaking falsely. But if he does not speak falsely, then we should believe what he claims. And again, if we believe what he claims, then we will be compelled not to believe what he claims. Hence if David speaks the truth, he refutes what he says since he is both a human being and does not speak falsely. But if he speaks falsely, of his own accord he has provided the grounds for not believing him. For who pays attention to a speaker of falsehoods? And so, since he claimed once that *every human being speaks falsely*, let it be assumed that David speaks falsely so that he

---

[5] Basil's scriptural allusion to David's search for truth is unclear.
[6] See 1 Sam 21.12–15.

confirms what he said. Or if it is assumed that he speaks the truth, then he refutes his own claim

But these are the musings of those who play games with language and glory in how their arguments take twists and turns before an uneducated audience. The truth, however, is not found in this way. Now those who are still in the grip of the human passions are called "human beings." But as for the man who has already transcended his carnal passions, who because of the perfection of his intellect has passed over to the angelic state, when he discusses human concerns, it is clear that he excludes himself from the rest of humanity. He did not speak falsely who said: *I said: "You are gods and all of you sons of the Most High. And yet you shall die like human beings"* [Ps 81.6–7]. *"You are gods."* Now if the designation "god" is appropriate for someone else, it is surely also appropriate for David. Indeed, "a son of the Most High" is the man who has been brought into affinity with God through virtue. And he does not "die like a human being," but rather he has God living in himself.   **4**   So then, he says: *I said in my bewilderment: "Every human being speaks falsely."* Let those who are disturbed by the passions of the flesh and yet raise their intellect to supercosmic realities heed these words. Destroying the thoughts of such people as well as the height of their heart that exalts itself against God[7] should be the common goal of all those who seek after piety.

What shall I return to the Lord for all that he returned to me? The cup of salvation I will take [Ps 115.3–4]. After he became aware of God's innumerable gifts—that he was brought into being from nothing, that he was formed from the earth and honored with reason, by virtue of which he can also bear the heavenly image; then, turning his attention to the economy for the human race, that the Lord gave himself as the ransom for us all[8]—he is at a loss and searches among all his possessions for a gift worthy of the Lord. So then, *What shall I return to the Lord?* "Neither sacrifices, nor whole burnt offerings, nor

[7]See 2 Cor 10.4–5.
[8]See Mt 20.28; Mk 10.45.

the service based on the ritual duties of the Law, but the entirety of my very own life." And for this reason he says: *The cup of salvation I will take.* Suffering in the contests of piety and resisting sin even unto death: this is what he calls the cup. And this would be the very thing that the Savior himself taught in the gospels: *Father, if it be possible, let this cup pass* [Mt 26.39]. And again to his disciples: *Are you able to drink the cup that I am to drink?* [Mt 20.22]. Now the cup signified the death that he would undergo for the salvation of the world. For this reason he[9] says: *The cup of salvation I will take.* That is, "I come thirsting for the perfection that martyrdom obtains, considering the tortures used in the contests of piety as rest for soul and body, not pains. So then," he says, "I shall make myself a sacrifice and offering to the Lord, since I consider all else inferior to the dignity of our Benefactor. Furthermore, I am ready to pay these promises with all the people as my witness. For *my vows I will pay to the Lord in the sight of all his people* [Ps 115.5]."[10]

Then there is an exhortation to his audience, not to be terrified of death. He says: *Precious in the sight of the Lord is the death of his devout ones* [Ps 115.6]. "Do not shrink," he says, "from the good fight, my people; do not flinch in the face of death. For it is not destruction, but a means to life; it is not complete annihilation, but a passage to honor." So then, it is the custom of greedy men to call those stones which gleam with brilliant colors "precious." But what is truly precious *is the death of his devout ones.* When a soul becomes pure in its manner of life, free from fleshly defilements, *without stain or wrinkle* [Eph 5.7], renowned in the contests of piety and wreathed with *the crown of righteousness* [2 Tim 4.8], and when because of all these

[9]That is, the Psalmist.

[10]Ps 115.5, whose wording parallels Ps 115.9, was marked with asterisks in the fifth column of Origen's *Hexapla.* This means that the line was found in the Hebrew yet was not included in the Septuagint translation and that it was contained in another Greek translation of the Old Testament (those by Aquila, Symmachus, and Theodotion). Basil's quotation of Ps 115.5 at this point in the homily (i.e., between Ps 115.4 and Ps 115.6) indicates that his version of Psalm 115 was the "mixed" Septuagint text, that is, the Septuagint with isolated readings from other versions based on Origen's fifth column that was widely used in the East in antiquity.

things it gleams with the beauty of virtue, it stands in the presence of the Lord and Judge of the universe in possession of the shining brilliance that comes from grace, which is more splendid than every precious stone. How is the death of such a human being not precious in the sight of the Lord?

So let us not mourn when devout men depart from here, but rather when people are born and enter into this life. For on the one hand, the entry into this world is inseparable from the ignominy of the filth, the stench, and the other things which none of those who govern our life would easily bear the sight of. Indeed, the entry which is our birth in the flesh has been established by the necessity of nature as inseparable from such things. But on the other hand, the departing and going away from here is precious and magnificent, yet not for all human beings, but only for those who live a devout and just life. So then, the death of human beings is precious, not their birth. For he says: *It is sown in ignominy, it is raised in glory* [1 Cor 15.43]. *It is sown in corruption, it is raised in incorruption* [1 Cor 15.42]. Therefore, compare birth and death, and stop mourning those who have been released from ignominy. When Jews died, their corpses were abominable.[11] When there is a death for Christ, the relics of his devout ones are precious. In the past it was said to the priests and Nazirites: "You shall not defile yourselves for any dead person."[12] And: "If anyone shall touch a dead body, he will be unclean until the evening."[13] And: "He shall wash his clothes."[14] But now, anyone who has touched the bones of a martyr receives some share of the holiness that comes from the grace inherent in the body. So then, *precious in the sight of the Lord is the death of his devout ones.* Do not prefer what is most ignominious to what is most precious. Do not make a wicked exchange, preferring the corrupt life to the incorruptible and blessed state. For besides the ignominious passions to which

[11]See Lev 11.11; Num 9.6; 19.11–16.
[12]See Lev 21.1; 21.11.
[13]See Lev 11.24; 11.39.
[14]See Lev 11.40.

most lovers of pleasure are subjected, there are also life's necessities, which bend the nobility of the soul, as if enslaving it, forcing it into servitude of the flesh. Where there is enslavement, there clearly is also ignominy. So then, one ought to flee that life which is inseparable from ignominy.

5 "And I do not make myself into anything great," he says, "when I pay you, Lord. Since *I am your slave* [Ps 115.7], I offer to you your own possession. After all, every creature is a slave of the Creator. So I am a slave not only by choice, but also by nature. For I am *the son of your maidservant* [Ps 115.7], whom the enemy seduced when she was innocent and quite childlike.[15] After instigating her rebellion against enslavement to you, he made her a slave to sin. But now I am returning and running back to my original Lord, and I acknowledge my enslavement of old. *You have broken through my bonds* [Ps 115.7]. You freed me from the bonds of sin by descending into hell and releasing humanity when it was in the bonds of death and detained in the inescapable prisons of hell."[16]

"It is for this reason that *to you I will sacrifice* [Ps 115.8] neither quadrupeds with the hoof divided who chew the cud, nor clean birds, nor fine flour mixed with oil, nor pure frankincense, nor the incense of the mixture.[17] For these are offered to you, Lord, from the earth. Instead I will offer that which is my very own personal possession and the offspring of my heart, namely, I will glorify you from my very own mind, as if from an altar. And I will sacrifice to you *a sacrifice of praise* [Ps 115.8], which is more precious to you than innumerable whole burnt offerings. For you, God, are self-sufficient and perfect. You do not demand the sacrifice of material goods, of which the affluent have more than their fair share; you demand instead confession from a good disposition and true heart, which is something that all can share in equally if they wish to do so."

[15]Here Basil refers to Eve.
[16]Here Basil alludes to the harrowing of hell; see also *Ps48* 9.
[17]See Ex 31.11, 35.19, 39.15, 40.27; Num 4.16; 2 Chr 13.11.

My vows I will pay to the Lord in the sight of all his people [Ps 115.9]. "When I offer a sacrifice of praise to you, I will not sacrifice in a secret place and a hidden corner as if I were ashamed, avoiding the complaints of the impious; instead I will perform a public sacrifice, associating with all the people who participate in the service. The midst of the most splendid Jerusalem[18] will be appointed as the place for sacrifice."

You who have abandoned the church and gather in profane houses, you who are the wretched fragments of the precious body, hear this: vows must be paid in the midst of Jerusalem,[19] that is, in the church of God. For according to the worship of old, each person was not allowed to construct his own altar, but a single one was designated for all who chose to sacrifice. But you raise an altar in opposition to the altar of your forefathers and kindle a strange fire upon it.[20] You are not chastened by the ancient pattern, as you are drawn to men of corrupted intellect and join in their madness.[21]

Flee the example that these men set, you people of the Lord. And do not separate yourselves from the portion of those who are being saved. Persevere in faith, and grow perfect in the precepts of the Lord, *to whom be glory and might for ever and ever. Amen* [1 Pet 4.11].

[18]See Ps 115.10.

[19]See Ps 115.10.

[20]See Lev 10.1, 16.1; Num 3.4, 17.2, 26.61.

[21]For a similar diatribe against those who abandon the church and gather in their own assemblies, see *Ps28* 3.

Homily on Faith

INTRODUCTION

Basil's homily *On Faith* is one of the classic expressions of his Trinitarian doctrine.[1] Here he provides a rich and at times lyrical summary of his views on the difficulty of knowing God and his concept of God as Father, Son, and Holy Spirit. According to one commentator, this homily is reminiscent of St Augustine's account of the vision which he and his mother experienced at Ostia in 387 (see *Confessions* 9.10.23–26).[2] Like Augustine, Basil takes the reader along on an intellectual ascent from the sensory material world through the levels of the immaterial spiritual world in order to reach its highest point, God himself. Once "there," Basil describes the Father, Son, and Holy Spirit, elaborating particularly upon the last to demonstrate his unity with the Father and Son. This makes *Fide* one of the key texts for understanding the development of Basil's pneumatology. In this homily the polemical tone found in his treatises *Against Eunomius* and *On the Holy Spirit*, as well as in certain homilies on Trinitarian subjects, is muted.[3] While the Trinitarian theology presented here was of course decisively shaped through debate with his opponents (and hints of these controversies pop up occasionally), this homily is nonetheless a positive presentation of his views unencumbered

---

[1]This *De fide* (CPG 2859) is to be distinguished from another *De fide* (CPG 2886) authored by Basil. The latter, also known as *Prologus viii*, is one of the prefaces of the *Moralia*. Translations can be found in W.K.L. Clarke, *The Ascetic Works of Saint Basil* (London: SPCK, 1925), 90–99, and M. Monica Wagner, *Saint Basil: Ascetical Works*, FOTC 9 (New York: The Fathers of the Church, Inc., 1950), 57–69.

[2]Hermann Dörries, *De Spiritu Sancto. Der Beitrag des Basilius zum Abschluss des trinitarischen Dogmas* (Göttingen: Vandenhoeck & Ruprecht, 1956), 98–9.

[3]See *Verb*, *Sab*, and *Trin* in this volume.

by the detailed argumentation demanded in polemical treatises. As such, this brief homily constitutes an excellent introduction to Basil's Trinitarian thought.

Basil begins this homily with a statement of one of the key elements of his theology, namely, how difficult it is to come to know and speak of God (§1).[4] Although piety demands that we fix our minds upon God without interruption, speaking about God is fraught with risk. For the human intellect has fallen far below the dignity of God and furthermore human speech is an imperfect vehicle for human thoughts about God. Given such inadequacies and the danger of diminishing the grandeur of God with our paltry words, it is best to keep silent. But since we are all endowed by nature with the desire to glorify God, we want to say something, even if no one can ever speak worthily about God. As the examples of Abraham and Moses show, the more we advance in knowledge of God, the more we realize our inability to speak about God in a fitting manner. He always eludes our grasp. Hence, since piety demands that we speak of God, we must do so insofar as we are able, accepting the fact that we can never speak of him exactly as he is.

At this point Basil leads his audience through an intellectual ascent. He exhorts us to leave behind all sense perceptions and earthly realities, to rise above the stars, to transcend the heavens and intellectually behold "there" the beauty of the heavenly powers. Passing even beyond these, we must transcend the entire created order in order to contemplate the divine nature itself. Once "there," Basil describes the divine nature with thirteen attributes that emphasize the utter transcendence of God. These attributes are a mixture of biblical and Platonist descriptions of God.[5] In fact, the entirety of §1 (especially the final paragraph in the translation

---

[4]For summaries of this homily, see Dörries, *De Spiritu Sancto*, 97–100; Volker Henning Drecoll, *Die Entwicklung der Trinitätslehre des Basilius von Cäsarea: Sein Weg vom Homöusianer zum Neonizäner* (Göttingen: Vandenhoeck & Ruprecht, 1996), 162–5; and Andrew Radde-Gallwitz, *Basil of Caesarea: A Guide to his Life and Doctrine* (Eugene: Cascade Books, 2012), 101–7.

[5]Drecoll, *Die Entwicklung*, 163.

below, which recounts the intellectual ascent) is conspicuous for its Platonist themes, though scholars continue to debate over his precise sources.[6] Whatever the philosophical antecedents, Basil has appropriated the idea of intellectual ascent to express in vivid terms the difficulty of coming to know God.

What we find "there," continues Basil, when we contemplate the divine nature is "Father, Son, and Holy Spirit, the uncreated nature, the lordly dignity, the natural goodness" (§2). Basil then proceeds to describe the attributes of the Father and Son. He first stresses the distinction between them. For example, the Father is "principle" (ἀρχή) and "cause" (αἰτία) of all, whereas the Son is wisdom, power, and indistinguishable image of God (see 1 Cor 1.24; Col 1.15). But Basil also emphasizes the distinction between the Son and creation: he is, for example, "he who exists before the ages, not a late acquisition" and "Maker, not something made" (§2). Because the Son falls on the divine side of the ontological gap between God and creation, this means that the Son "is everything that the Father is" (§2). As Basil puts its, they share the same "distinctive features" (ἰδιότητας) that characterize the divine nature.[7] The Son by nature possesses the

[6]Scholars such as Paul Henry, *Études plotiniennes I. Les états du texte de Plotin* (Paris: Descleé de Brouwer et Cie; Bruxelles: L'édition universelle, 1938), 160, 161, 165–6, and 175–8, and Hans Dehnhard, *Das Problem der Abhängigkeit des Basilius von Plotin* (Berlin: De Gruyter, 1964), 9, 11, and 57–61, argued that here Basil drew directly upon Plotinus. Not all have agreed with this assessment. For example, W. Theiler, in a review of Dehnhard's book (*Byzantinische Zeitschrift* 41 [1941]: 169–76, especially pp. 171–3), suggested Porphyry as Basil's source. Salvatore Lilla, "Le fonti di una sezione dell'omelia *De fide* di S. Basilio Magno," *Augustinianum* 30 (1990): 5–19, denied Porphyry's influence on Basil here, and sees rather an eclectic use of Platonist sources including Plotinus, Plato himself, Maximus of Tyre, and the Corpus Hermeticum. In contrast to these positions, John M. Rist, "Basil's 'Neoplatonism': its Background and Nature," in Paul Jonathan Fedwick, ed., *Basil of Caesarea: Christian, Humanist, Ascetic. A Sixteen-Hundredth Anniversary Symposium* (Toronto: The Pontifical Institute of Mediaeval Studies, 1981), 137–220, at 202–5, has denied all claims of Neoplatonist influence on Basil in *Fide* 1, seeing only vague terminological parallels with Platonism, too vague to suggest Basil's direct use of Platonist material.

[7]On "distinctive features" (and its equivalent "distinguishing marks"), see Drecoll, *Die Entwicklung*, 107–10; Andrew Radde-Gallwitz, *Basil of Caesarea, Gregory of Nyssa, and the Transformation of Divine Simplicity* (Oxford: Oxford University Press,

glory and dignity of divinity just as the Father does by nature. He has not received the attributes he possesses by grace, as is the case for creatures. They are his by nature. Having shone forth "from the Father's substance" (note the allusion to the original Nicene Creed of 325[8]), the Father and Son share the same nature and the Son is the Father's "equal in goodness, his equal in power, sharing in his glory" (§2).

Basil then briefly turns to the "economy of human salvation," but only to affirm that the incarnate Christ's displays of subordination to the Father should not be seen as signs of the Son's lesser divinity. Rather, these exhibit his loving condescension to human frailty for the purpose of the salvation of humanity. As elsewhere in his corpus, Basil undoubtedly included these lines, which deny that the Son loses or damages his divinity in the incarnation, with an anti-Eunomian intent.[9] Basil is adamant that nothing can negate the Son's natural equality with the Father.

The remainder of the homily is dedicated to the Holy Spirit (§3).[10] The intellect finds the Holy Spirit "there" where the Father and Son are. He too possesses the essential properties of the divine nature: goodness, uprightness, holiness, and life. Basil stresses that, unlike creatures, the Holy Spirit possesses these attributes by nature; they are inseparable from him as heat is inseparable from fire. The Spirit's unity with the Father and Son is also demonstrated by the fact that "he is proclaimed in the singular," that is, Scripture speaks of a single Holy Spirit just as it speaks a single Father and a single Son. Thus Scripture's customary way of speaking of the Spirit indicates

2009), 132–7; and Mark DelCogliano, *Basil of Caesarea's Anti-Eunomian Theory of Names: Christian Theology and Late-Antique Philosophy in the Fourth-Century Trinitarian Controversy*, VCS 103 (Leiden: Brill, 2010), 189–260.

[8]The original Creed issued at the Council of Nicaea in 325 stated that the Son was "begotten from the Father, that is, from the substance of the Father." The revised version of the Nicene Creed adopted at the Council of Constantinople in 381 removed the explanatory, "that is, from the substance of the Father."

[9]See also *Chr* 2 and *Trin* 4.

[10]For an analysis of Basil's pneumatology in §3, see Radde-Gallwitz, *Basil of Caesarea*, 102–7.

that the Spirit is to be differentiated from the multitude of created *ministering spirits* (Heb 1.14) and joined with the Father and Son. An additional argument is advanced in favor of the Spirit's unity with the Father and Son: the attributes of the Spirit, which belong to him by nature, are not depleted or exhausted when they are shared with creatures. The Spirit gives sanctification and life to creatures (both angels and human beings); he loses nothing when creatures participate in him, when they are sanctified and given life by him. Here Basil is using an argument for the divinity of the Holy Spirit based on the idea that God is the Undiminished Giver. Only God can give of his own possessions, of his own self, without diminishment; created and material things cannot be distributed without depletion. The Holy Spirit exhibits this same divine characteristic of undiminished giving. Therefore, Basil argues that "the Spirit bestows his own grace upon all while remaining undiminished and undivided" (§3) in order to affirm the Spirit's unity with the Father and Son.[11]

Next, Basil takes up the role of the Spirit in the economy of salvation. He "inspires the prophets, gives wisdom to lawmakers, consecrates priests," and so forth "through rebirth from above" (§3). The Spirit is especially responsible for the conversion of the apostles, making these weak men strong, these poor men rich, these ignorant men wise. The homily concludes with descriptions of some other attributes of the Spirit which demonstrate that he is divine: omnipresence and agency. Andrew Radde-Gallwitz has identified three pneumatological moves that Basil makes in this last section of the homily.[12] First, Basil articulates the implications of the doctrine of divine simplicity, the idea that God is indivisible into parts and thus fully present everywhere. The Spirit's omnipresence is a function of his simplicity and demonstrates his unity with the Father and

[11]On the Undiminished Giver argument, see Lewis Ayres, "The Holy Spirit as Undiminished Giver: Didymus the Blind's *De Spiritu Sancto* and the Development of Nicene Pneumatology," in D. Vincent Twomey and Janet E. Rutherford, eds., *The Holy Spirit in the Fathers of the Church. The Proceedings of the Seventh International Patristic Conference, Maynooth, 2008* (Dublin: Four Courts Press, 2011), 57–72.

[12]See Radde-Gallwitz, *Basil of Caesarea*, 104–7.

Son. Second, scriptural passages which speak of the Spirit's activity show that he is not merely a mode or facet of God. For Basil, when Scripture proclaims that the Spirit acts as he wills (see 1 Cor 12.11), it demonstrates that the Spirit is not one of subordinate ministering spirits (see Heb 1.14) who do not act according to their own will, but rather a divine agent with the authority to act who is not identical to either the Father or the Son. Third, just as the Son's being sent in the incarnation does not damage or lessen his divinity, so too the Spirit's being sent for the economy does not lessen or preclude his divinity. Hence, in Basil's view the scriptural language of sending can be taken, for both the Son and the Spirit, as indicative of both the willed actions of the individual divine persons and the action of God. It is another way of demonstrating the Spirit's unity with the Father and Son. With these reflections, the homily ends.

Authenticity. The authenticity of this homily is certain and has never been doubted. It is one of the homilies of Basil's that Rufinus of Aquileia translated in the early 400s.[13] It is also widely attested in the best manuscripts of Basil's homilies.[14] Nothing within the homily itself suggests that Basil is not its author.

Context and Date. There is little in this homily to suggest a particular context or a firm date. Hermann Dörries demonstrated that it has several descriptions of the Spirit in common with *Spir.* 9.22, which may indicate that both works were composed around the same time, about 375.[15] Jean Gribomont appears to have endorsed this suggestion.[16] But these parallels are susceptible to other explanations. Basil could also be articulating ideas about the Spirit that either would later find expression in *Spir.* or were repeated after this treatise was already written. Furthermore, the anti-Eunomian and anti-Pneumatomachian themes found in this homily echo

[13]PG 31.1781–1785.
[14]See BBV ii.1069–72.
[15]Dörries, *De Spiritu Sancto*, 99–100.
[16]Jean Gribomont, *In Tomum 31 Patrologiae Graeae ad editionem operum rhetoricorum, asceticorum, liturgicorum Sancti Basilii Magni Introductio* (Turnhout: Brepols, 1961), 5.

similar discussions of the Trinity elsewhere in Basil's corpus. But this homily's lack of explicit polemics makes a more precise dating impossible. However, the relatively brief, summary treatment of the Father and Son and the great attention given to the Holy Spirit would seem to suggest that the last was a topic of current interest and significance, so a date from 372 onwards may be more likely. In any event, the most that can be said with any confidence is that *Fide* probably postdates *Against Eunomius* (364–365) but precedes *On the Holy Spirit* (around 375).

Jean Bernardi identified this homily as the one preached by Basil on the festival of the martyr Eupsychius (celebrated on September 7) in 372, which a certain monk heard and complained about to Gregory of Nazianzus that Basil had "slurred" the Spirit.[17] This is an interesting suggestion and nothing in the homily itself precludes this possibility.[18] Yet at the same time nothing in the homily itself compels acceptance of Bernardi's identification. Surely not every word Basil preached on the Spirit is extant, and *Fide* need not be the homily that led the monk to denounce Basil to Gregory. And so, Bernardi's suggestion is unprovable though not impossible.

Translation. The following translation is based on Julien Garnier's edition as reprinted in De Sinner ii.182–187 (=PG 31.464–472).[19] In crafting my translation, I benefited from the Latin translations of Rufinus and Garnier, as well as from the (at times quite free) nineteenth-century English translation of Hugh Stuart Boyd.[20]

---

[17] Jean Bernardi, *La prédication des pères cappadociens* (Paris: Presses universitaires de France, 1968), 85–86; see also Paul Jonathan Fedwick, "A Chronology of the Life and Works of Basil of Caesarea," in idem, ed., *Basil of Caesarea: Christian, Humanist, Ascetic. A Sixteen-Hundredth Anniversary Symposium* (Toronto: The Pontifical Institute of Mediaeval Studies, 1981), 3–19 at 10 n. 39. The complaint of the monk is recorded in Gregory of Nazianzus, *Letter* 58.

[18] See Radde-Gallwitz, *Basil of Caesarea*, 100–1.

[19] CPG 2859.

[20] Hugh Stuart Boyd, *The Fathers not Papists; or Six Discourses by the Most Eloquent Fathers of the Church. With Numerous Extracts from Their Writings. Translated from the Greek. A New Edition Considerably Enlarged* (London: Samuel Bagster, 1834), 86–99.

Translation

1 It is pious to keep God in mind without ceasing, and the soul who loves God finds no satiety in this, but it is audacious to expound upon God in speech. For our mind has fallen quite far from the dignity of the true realties and moreover our speech communicates our thoughts obscurely. So then, if our mind is so distant from the grandeur of the true realities and our speech is even more inadequate than our mind, how are we not compelled to keep silent, so that the wonders of theology do not seem to be diminished by the poverty of our words?[1]

So then, while the desire to glorify God is naturally planted in all rational beings, the ability speak worthily of God is similarly lacking in all of them. As far as eagerness for piety is concerned, we are different from one another. But no one is so blind and self-deceived that he thinks he has ascended to the height of comprehension. Rather, the more someone seems to advance in knowledge, the more he realizes his incapacity. Such was Abraham. Such was Moses. When they were allowed to see God (insofar as it is possible for a human being to see him), precisely at that moment each belittled himself: Abraham called himself *dust and ashes* [Gen 18.27] and Moses said that he was *weak in speech and slow-tongued* [Ex 4.10]. Because of the incapacity of his tongue, he realized that he could not use it to express his sublime thoughts.

But since every ear is now open to receive theological instruction and the church finds no satiety in hearing such things (thereby confirming the word of Ecclesiastes: *the ear is not filled with hearing* [Eccl 1.8]), we must speak insofar as we are able. We will not speak of the full extent of God's greatness but to the extent that it is possible for us.[2] For though our eyes cannot take in the entire region between heaven and earth, still we do not refuse to gaze upon it to the extent

[1] Cf. *Ep.* 7 and *Chr* 1, where Basil also speaks of language as an imperfect vehicle for human thoughts about God.

[2] Gk. οὐχ ὅσος ἐστιν ὁ θεὸς, ἀλλ᾽ ὅσον ἡμῖν ἐφικτόν.

that we can. In a similar fashion, let us now fulfill the demands of piety with words inadequate to the task, but let us concede victory to the majesty of the true nature over against all speech. For not even the tongues of angels (however many there are), nor those of archangels, gathered together with every rational nature, are able to reach its smallest part, much less to make themselves equal to the whole of it.

Now if you want to say or hear something about God, break free from your body, break free from your sense perceptions, leave behind the earth, leave behind the sea, rise above the air, fly past the hours of day, the cycles of the seasons, the rhythms of the earth, climb above the aether, pass beyond the stars, their marvels, their harmonious order, their immense size, the benefits they supply to all, their good arrangement, their splendor, their position, their motion, their constellations and oppositions.[3] Once you have passed beyond all things in your thoughts, transcended the heaven, and risen above it, behold the beauty there with your mind alone: the heavenly armies, the choirs of angels, the dignities of archangels, the glories of the dominions, the preeminence of the thrones, the powers, the principalities, the authorities.[4] Once you have flown past all these things, transcended the entire created order in your thoughts, and raised your intellect far beyond these, contemplate the divine nature: permanent, immutable, inalterable, impassible, simple, incomposite, indivisible, *unapproachable light* [1 Tim 6.16], ineffable power, uncircumscribed greatness, supereminent glory, desirable goodness, extraordinary beauty that ravishes the soul pierced by it but that cannot be worthily expressed in speech.

2 There we find Father, Son, and Holy Spirit, the uncreated nature, the lordly dignity, the natural goodness. The Father is the principle of all, the cause of being for whatever exists, the root of the living.

---

[3]Literally, "how with respect to one another they have relations and distinctions."

[4]See Col 1.16.

From him proceeded the source of life;[5] the *wisdom*, the *power* [1 Cor 1.24], and the indistinguishable *image of the invisible God* [Col 1.15]; the Son who was begotten from the Father; the living Word; he who is both *God and with God* [Jn 1.1]; he who is,[6] not adventitious; he who exists before the ages, not a late acquisition; he who is Son, not something possessed; he who is Maker, not something made; he who is Creator, not creature; who is everything that the Father is. Note that I have said: "Son and Father." Please keep in mind these distinctive features[7] of theirs.

So then, the Son, while continuing to be Son, is everything that the Father is, according to the statement uttered by the Lord himself: *All that the Father has is mine* [Jn 16.15]. For surely all things whatsoever present in the archetype belong to the image of that archetype. The Evangelist says: *We have beheld his glory, glory as of the Only-Begotten from the Father* [Jn 1.14]. In other words, that marvelous glory was not given to him as a gift or by grace, but the Son possesses the dignity of the Father's divinity on account of their community in nature. For "receiving" is a trait shared with the created order, but "having by nature" is proper to the one who is begotten. So then, as Son, he naturally possesses what belongs to the Father; as Only-Begotten, he contains within himself all that is the Father's, with none of it being passed down to another. Therefore, the very designation "Son" teaches us that he shares in the nature [of the Father], not created by a command but having shone forth from the Father's substance and been conjoined to him instantaneously beyond all time, his equal in goodness, his equal in power, sharing in his glory. And indeed what is he but the seal and image that reveals within himself the whole Father?

Now whatever he says to you afterward on the basis of[8] his corporeal constitution as he is engaged in the economy of human salvation that he revealed to us through his manifestation in the

[5]See Jn 4.14.
[6]See Ex 3.14; Jn 8.58.
[7]Gk. ἰδιότητας.
[8]Literally, "from."

flesh, when he claims that he was sent,[9] that he is not able to act on his own,[10] that he is given a command,[11] and all such things: do not take these as an opportunity for disparaging the divinity of the Only-Begotten. For his condescension to your frail human condition ought not be taken as a diminishment of the dignity of the Almighty. Instead, understand his nature in a way that is appropriate for God and take his more lowly statements as about the economy. If we were to speak on these matters now with any accuracy, we would have to jettison our original plan altogether and introduce into our discussion a countless number of words.

3 So let's return to the subject. The mind which can be purified of the material passions, and leave behind every intelligible creature, and swim like a fish from the depths to the surface above, that mind, when it becomes purified of the created order, will see the Holy Spirit there where the Son is and where the Father is. He too has everything essentially by nature: goodness, uprightness, holiness, life.[12] For it says: *your good Spirit* [Ps 142.10]. And again: *Upright Spirit* [Ps 50.12]. And again: *the Holy Spirit* [Ps 50.13]. And the Apostle: *The law of the Spirit of life* [Rom 8.2]. None of these is acquired by him nor added adventitiously later. Instead, just as heat is inseparable from fire and radiance from light, so too are holiness, giving life, goodness, and uprightness inseparable from the Spirit.

There now stands the Spirit—there, in that blessed nature—not counted with the multitude, but contemplated in the Trinity. He is proclaimed in the singular,[13] not included among the creatures. For as the Father is one and the Son is one, so too the Holy Spirit is one. But *the ministering spirits* [Heb 1.14] arranged in their respective ranks display to us an innumerable multitude. Therefore, do not seek within the created order that which is above the created order.

[9]See Jn 20.21.
[10]See Jn 5.30.
[11]See Jn 14.31.
[12]See *Ep.* 159.
[13]Gk. μοναδικῶς.

Do not bring that which sanctifies down to the level of those who are sanctified. The Spirit fills angels, fills archangels, sanctifies the powers, gives life to all things. The Spirit, though divided among all creatures and participated in by the different ones in different ways, is yet not at all diminished by those who participate in him. Though he bestows his grace on all, yet he is not expended among those who participate in him. On the contrary, those who receive him are filled while he loses nothing. Indeed, just as the sun, though it shines on various bodies and is participated in by these bodies in various ways, and yet is not dimmed by those bodies which participate in it, so too the Spirit bestows his own grace on all while remaining undiminished and undivided.

He enlightens all so that they may comprehend God, inspires the prophets, gives wisdom to lawmakers, consecrates priests, empowers kings, perfects the just, exalts the prudent, is active in gifts of healing, gives life to the dead, frees those in bondage, turns foreigners into adopted sons. All these things he accomplishes through the rebirth from above.[14] When he received the tax collector who believed, he turned him into an Evangelist.[15] When he came among fishers, he made one of them into a Theologian.[16] When he found the persecutor repenting, he produced the Apostle to the gentiles,[17] the preacher of the faith, *the vessel of election* [Acts 9.15].[18]

Through him the weak are strengthened, the poor enriched, those unskilled in speech are made wiser than the wise. Paul was weak, but through the presence of the Spirit, the handkerchiefs that had touched his body healed those who received them.[19] Peter too was beset by bodily weakness, but through the indwelling grace of the Spirit, the shadow his body cast expelled the sicknesses of the infirm.[20] Peter and John were poor (for they had neither silver or

[14]See Jn 3.3.
[15]See Mt 9.9. Basil refers to Matthew.
[16]See Mt 4.19. Basil refers to John.
[17]See Rom 11.13; 1 Tim 2.7.
[18]Basil refers to Paul.
[19]See Acts 19.12.
[20]See Acts 5.15.

gold), but they bestowed health, which is more precious than heaps of gold. For though the lame man had received gold from many people, he still remained a beggar; but when he received grace from Peter, he stopped begging, leapt like a deer, and praised God.[21] John knew nothing of the wisdom of the world, but in the power of the Spirit he uttered words which no wisdom can comprehend.

The Spirit remains in heaven and fills the earth. He is everywhere present and nowhere contained. In his entirety he indwells each point and is with God in his entirety. He does not administer his blessings as a servant,[22] but he distributes the gifts with authority.[23] For it says: *he distributes to each one individually as he wills* [1 Cor 12.11]. He is sent[24] for the economy, but *acts* [1 Cor 12.11] on his own authority.[25] Let us pray that the Spirit be present to our souls and never abandon us, by the grace of our Lord Jesus Christ, *to whom be glory and might for ever and ever. Amen* [1 Pet 4.11].

[21]See Acts 3.1–10.
[22]See Heb 1.14.
[23]Gk. αὐθεντικῶς.
[24]See Jn 14.26, 15.26, 16.7.
[25]Gk. αὐτεξουσίως.

Homily on the Beginning of
the Gospel of John
(Jn 1.1–2)

*In the beginning was the Word, and the Word was
with God, and the Word was God. This one was in the
beginning with God.*

INTRODUCTION

Basil saw John 1.1 as an affirmation of the pro-Nicene doctrine of
the Trinity.[1] Or rather, he saw in John 1.1 a refutation of a number
of mistaken ideas about the Trinity held by his opponents and a
succinct confirmation of his own doctrine. He dealt with this verse
a number of times in his extant corpus, but this homily is by far
his most extensive and most developed discussion.[2] Here Basil
marshals the verse to refute key elements not only of the Heteroousian theology of Eunomius,[3] but also of the modalist theology

[1]See Mark DelCogliano, "Basil of Caesarea on John 1.1 as an Affirmation of
Pro-Nicene Trinitarian Doctrine," [forthcoming]. What follows below is drawn from
this study. On the label "pro-Nicene," see Lewis Ayres, *Nicaea and its Legacy: An
Approach to Fourth-Century Trinitarian Theology* (Oxford: Oxford University Press,
2004), 236–40.

[2]See also *Eun.* 2.14–15; 2.17; *Mam* 4; *Trin* 4; *Sab* 1; *Spir.* 6.14.

[3]On Eunomius and Heteroousian theology, see Thomas A. Kopecek, *A History of
Neo-Arianism* (Cambridge: The Philadelphia Patristic Foundation, Ltd., 1979); Rich-
ard Paul Vaggione, *Eunomius of Cyzicus and the Nicene Revolution* (Oxford: Oxford
University Press, 2000); Michel R. Barnes, *The Power of God: Δύναμις in Gregory of
Nyssa's Trinitarian Theology* (Washington, DC: The Catholic University of America

of Marcellus of Ancyra.[4] This method of argumentation is entirely consistent with his approach elsewhere in his corpus. Neither appealing to authoritative creedal statements nor employing technical terms like the Nicene *homoousios*, Basil aims to demonstrate that his opponents' theology contradicts Scripture.[5] And so, in John 1.1 Basil found a kind of encapsulation of his theology of the Trinity that directly refuted the positions of its key opponents on opposite ends of the theological spectrum. Rarely in the history of ecclesiastical debates has a theologian used a single verse of Scripture with such versatility.

In particular, Basil sees John 1.1 as an affirmation of four pro-Nicene doctrines about the Trinity. The first three are anti-Eunomian. The first is the eternity of the Word, which implies the Son's co-eternity with the Father. Like most non-Nicene theologians, Eunomius held that if the Son had been begotten from the Father, it implied that the Father pre-existed the Son.[6] Hence they are not co-eternal. The second affirmation of John 1.1 is that the begetting of the Son from the Father takes place without any passion (πάθος), that is, without suffering and change. Eunomius de-emphasized Father-and-Son language because he maintained that these terms connotated passion, suggesting that the Father's begetting of the Son was

Press, 2001), 173–219; Andrew Radde-Gallwitz, *Basil of Caesarea, Gregory of Nyssa, and the Transformation of Divine Simplicity* (Oxford: Oxford University Press, 2009), 87–112; and Mark DelCogliano, *Basil of Caesarea's Anti-Eunomian Theory of Names: Christian Theology and Late-Antique Philosophy in the Fourth-Century Trinitarian Controversy*, VCS 103 (Leiden: Brill, 2010), 1–134.

[4]On Marcellus' theology, see Ayres, *Nicaea and its Legacy*, 62–9; R.P.C. Hanson, *The Search for the Christian Doctrine of God: The Arian Controversy 318–381 AD* (Edinburgh: T & T Clark, 1988), 217–35; Klaus Seibt, *Die Theologie des Markell von Ankyra* (Berlin: De Gruyter, 1994); Markus Vinzent, *Markell von Ankyra: Die Fragmente [und] Der Brief an Julius von Rom*, VCS 39 (Leiden: Brill, 1997); and Joseph T. Lienhard, *Contra Marcellum. Marcellus of Ancyra and Fourth-Century Theology* (Washington, DC: The Catholic University of America Press, 1999), 49–68.

[5]See Jean Bernardi, *La prédication des pères cappadociens* (Paris: Presses universitaires de France, 1968), 87.

[6]See *Apologia* 12. There is an English translation of Eunomius' *Apologia*, together with an edition of the Greek text, in Richard Paul Vaggione, *Eunomius: The Extant Works* (Oxford: Oxford University Press, 1987).

somehow corporeal.[7] This of course goes against the idea of divine incorporeality, and it led Eunomius to favor the names "Unbegotten" and "Begotten" in preference to "Father" and "Son," and also to interpret begetting as an act analogous to creating. In contrast, Basil maintains that the divine begetting, which for him is something distinct from creating, can and must be understood as without involving any passion.[8] The third affirmation is the Son's essential likeness to the Father. According to Eunomius' theory of names, those names uniquely applied to God revealed substance, and thus Eunomius argued that the "unbegotten" Father and the "begotten" Son were two different substances.[9] Hence they did not share a single divine substance and were essentially unlike each other. The fourth and last affirmation is anti-Marcellan, that the Father and Son are distinct in number, or to use later terminology, two distinct persons. Marcellus, like Eunomius, downplayed Father-and-Son language, preferring to speak of God and his Word, but in contrast to Eunomius he stressed the unity of God to such an extent that the distinct existence of the Word was compromised. Hence through his interpretation of John 1.1 Basil presents his Trinitarian theology as the middle way between the extremes of the Heteroousian theology of Eunomius and the modalism of Marcellus.[10]

Basil begins the homily by praising the gospels as "nobler" than all the other books of Scripture, and the Gospel of John as preeminent among the four gospels (§1).[11] In the other books of Scripture the Spirit communicates with us through his servants, whereas in the gospels the Lord himself speaks to us. In this homily Basil simply asserts that John is "the most resounding" (§1) of the preachers of the gospels, but we learn the reason for this

[7]See *Apologia* 16–17.

[8]See *Eun.* 2.5–6 and 2.22–24.

[9]See DelCogliano, *Theory of Names*, 25–48.

[10]The same tactic is found in *Ep.* 69.2, 210.4, 226.4, and *Sab.*

[11]For another summary of this homily, see Volker Henning Drecoll, *Die Entwicklung der Trinitätslehre des Basilius von Cäsarea: Sein Weg vom Homöusianer zum Neonizäner* (Göttingen: Vandenhoeck & Ruprecht, 1996), 165–7.

judgment from *Against Eunomius*. While the other gospels speak
of the divine economy, God's actions in the world through Christ,
John provides theology, an account of God in himself.[12] And for
Basil, the first words of the Prologue are also the most important
for understanding the theology of the eternal Word which the
Gospel of John reveals: *In the beginning was the Word, and the
Word was with God, and the Word was God* (Jn 1.1). Basil notes
that even non-Christians marvel at these words and insert them
in their treatises.[13] Therefore, we who are "truly disciples of the
Spirit" should make every effort to understand the deep insight
which these words convey, even though this endeavor is difficult
to achieve because of their profundity.

This difficulty arises with the very first words: *In the beginning
was the Word*. For who can understand the details of the beginning of
all things? Basil suggests that these words were preemptively uttered
by the Spirit against the Eunomians, who Basil claims encapsulated
their beliefs in catch phrases such as: "If he was begotten, he was not"
(εἰ ἐγεννήθη, οὐκ ἦν), "Before his begetting, he was not" (πρὸ τοῦ
γεννηθῆναι, οὐκ ἦν), and, "He received his subsistence from nothing"
(ἐξ οὐκ ὄντων τὴν ὑπόστασιν ἔλαβε). These phrases are reminiscent
of sayings attributed to Arius: "There was a point when he was not"
(ἦν ποτε ὅτε οὐκ ἦν), "He was not before he was begotten" (οὐκ ἦν
πρὶν γένηται), and "From nothing he came into existence" (ἐξ οὐκ
ὄντων ἐγένετο). In fact, these three statements had been anathematized in the original Nicene Creed of 325. While Eunomius himself
did not use these formulas, he did say that the substance of the Son
"was begotten but did not exist before its own constitution."[14] Basil
believed that Eunomius meant the same thing as Arius, namely, that
first the Father was alone and only afterwards brought the Son into

[12]*Eun.* 2.15.

[13]One non-Christian who esteemed the prologue of John and quoted it is the
philosopher Amelius, a leading member of the school of Plotinus; see Eusebius,
Preparation for the Gospel 11.19.1. Cf. Eusebius, *Preparation for the Gospel* 11.17–18; and
Augustine, *Confessions* 7.9.13–14.

[14]*Apologia* 12.

existence, such that they were not co-eternal.[15] Thus Basil appeals to John 1.1 to prove their co-eternity, the first affirmation.

To do this, Basil investigates the meaning of the word *beginning* in John 1.1. He first seeks to determine what sort of beginning this is. He notes that most beginnings are merely relative to something else. For example, *the fear of the Lord is the beginning of wisdom* (Prov 9.10). All such beginnings are not absolute, since something precedes them. But there is also an absolute beginning (§2). Here Basil does not mean the creation of time and the physical, visible world, as recounted in Genesis, but the beginning of the spiritual universe.[16] When the human mind strives to imagine something "before" this absolute beginning, it fails. There is nothing "before" this absolute beginning: there is only the timeless present of eternity.

Basil next turns to the significance of the word *was*, which he sees as corroborating his interpretation of *beginning*. If the Word was at the absolute beginning, if the Word already existed at the absolute beginning, then there never was a point at which the Word did not exist. The Father's begetting of the Son cannot be regarded as a kind of temporal event for which there is a before and after. Rather, it is something which belongs to the timeless present of eternity. Accordingly, the slogans, "there was a point when he did not exist" and "he did not exist before he was begotten" are wrong because they assume that the Son's birth was a kind of temporal event with a before and after. The terms "when" and "before" are meaningless in eternity. Since the Word already existed at the absolute beginning, the human mind cannot imagine a point "before" this, "when" the Word did not exist. Thus John 1.1 shows that the Word must be eternal, co-eternal with the Father.

Basil next turns to the second and third affirmations of pro-Nicene theology, the Father's begetting of the Son without passion and the Son's essential likeness to the Father (§3). Here he bases his arguments on the name *Word* (*Logos*) in John 1.1. First, Basil seeks

[15] *Eun.* 2.11–14.
[16] See *Hex.* 1.5–6.

to identify what sort of *logos* existed at the absolute beginning. Was it a human word? An angelic word? Since both angels and humanity were created after the absolute beginning, neither a human nor an angelic word could have been *in the beginning*. Accordingly, the term *logos* must be understood "in a way appropriate to God," just as other names applied to the Only-Begotten elsewhere in the Gospel of John are understood. When he is called *light* (Jn 1.4), he is not understood to be that perceptible light seen with the eyes; nor when he is called *life* (Jn 11.25) is he understood to be that life shared with irrational creatures. The name *Logos* must be understood similarly.

So why is the Son called the *Logos* here? Basil says that it is to teach that the Son is begotten from the Father as a spoken word proceeds from the intellect. A bit earlier Basil had noted the well-known Stoic distinction between the expressed *logos*, or the spoken word, and the internal *logos*, or the thought in the mind.[17] The spoken word expresses the thought in the mind. And so, just as the human intellect gives birth to a spoken word without any passion, suffering, or change in the mind, so too the Father gives birth to the Son. This second affirmation is closely connected with the third. The content of what we express in spoken words reflects the content of the thoughts in our mind. According to Basil, there is a one-to-one correspondence between the interior *logos* and the expressed *logos*. So too it is with the Father's begetting of the Son. As the *Logos*, the Son is expressed by the Father and corresponds fully to what the Father is. As the word that comes from the human mind contains within itself all the power of that mind, so too the Son, as the *Logos*, comes from the Father with all the Father's power. Thus the Son is essentially like the Father. If John 1.1 had said "In the beginning was the Son," Basil grants that it would be permissible to think of the Father's begetting of the Son as involving time, passion, and suffering, since the word "son" has such associations. But the use of the term *Logos* precludes those associations since a spoken word proceeds from the mind timelessly and without change.

[17] See SVF 2.223.

Basil then turns to the next clause of John 1.1, *And the Word was with God* (§4). After devoting a few lines the idea that the Word is not in a place but *with God* since just like the Father he is infinite and uncircumscribed, Basil proceeds to the anti-Marcellan fourth affirmation, that Father and Son are distinct individuals. The important word here is the preposition *with* (πρός). The fact that the Word is *with God* shows that the Son is distinct from the Father. If John 1.1 had said that the Word was "in" God, then it would lend support to the Marcellan position that Father and Son are really one individual existent. But the wording of John 1.1 proves that they are distinct in number.[18]

The next section of the homily deals briefly with the third clause of John 1.1 and John 1.2, *The Word was God. This one was in the beginning with God* (§4). Basil sees these lines as more or less repeating or confirming what the first two clauses of John 1.1 taught. But he does explore the significance of the demonstrative pronoun *this one* (οὗτος, often translated "he"), which was normally used in Greek to indicate someone near at hand, someone to whom the speaker could point. Basil advises his audience not to look outside themselves to find *this one*, but to enter the hidden recesses of their own souls. There they will find God the Word who was in the beginning and always with God his Father.

The homily concludes with an exhortation to use the words of John 1.1–2 as bulwark against those who blaspheme against the Only-Begotten and deny his eternal co-existence with the Father. The four uses of *he was* in these verses, Basil assures us, will destroy the "he was not" of the Eunomians. He encourages his audience to keep these foundations of the faith he has taught them undisturbed by blasphemers. Yet Basil says that he has taught his audience enough today, and does not want to render what he has taught unprofitable by continuing to preach. So on another day he will build the remaining doctrines of the faith upon these foundations when they have digested today's teaching.

[18]See *Sab* 1.

Authenticity. The authenticity of this homily is certain and has never been doubted. It is widely attested in the best manuscripts of Basil's homilies.[19] Nothing within the homily itself suggests that Basil is not its author.

Context and Date. It is reported in the opening paragraph that the prologue of the Gospel of John has just been read (§1). So this homily may have been preached in a liturgical context. Jean Gribomont saw the last lines of the homily, when Basil says that he has preached enough for the day and will resume on another day, as an indication that it was delivered to the catechumens during Lent.[20] This may well be the case, though nothing else in the homily seems to indicate this.

Previous attempts to date the homily are unsatisfactory. Based on the anti-Eunomian arguments in the homily Jean Gribomont places it during Basil's time as presbyter, that is 362–370.[21] But Basil's anti-Eunomian interests were not limited to his presbyterate. As noted above, anti-Eunomian themes are found in homilies from early and late in his career.[22] Jean Bernardi dated the homily to early in Basil's episcopacy, that is, 370–372, for two reasons.[23] First, he found Basil's words at the end of the homily, where he exhorts his audience to reflect on his teachings and states his readiness to bring his teachings to a conclusion when time permits, as expressive of a tone more suited to a bishop than a priest. The reasoning here is weak; Gribomont's interpretation of the final words of the homily has more plausibility, even though it remains uncertain. Second, Bernardi suggests that *Verb* must precede *Fide*, which he dated to September 7, 372,[24] because the account of the Trinity in *Verb*, which

[19] See BBV ii.1125–8.

[20] Jean Gribomont, *In Tomum 31 Patrologiae Graeae ad editionem operum rhetoricorum, asceticorum, liturgicorum Sancti Basilii Magni Introductio* (Turnhout: Brepols, 1961), 5

[21] Gribomont, *In Tomum 31*, 5

[22] See pp. 217–218 above. Homilies preached during his episcopacy with anti-Eunomian themes include *Fide*, *Sab*, and *Trin*.

[23] Bernardi, *La prédication*, 86–87.

[24] See above p. 233.

discusses only the Father and Son, is less precise and less complete than the account of the Trinity in *Fide*, which discusses Father, Son, and Holy Spirit. But the omission of a discussion of the Holy Spirit in *Verb* is surely the result of the homily's being an exegesis of John 1.1–2, which does not mention the Spirit. Thus the homily does not suggest a less developed Trinitarian theology that warrants placing it before *Fide*.[25]

In terms of relative chronology, *Verb* seems to be later than *Against Eunomius* (dated to 364–365) because Basil's exegesis of John 1.1 is more developed in the homily than in his anti-Eunomian treatise.[26] In the treatise John 1.1 is given solely an anti-Eunomian interpretation, whereas in the homily it is given additional anti-Eunomian interpretations plus an anti-Marcellan interpretation. Now we would not expect to find anti-Marcellan themes in a treatise dedicated to refuting Eunomius, and this may explain the scope of the exegesis of John 1.1 there. Yet at the same time it seems as if in the homily Basil has purposely, based on further reflections, expanded upon the anti-Eunomian exegesis of John 1.1 in the treatise by extending it to include more anti-Eunomian elements plus an anti-Marcellan component. Unfortunately, while this relative chronology seems probable, it suggests only a wide range of dates for the homily, 365–378. And yet, while Basil was aware of Marcellus and his modalist theology from the beginning of his ecclesiastical career, we know that it was only as a bishop, for purposes of achieving ecclesiastical unity, that he began in earnest to refute Marcellus, often under the codename "Sabellius," the purported heresiarch of modalism.[27] So perhaps it was at some point in the period of his episcopacy that he extended his anti-Eunomian exegesis of John 1.1 to include an anti-Marcellan theme. Thus we may plausibly narrow the range of

[25]See also my comments on Bernardi's dating of *Fide* above on p. 233.

[26]See Drecoll, *Die Entwicklung*, 165.

[27]On Basil's engagement with the theology of Marcellus, see Joseph T. Lienhard, "Basil of Caesarea, Marcellus of Ancyra, and 'Sabellius,'" *Church History* 58 (1989): 157–67, which serves as the basis for that author's *Contra Marcellum*, 199–208. On "Sabellius" as a codename for "Marcellus," see idem, *Contra Marcellum*, 210–2.

possible dates a bit, to 370–378, without, however, denying that it could have also been preached from 365 onward.

Translation. The following translation is based on Julien Garnier's edition as reprinted in De Sinner ii.187–194 (=PG 31.472–481).[28] In crafting my translation, I benefited from Garnier's Latin translation and an unpublished English translation by Timothy McConnell, as well as the excerpts translated into English by Blomfield Jackson.[29]

Translation

1   Every statement of the gospels is nobler than the other teachings transmitted by the Spirit. For in the latter he spoke to us through his servants the prophets, whereas in the gospels the Master conversed with us in his own person.[1] Now among his preachers of the gospel, the most resounding is John, the son of thunder,[2] whose utterances overwhelmed every ear and bedazzled every mind.[3] We have just heard read to us the prologue of the book of his gospel: *In the beginning was the Word, and the Word was with God, and the Word was God* [Jn 1.1]. I know that many of those who are external to the word of truth and take pride in worldly wisdom also marveled at these words and even dared to insert them into their own treatises.[4] After all, the devil is a thief, and what is ours he divulges to his own mouthpieces!

So then, if carnal wisdom marveled so greatly at the force of these words, what should we do, seeing that we are disciples of the Spirit? Should we pay them scant attention and conclude that the power existing in them is negligible? Who is so obtuse that he is not

[28]CPG 2860.
[29]"Prolegomena. Sketch of the Life and Works of Saint Basil," NPNF 2.8, lix–lx.

[1]Gk. αὐτοπροσώπως.
[2]Mk 3.17.
[3]Basil's esteem for John as a theologian and praise of his gospel echoes Origen, *Commentary on the Gospel of John* 1.20–23. See also *Eun.* 2.15.
[4]That is, non-Christian philosophers outside the church.

awestruck at the great beauty of the insight they offer and the truly unimaginable profundity of the doctrines they convey? So obtuse that he does not yearn to attain a true comprehension of them? Now marveling at beautiful things is not difficult, but attaining an accurate comprehension of the things at which one marvels is hard and nearly impossible. For example, there is no one who does not praise the sun when it can be seen, paying homage to its greatness and beauty, the symmetry of its rays, and its shining light. Yet if anyone were to try to fix the gaze of his eyes directly on that orb, not only would he fail to see what he hoped to see, but he would also ruin the sharpness[5] of his eyes.

I think that the mind has a similar experience when it tries to give an accurate explanation of the following words: *In the beginning was the Word.* Who can worthily understand what pertains to *the beginning*? What sort of power of words might be found that is equal to communicating what is known about it? Intending to hand on to us what pertains to the theology of the Son of God, he gave the account no other beginning than the beginning of all things. The Holy Spirit knew those who would cling to the glory of the Only-Begotten. He foreknew those who would utter sophistical arguments against us, which they concocted to dishearten those who heard them. Here's one: "If he was begotten, he was not." Also: "Before his begetting, he was not." And: "He received his subsistence from nothing."[6] Such statements are uttered by tongues honed sharper than every double-edged sword through the use of plausible arguments.[7]

Therefore, lest anyone have a basis for saying such things, the Holy Spirit takes the initiative through the gospel, saying: *In the beginning was the Word.* If you hold fast to this statement, you will

[5] Gk. ἀκρίβεια, literally, "accuracy."

[6] These statements are reminiscent of sayings attributed to Arius which were anathematized in the original Nicene Creed of 325: "There was a point when he did not exist," "He did not exist before he was begotten," and "From nothing he came into existence." Hence Basil suggests that Eunomius' Heteroousian theology is nothing more than the Arianism condemned at the Council of Nicaea.

[7] Gk. πιθανολογία, "the use of plausible arguments." In *Eun.* 1.1 Basil accuses Eunomius of using plausible arguments.

never suffer any evil from those practitioners of evil arts.[8] If one of them says, "If he was begotten, he was not," then retort: *In the beginning he was.* "But," he continues, "how could he exist before his begetting?" Do not let go of *he was.* Do not forsake *in the beginning.* The very tip of the beginning cannot be comprehended. What is beyond the beginning cannot be found.

Do not let anyone deceive you through the multivalence of the term. For in this life there are many beginnings of many things, but there is one beginning for all things that is beyond them all. *The beginning of the good way* [Prov 16.7], the proverb says. But the beginning of the way is the first movement by which we begin our journey, and you can find something before this first movement. Also: *The fear of the Lord is the beginning of wisdom* [Prov 9.10; Ps 110.10]. But something else also precedes this beginning, namely, the preliminary instruction that is the beginning of the acquisition of the arts. So then, the fear of the Lord is a preliminary step to wisdom. But there is even something prior to this beginning, namely, the state of the soul that is not yet wise and has still to acquire the fear of God. The civic magistrates who hold the eminent positions of power are also called beginnings.[9] But these beginnings are the beginnings[10] of particular people and each is a beginning[11] only in relation to a particular domain. And indeed the point is the beginning of the line, the line is the beginning of the surface, and the surface is the beginning of the body. And the letters are the beginnings of a word when they are put together.

2 The beginning is certainly not like this. For it is linked with nothing, bound to nothing, considered along with nothing, but rather utterly free, autonomous, unbound from relation to another, insurmountable to the mind. It is impossible to transcend it in thought.

---

[8]Again, Basil refers to the Eunomians; see *Eun.* 1.9.
[9]The Greek word for "beginning," ἀρχή, could also mean "ruler."
[10]That is, "rulers."
[11]That is, "ruler."

It is impossible to discover anything beyond it. For if you strive to pass beyond *the beginning* with your intellect's imagination, you will find that it has raced ahead of you, waiting for your thoughts to catch up to it. Allow your intellect to go as far as it wishes and reach for the heights. Then after countless wanderings and much stumbling around, you will find that it returns to itself again because it could not make *the beginning* lower than itself. Accordingly, *the beginning* is always beyond and greater than what can be conceived.

In the beginning was the Word. What a marvel! How all these words are linked with one another and accorded equal honor! *He was* is equivalent in meaning to *in the beginning*. Where is the blasphemer? Where is the tongue that fights against Christ? I mean, the tongue that says, "There was a point when he was not."[12] Listen to the gospel: *In the beginning he was.* If he was in the beginning, at what point was he not? Shall I groan at their impiety or loathe their stupidity? "But before his begetting, he was not." Do you really know when he was begotten, such that you can apply the word "before" to that time? For the term "before" is temporal, placing one thing before another in terms of how old it is. How is it logical that the maker of time has a begetting that is subject to temporal designations?

In the beginning he was. Unless you discard *he was*, you will leave no opening for their wicked blasphemy to slip in. For just as sailors mock the waves whenever they find themselves rocked between two anchors, so too, when this wicked tumult is stirred up by the vehement spirits of wickedness and violently shakes the faith of the many, you for your part can laugh at it, if you have your soul harbored in the secure port of these words.

3   Our mind now seeks who it was that was *in the beginning*. He says: *the Word.* What kind of word? The word of human beings? The word of the angels? After all, the Apostle intimated that the angels have their own language when he said: *If I should speak in the languages of men or angels* [1 Cor 13.1]. But "word" has a twofold

---

[12]Here Basil cites the actual saying attributed to Arius. See n. 6 above.

meaning. The first is the word expressed with the voice,[13] which perishes after it is produced in the air. The second is the internal word[14] which subsists in our hearts, the mental word.[15] But the other is the articulated word.[16]

See that you are never deceived by the homonymy of the term. For how could the word of human beings be in the beginning, when humanity received the beginning of its existence at some point afterward? Before humanity, there were the beasts. Before humanity, there were cattle, all the quadrupeds both terrestrial and aquatic, birds of the sky, stars, sun, moon, plants, seeds, earth, sea, sky. Therefore, the word of human beings was not in the beginning, but neither was the word of the angels. For all creation is posterior to the ages, having received the beginning of its existence from the Creator. And as for the word in the heart, it too is more recent than each of the things we have enumerated.

Accordingly, take "word" in a way appropriate to God. When you were told about the Only-Begotten, it was said that he was *the Word*. And so, just as a little afterwards it says *light* [Jn 1.4], as well as *life* and *resurrection* [Jn 11.25], and when you heard *light* you did not reduce it to the perceptible light that can be seen with the eyes, and when you heard *life* you did not think of that life which we share with irrational creatures, so too, when you hear *Word*, guard against letting your weakness of mind drag you down to lowly and humble senses of the term. Rather, seek out its intended sense.

Why *Word*? So that it may be understood that it proceeds from the intellect. Why *Word*? Because he was begotten without passion. Why *Word*? Because he is the image of his begetter, showing in himself the whole of the begetter, not divided from him in any way and existing perfect in himself, just as our word also reflects the whole of our thought. For what we express in words is that which we think

---

[13]Gk. ὁ διὰ τῆς φωνῆς προφερόμενος.
[14]Gk. ὁ ἐνδιάθετος.
[15]Gk. ὁ ἐννοηματικός.
[16]Gk. ὁ τεχνικός λόγος.

in our heart, and that which is spoken is a reflection of the thought in the heart. For *out of the abundance of the heart* [Mt 12.34; Lk 6.45] the word is expressed. Indeed, our heart is like a fountain and the expressed word is like a stream flowing from this fountain. So then, the outflow is like the initial upsurge, and when something appears, it is similar to what it was when hidden.

So then, he said *Word* so that he could communicate to you the Father's passionless begetting and teach you the theology of the perfect existence of the Son, and through these demonstrate the Son's non-temporal conjunction with the Father. After all, our word, as something begotten of the intellect, is also begotten without passion. For it is neither severed nor divided from the intellect, nor does it flow out from and leave the intellect. On the contrary, while the whole of the intellect remains in its proper state, it brings the word into existence, whole and complete. And the word that comes forth contains within itself all the power of the intellect that has begotten it. So then, take as much as is pious from the term "word" for the theology of the Only-Begotten. Reject whatever you find in it that appears unconducive and unsuitable, and transcend every contrivance.

In the beginning was the Word. Now if he had said, "In the beginning was the Son," the notion of passion would have been introduced along with the designation "Son." For in our case, that which is begotten is begotten in time and begotten with passion. For this reason, in anticipation he said *Word*, preemptively correcting inappropriate suppositions so that your soul could be kept unharmed.

4 *And the Word was with God.* Once again, he says *he was* on account of those who blaspheme by saying that he was not. Where was the Word? Not in a place. For that which is uncircumscribed is not contained in a place. But where was he? *With God.* Not that the Father is understood to be in a place, or the Son in some marked off space and definite, circumscribed area. On the contrary, the Father is infinite and the Son is infinite. Whatever place you can conceive of, wherever you can go in your spirit, you will find it filled with

God, and everywhere you will find the co-extensive subsistence of the Son.

And the Word was with God. Marvel at the accuracy of each term! He did not say, "The Word was in God," but rather *with God*, so that he could communicate the distinctness of his subsistence.[17] He did not say "in God," lest he give a pretext for a conflation of his subsistence [with the Father's]. For the wicked blasphemers who attempt to mix them all together claim that Father and Son and Holy Spirit are a single subject and apply different designations to the one reality.[18] This impiety is wicked and should be avoided no less than that of those who blaspheme by saying that the Son of God is unlike the God and Father according to substance.[19]

And the Word was with God. Next, after employing the term "Word" to communicate the passionlessness of his begetting, he at once eliminates any potential harm that might come to us from "Word." And so, as if snatching him away from the distortions of blasphemers, he tells us what the Word is: *The Word was God.* Do not quibble with me about the verbal distinctions. Do not attribute a blasphemy to the teaching of the Spirit by appeal to your evil arts. You have the verdict; submit yourself to the Lord.

The Word was God. This one was in the beginning with God. Once again, in a few words he sums up his whole theology, which the Evangelist handed on to us about the Only-Begotten. Who is *this one*? *This one* is God the Word. After articulating to you how to think about him, as if impressing upon your soul what you did not know through his teaching and causing Christ the Word to dwell in your heart, he says: *This one.* What is *this one*? Do not look outside yourself, searching for what the demonstrative pronoun[20] indicates, but enter into the hidden recesses of your own soul. There once you have identified and marveled at the God whom you have learned was

[17] Gk. τὸ ἰδιάζον τῆς ὑποστάσεως. See *Sab* 1 for a similar use of Jn 1.1.

[18] This is the modalist, or Sabellian, position, associated with Marcellus of Ancyra.

[19] This is the Heteroousian position, associated with Eunomius.

[20] That is, *This one.*

in the beginning, who proceeded as Word, who is with God, once you have worshipped your own Master who dwells in you through this teaching, realize that *this one* was *in the beginning*, that is, he is always *with God* his Father.

Please save these few words, imprinting them like a seal upon your memory. They will be for you an impregnable wall against the attacks of those who plot against you. They are the secure bulwark of souls against those who assault them. If anyone should come to you and say, "When he was not, he was begotten. For if he was, how could he be begotten?," repulse this blasphemy against the glory of the Only-Begotten as nothing less than a statement of the demons. Return to the words of the gospel and remain there: *In the beginning was the Word, and the Word was with God, and the Word was God. This one was in the beginning with God.* Say *he was* four times and you will quash their "he was not."

Let these foundations of the faith remain unshaken. We will build the remaining [doctrines of the faith] upon them, God willing. For it is not possible to discuss everything with you all at once, at least if we don't want to make what we have spent so much labor putting together for your benefit a waste of your time by prolonging this homily too much. For when the mind becomes exhausted from grasping many things all at once, it suffers much like the stomach that is surfeited through excessive eating and unable to digest what has been eaten. So then, I pray that you find sweetness in what you have tasted and receive benefit from what you have been given to digest. I stand ready to serve you the remaining [doctrines of the faith], in our Lord Jesus Christ, *to whom be glory and might for ever and ever. Amen* [1 Pet 4:11].

Homily On Not Three Gods Against Those Who Calumniate Us, Claiming That We Say That There Are Three Gods

Introduction

In this short homily, preached on the feast day of unnamed martyrs, Basil relates that he has been accused of tritheism because he refuses to classify the Holy Spirit among the creatures.[1] In other words, his Trinitarian doctrine of three equal and irreducible divine persons—Father, Son, and Holy Spirit—has been misinterpreted or misunderstood by his opponents as crude polytheism. Basil does not hide his distress and sorrow over the contentious situation, sadly reporting that his audience has been infiltrated by "spies" interested only in catching him in saying something that could be used to calumniate him. He denies that his understanding of the Trinity is tantamount to tritheism and anathematizes those who say the Holy

[1] The Greek title of this homily varies in the mss. See BBV ii.1122–3. The two most common titles are some form of: περὶ τοῦ μὴ δεῖν τρεῖς θεοὺς καταγγέλλεσθαι ("On the inappropriateness of proclaiming three gods"), and: πρὸς τοὺς συκοφαντοῦντας ἡμᾶς, ὅτι τρεῖς θεοὺς λέγομεν ("Against those who calumniate us, [claiming] that we say there are three gods"). The latter was used by Julien Garnier in the Maurist edition of Basil's works. An ancient Syriac translation of this homily calls it the *Second Homily on Faith* (the first being *Fide*). The shorter title, *On Not Three Gods*, is inspired by Gregory of Nyssa's *Ad Ablabium, quod non sint tres dei*. Note that *Trin* and *Ad Ablabium* have little, if anything, in common other than the theme of defending against tritheism. The Introduction to this homily is adapted from my study, "Basil of Caesarea's Homily *On Not Three Gods* (CPG 2914): Problems and Solutions," *Sacris Erudiri* 50 (2011): 87–131.

Spirit is a creature. He even says, with full confidence in the orthodoxy of his views and with not a little rhetorical flourish, that he is ready to suffer torments for what he believes, just as did the martyrs in the presence of whose relics he preaches. Thus in this homily we encounter Basil late in his career—the homily is most plausibly dated from the mid to late 370s—articulating and defending his views, in the heat of battle as it were, and thus providing us with essential evidence for understanding the contours and development of his Trinitarian theology.[2]

The charge of tritheism was most likely imputed to Basil by the followers of Eustathius of Sebasteia, his former mentor in ascetical matters.[3] In the years 372–375 Basil's association with Eustathius became increasingly problematic when allies such as Meletius of Antioch and Theodotus of Nicopolis began to question the orthodoxy of Eustathius' views on the Holy Spirit. In the summer of 372 or 373 Basil met with Eustathius and more or less compelled him to sign a declaration of his orthodoxy.[4] In time Eustathius repudiated the declaration he signed, and he and Basil distanced themselves from one another as their conflict became increasingly acrimonious. Finally, Eustathius accused Basil of Sabellianism, which emphasized

[2]For brief comments on the historical context, see: Louis-Sébastien Le Nain de Tillemont, *Mémoires pour servir à l'histoire ecclésiastique des six premiers siècles* (Venice: Pitteri, 1732), ix.263; Gustave Bardy, "L'homélie de saint Basile *Adversus eos qui calumniantur nos*," *Recherches de science religieuse* 16 (1926): 21–28 at 22–23; and Hermann Dörries, *De Spiritu Sancto. Der Beitrag des Basilius zum Abschluss des trinitarischen Dogmas* (Göttingen: Vandenhoeck & Ruprecht, 1956), 100, n. 2.

[3]On Eustathius, see V.C. De Clerq, "Eustathius of Sebaste," in NCE 5:456–7; S. Salaville, "Eustathe de Sébaste" and "Eustathiens," in DThC 5.2:1565–74; Jean Gribomont, "Eustathe de Sébaste," in DSpir 4.2:1709–12; idem, "Eustathe de Sébaste," in DHGE 16:26–33 (=idem, *Saint Basile Évangile et Église: Mélanges*, Spiritualité Orientale 36 [Bégrolles-en-Mauges: Abbaye de Bellefontaine, 1984] t. 1, 95–106). On Basil's relationship and conflict with Eustathius of Sebasteia, see Philip Rousseau, *Basil of Caesarea* (Berkeley: University of California Press, 1994), 239–54; Lewis Ayres, *Nicaea and its Legacy: An Approach to Fourth-Century Trinitarian Theology* (Oxford: Oxford University Press, 2004), 225–6; and John Behr, *The Nicene Faith* (Crestwood, NY: St Vladimir's Seminary Press, 2004), 109–10.

[4]*Ep.* 99.2 (on the date of this letter, see p. 155 n. 19 above). The document Eustathius signed is preserved as Basil, *Ep.* 125.

the unity of the triune God in a way that failed to account for the real and permanent distinctions between Father, Son, and Holy Spirit. Basil broke definitively with Eustathius in 375, tagging him a "Pneumatomachian"—that is, a fighter against the Spirit.[5] Though Eustathius seems to have died around 377, his enmity with Basil was kept alive by his followers.

It is surely odd that the Eustathian Pneumatomachians would accuse Basil of both Sabellianism and polytheism. These characterizations of Basil's Trinitarian theology seem diametrically opposed. But after Basil's death the same group would level the same charges against Gregory of Nyssa.[6] If there is any substance to these accusations, if they are not just the result of shifting polemical tactics, perhaps the interpretation of Johannes Zachhuber is correct. He has suggested that Basil's Trinitarian theology was simultaneously susceptible to interpretations both Sabellian and polytheistic precisely because of his insistence upon the complete co-ordination and equality of the persons.[7] In other words, Basil identified the principle of unity in the Trinity, or so claims Zachhuber, as equality *qua* substance, not as derivation *qua* substance as previous theologians had done. The Trinitarian persons, as Basil put it, have the identical "formula of substance" (λόγος τῆς οὐσίας) and thus share a "commonality of substance" (τὸ κοινὸν τῆς οὐσίας).[8] This means that those terms predicated in common of the persons—such as "goodness" and "light"—name the commonality of substance and should

[5] *Ep.* 223.

[6] *Ad Eustathium* 2. On this treatise, see Andrew Radde-Gallwitz, "Ad Eustathium de sancta trinitate," in Volker Henning Drecoll and Margitta Berghaus, eds., *Gregory of Nyssa: The Minor Treatises on Trinitarian Theology and Apollinarianism*, VCS 106 (Leiden: Brill, 2011), 89–109.

[7] Johannes Zachhuber, *Human Nature in Gregory of Nyssa: Philosophical Background and Theological Significance*, VCS 46 (Leiden: Brill, 2000), 57–61.

[8] See *Eun.* 1.19. See Mark DelCogliano and Andrew Radde-Gallwitz, *St. Basil of Caesarea: Against Eunomius*, FOTC 122 (Washington, DC: The Catholic University of America Press, 2011), 50–1; and Andrew Radde-Gallwitz, *Basil of Caesarea, Gregory of Nyssa, and the Transformation of Divine Simplicity* (Oxford: Oxford University Press, 2009), 154–5. Note that in his corpus Basil does not clearly state that the Holy Spirit shares a common formula of substance together with the Father and Son.

be taken in the same sense for all three. In contrast, those terms predicated uniquely of the three name the distinguishing marks of their individual *hypostases*. According to Zachhuber, if Basil's understanding of Trinitarian equality *qua* substance is not also properly qualified with this distinction between *ousia* and *hypostasis*, "this would necessarily result in either tritheism or Sabellianism: in the former case the three persons would be independent principles, in the latter, simply aspects of one divine being."[9] Hence the accusations against Basil made by the Eustathian Pneumatomachians may have been based upon an imperfect or limited understanding of his Trinitarian theology.

Basil begins *On Not Three Gods* with a lament about the present disunity of the church, encouraging his audience to seek unity (§1). The Lord bestowed love and peace, but these have now been replaced by hatred. Everyone is more concerned with fighting for his own interests than with reconciliation. Nonetheless, Basil applauds those who have presently gathered together in unity, as it is impossible to build up the church without the bonds of peace and love, and he finds consolation in their support. He notes that the present festival—a feast of certain unnamed martyrs, as we learn later in the homily—was instituted by their fathers to foster love and unity, allowing for the renewal of old friendships and furnishing an opportunity for new ones (§2). But this tradition is now more or less abandoned since most of those present are "spies" seeking to catch Basil saying something that they can use to calumniate him.

Basil reports that his opponents, who have spies in the audience, are charging him with tritheism (§3). In the remainder of the homily, he refutes this Pneumatomachian charge, not by making an anti-Pneumatomachian defense of the Holy Spirit's divinity as one might expect, but by making an anti-Heteroousian defense of his Trinitarian theology.[10] He first notes that he is merely following the faith of

⁹Zachhuber, *Human Nature*, 58

¹⁰On this tactic, see DelCogliano, "Basil of Caesarea's Homily *On Not Three Gods*," 105–115.

the fathers, who themselves are merely following Christ, alluding to the baptismal command of Matthew 28.19. So those who accuse him of tritheism are actually impugning the Lord himself! Furthermore, as Paul said in Ephesians 4.5, there is one Lord. Calling both Father and Son "Lord" does not divide the divine Lordship between two gods. Here Basil's teaching assumes his distinction between terms predicated in common of Father and Son and terms predicated uniquely of Father and Son that he developed in the *Contra Eunomium*. There Basil insists that those terms predicated in common of the Father and Son have the same signification, and that they name what he calls "the commonality of the substance" (τὸ κοινὸν τῆς οὐσίας).[11] The commonality of substance does not mean that there is "a kind of doling out and division (διανομήν τινα καὶ καταδιαίρεσιν) of pre-existent matter into the things that come from it," but rather that "one and the same formula of being is observed in both [Father and Son]."[12] As mentioned above, Basil employs the phrase "formula of being" (and its equivalent "formula of substance") to signify the sense in which God is one; it is that which accounts for divine unity.[13] And so, a term predicated in common of Father and Son signifies a property of the common nature or substance shared by Father and Son. Though predicated of both Father and Son, "Lord" signifies the single divine sovereignty and omnipotence, which the Father entrusted to the Son.[14] Father and Son share a single lordship and a single divinity; they are neither two lords nor two gods. And so, Basil deploys his logic of common terms to demonstrate his belief in divine unity against the charge of tritheism.

Basil then reveals the basis for the charge of his opponents: it is because he refuses to categorize the Holy Spirit as a created, servile spirit. Indeed, says Basil, he refuses to budge from his position. He will adamantly stand up for his beliefs, as did the martyrs whose

[11]*Eun* 1.19, 27 and 38–39 (SChr 299:240 Sesboüé).
[12]*Eun* 1.19, 28–29 and 33–34 (SChr 299:240 Sesboüé).
[13]See p. 261.
[14]*Eun* 2.3. Sovereignty characterizes the divine nature; see *Eun* 3.2.

bodies lie in the church. But this does not make him a tritheist. Basil then reports that his opponents even take the name "Paraclete," a name just mentioned in a reading that included John 15.26, as indicative of the Spirit's lowly status. Basil refutes this silly notion by noting on the basis of John 14.16 that Christ too bears the name "Paraclete." Here again he relies upon the same logic of common terms: the term does not indicate the lowly status of the Spirit since the Son is also designated by this term. Thus it is a term that signifies the common divine substance, in which the Son and Spirit share.

The deployment of the same logic of common terms to demonstrate divine unity is continued in what follows. Both Father and Son are designated "God," "perfect God," and "incorporeal." Each of these terms signifies a property of the common divine nature. Here Basil also lists terms applied uniquely to each, "unbegotten" and "Father," and "only-begotten," "Son," "Representation," and "Image." Such terms name the distinguishing marks of each, that is, the individuating properties of the Father and Son.[15] "Father" and "Son" are not mere names, but truly signify who the Father and Son are. Once again, the logic of common terms is employed to argue for divine unity, this time alluding also to the distinction between terms predicated in common and terms predicated uniquely of each.

The remainder of the homily deals with various possible objections to Basil's account of divine unity, that Father and Son are equally God, and yet one God. The major potential objection identified by Basil is the divine begetting. As Eunomius and others before him had argued, the fact of the divine begetting suggests that the Son's divinity is inferior to the Father's. In other words, Eunomius preserves divine unity by ascribing full divinity to the unbegotten

---

[15]On "distinguishing marks" (and its equivalent "distinctive feature"), see Volker Henning Drecoll, *Die Entwicklung der Trinitätslehre des Basilius von Cäsarea: Sein Weg vom Homöusianer zum Neonizäner* (Göttingen: Vandenhoeck & Ruprecht, 1996), 107–10; Radde-Gallwitz, *Divine Simplicity*, 132–7; and Mark DelCogliano, *Basil of Caesarea's Anti-Eunomian Theory of Names: Christian Theology and Late-Antique Philosophy in the Fourth-Century Trinitarian Controversy*, VCS 103 (Leiden: Brill, 2010). 189–260.

Father alone and denying the begotten Son a share in it. In what follows Basil is concerned to give an account of the divine begetting which preserves his account of the divine unity of the Father and Son. He begins by stressing the incomprehensibility of the divine begetting, saying that there is no source among things created from which one can acquire knowledge of it. By stressing the incomprehensibility of the divine begetting Basil seeks to eliminate the basis for Heteroousian claim that, in a way analogous to human begetting, the divine begetting necessarily implies the Son's inferiority. Then Basil briefly appeals to John 1.1 as proof that the Word was always God, again emphasizing the eternity of the Son (§4). This was Basil's favorite text for making this point.[16]

Then Basil segues into an interlude on the incarnation. While this may seem to be an odd move, it appears that in Basil's mind discussion of the eternal begetting of the Son and the birth of the incarnate Word from Mary went hand in hand, forming a kind of natural progression.[17] Basil repeatedly mentions the paradox of God becoming human. One of his main points is that in the incarnation the divinity of the Word is preserved intact, not diminished or destroyed in any way. In the incarnation, the "true reality" of God is preserved. He was and remains God, but became human. Basil characterizes the idea that the Word's divinity is destroyed in the incarnation as heretical and Manichaean. The remainder of the section on the incarnation spells out the divine accomplishments achieved through it: conquering death and giving life. Thus Basil eliminates another one of the Heteroousians' chief arguments for the substantial inferiority of the Son, the incarnation.

After the discussion of the incarnation, Basil briefly returns to the subject of the ineffability of the divine begetting before dealing with two final objections to the divine unity of the Father and Son. The first is concerned with whether the Son is more honored than the Father because he sits at the right hand of the Father. This issue

---

[16]*Eun.* 2.14–15; *Verb*; *Mam* 4; *Spir.* 6.14.
[17]See *Chr* 1–2.

is similar to a view rejected by Basil in the statement of faith he composed and had Eustathius of Sebasteia sign to affirm his pneumatological orthodoxy.[18] Basil affirms that the Father and Son share the same honor because the Son has received honor from his Father and the Father freely bestowed honor upon the Son. Once again, echoing an earlier section of the homily, Basil affirms that "God" is a name predicated in common of the Father and Son, showing their divine unity.

The final section of the homily counters a possible objection to Basil's account of divine unity based on the meaning of the name "father." Basil acknowledges that human fatherhood is inseparable from temporality, effort, ignorance, and an inability to effect one's will, but emphasizes that divine fatherhood is not marked by these traits. These traits of human fatherhood should be used neither to understand divine fatherhood nor to suggest that the Father and Son are not unified in their divinity. With this, the homily rather abruptly concludes.

One of the remarkable features of this homily is that it exhibits verbal parallels with two non-Basilian texts composed after Basil was dead. I have argued elsewhere that both these later texts and Basil are quoting from a common source that is no longer extant.[19] From midway through §3 to midway through §4 there is a long, more-or-less verbatim parallel with the *Historia ecclesiastica* once attributed to Gelasius of Cyzicus, and in §4 there is a short verbatim parallel with an anonymous homily entitled *Oratio in resurrectionem domini*. These parallels are marked in the translation below with guillemots («...»). Because these sources are not so seamlessly integrated as they could have been and are stylistically inferior to the earlier part

---

[18]*Ep* 125.3. The relevant portion reads: "one must flee ... those who alter the sequence that the Lord handed down to us and rank the Son before the Father and set the Holy Spirit before the Son" (φεύγειν δεῖ καὶ τοὺς τὴν ἀκολουθίαν ἣν παρέδωκεν ἡμῖν ὁ κύριος ἐναμείβοντας ... καὶ υἱὸν μὲν προτάσσοντας τοῦ πατρός, υἱοῦ δὲ τὸ πνεῦμα τὸ ἅγιον προτιθέντας; Yves Courtonne, *Saint Basile: Lettres*. 3 vols. [Paris: Société d'édition 'Les Belles Lettres', 1957–1966], vol. ii, p. 34). See also *Ep.* 52.4.

[19]DelCogliano, "Basil of Caesarea's Homily *On Not Three Gods*," 115–130.

of the homily from Basil's own pen, it can give the impression that *Trin* lacks integrity and jumps from topic to topic. But in fact Basil utilizes these sources as essential elements of his anti-Heteroousian defense against the charge of tritheism.

Authenticity. The homily *Trin* was considered authentic by scholars until the 1720s when the Maurist edition of Basil's *opera omnia* was published.[20] In his Preface to this edition Julien Garnier argued that this homily should be placed among those works spuriously attributed to Basil.[21] As was the case for *Lak*, his arguments against authenticity are made on stylistic grounds.[22] The logic of such arguments assumes that Basil is flawless when it comes to composing Greek.[23] Therefore, any departures from impeccable Greek are deemed sufficient evidence for denying authorship to Basil. Garnier cites several inferior passages to prove his point. But as mentioned above his stylistic arguments are too subjective to serve as useful criteria for determining authenticity. Even though he denies authorship of this homily to Basil, nonetheless Garnier admits that it contains much that is worthy of Basil. He attributes this fact to the true author being a conscious imitator of Basil, in particular of *Sab*. Garnier's opinion continued to influence scholars well into the twentieth century.[24]

---

[20] The history of scholarship on the authenticity of *Trin* is discussed in more detail in DelCogliano, "Basil of Caesarea's Homily *On Not Three Gods*," 89–93. The following section abbreviates this account.

[21] "Praefatio," §VII, 20–21 (De Sinner ii.xxii–xxvi; PG 31.43–49).

[22] See pp. 190–191 above. See also pp. 89–90 and 216.

[23] In his discussion of *Trin* Garnier once again articulates his fallacious assumptions: "In Basil everything is expressed with words that are proper and appropriate to the matter at hand. . . . His oratory is so natural that you hear nothing save what you expect; but all things are connected with each other so aptly and so fittingly that it is necessary to confess that they could not have been said better or more fittingly" ("Praefatio," §VII, 20; De Sinner ii.xxii; PG 31.44).

[24] For example, though citing Gribomont's assessment of the genuineness of *Trin*, M. Geerard, *Clavis Patrum Graecorum. Volumen II. Ab Athanasio ad Chrysostomum* (Turnhout, 1974), p. 167 still ranked it among the Basilian *dubia*. The 1998 *CPG Supplementum* (ed. M. Geerard and J. Noret) drops this classification.

In 1904 Karl Holl was the first to argue that this homily should be restored to Basil.[25] Following the lead of Holl, in 1926 Gustave Bardy dedicated an article to demonstrating that *Trin* was authentic.[26] Both Holl and Bardy argued their case on the basis of the evidence of numerous parallels between *Trin* and Basil's indisputably genuine writings. These arguments for authenticity were accepted by Hermann Dörries,[27] as well as by the noted Basilian scholars Jean Gribomont[28] and Paul Jonathan Fedwick.[29] More recently, I have corroborated and expanded upon these arguments for the homily's authenticity.[30] It is also now clear that this homily is widely attested in the best manuscripts of Basil's homilies.[31] And so, now the general consensus is that, on the basis of external and internal evidence, nothing precludes Basil's authorship of this homily and in fact everything points to its genuineness.[32]

Context and Date. As discussed above, this homily is a response to Pneumatomachian supporters of Eustathius of Sebasteia who had infiltrated Basil's audience on the festival of certain unnamed martyrs. Since it cannot be determined whether Eustathius was still alive, the homily is most plausibly dated from the mid to the

[25]Karl Holl, *Amphilochius von Ikonium in seinem Verhältnis zu den grossen Kappadoziern* (Tübingen / Leipzig: J.C. Mohr, 1904), 143 n. 1.

[26]"L'homélie de saint Basile *Adversus eos qui calumniantur nos*," *Recherches de science religieuse* 16 (1926): 21–8.

[27]*De Spiritu Sancto. Der Beitrag des Basilius zum Anschluß des trinitarischen Dogmas* (Göttingen: Vandenhoeck & Ruprecht, 1956), 100–2.

[28]*In Tomum 31 Patrologiae Graecae ad editionem operum rhetoricorum, asceticorum, liturgicorum Sancti Basilii Magni Introductio* (Turnhout: Brepols, 1961), 7.

[29]Paul Jonathan Fedwick, "A Chronology of the Life and Works of Basil of Caesarea," in idem, ed., *Basil of Caesarea: Christian, Humanist, Ascetic. A Sixteen-Hundredth Anniversary Symposium* (Toronto: The Pontifical Institute of Mediaeval Studies, 1981), 3–19 at 10.

[30]DelCogliano, "Basil of Caesarea's Homily *On Not Three Gods*."

[31]See BBV ii.1122–5.

[32]Drecoll, *Die Entwicklung*, 161–2, cautiously dissents from this majority position. While admitting, mostly on external criteria, that there is "no definitive argument against authenticity," he believes that *Trin* remains suspect. At the same time, of those homilies whose authenticity Drecoll believes to be suspect, he holds *Trin* among those most likely to be Basil's.

late 370s. In §2 Basil notes that he is preaching on the occasion of a synod, the purpose of which he describes at length. In §3 he mentions that he is preaching in the presence of the relics of martyrs. These two facts suggest that the synod was held in conjunction with the feast day of the martyrs. We know that each year on September 7 Basil convoked a synod at Caesarea that coincided with the festival of the martyrs Eupsychius, Damas, and their companions, who had been martyred in Caesarea under Julian the Apostate.[33] So perhaps *Trin* was preached on the occasion of this celebration.[34] That on this feast day Basil would preach on other topics besides the martyrs, and specifically on Trinitarian matters, is known from a letter of Gregory of Nazianzus.[35] Therefore, *Trin* was most likely preached in the mid to late 370s, possibly on September 7 as part of the celebration of the Caesarean martyrs.

Translation. The following translation is based on Julien Garnier's edition as reprinted in De Sinner ii.867–872 (=PG 31.1487–1496).[36] In crafting my translation, I benefited from Garnier's Latin translation.

TRANSLATION

1   It is a great consolation for those[38] who are distraught over being hated that they are hated together with the Lord. *If the world hates you,* he says, *know that it hated me before it hated you* [Jn 15.18]. Therefore, if the Beloved[39] was hated, is it a cause for great concern if

---

[33]*Ep.* 100, 142, 176, 200, 252, and 282. On those martyred at Caesarea under Julian, see Sozomen, *Historia Ecclesiastica* 5.4 and 5.11. There was also a synod held in conjunction with the celebration of (unnamed) martyrs in Phargamos; see *Ep.* 95.

[34]Jean Bernardi, *La prédication des pères cappadociens* (Paris: Presses universitaires de France, 1968), 78, notes that, while no homilies on the martyrs Eupsychius, Damas, and their companions are extant, it is inconceivable that Basil did not preach regularly on their festival day. Bernardi suggested that *Fide* was preached on this feast in 372; see p. 233 above.

[35]*Ep.* 58.
[36]CPG 2914.

[1]Omitting ψυχαῖς, an addition by Garnier.
[2]Gk. ὁ ἀγαπητός. Cf. Mt 3.17, 17.5; Mk 1.11, 9.7; Lk 3.22.

we are deemed worthy of being hated by men who possess an abundance of hatred? I cannot even speak when I remember those who sorrow because they pierce my heart. And a stream of tears chokes my voice, when I ponder that, even though the Lord has bestowed love and peace upon us, we do not seek what he has bestowed. His gift is hidden from our eyes and is nowhere to be found. Love has been bestowed, but we live by fighting. Unity was granted, but hatred has been kindled. We have stoked a great conflagration of hatred for each other. Each of us bewails his own plight, but we do nothing to be reconciled with one another. Who will grant me the whole inhabited world as my stage, a voice louder than a trumpet, the lamentations of Jeremiah, and an abundance of tears, so that with these tears I can shatter the heart crushed by grief, heap the dust that is now dishonorably heaped upon us, and mourn for our common misfortune, namely, that love, the root of the commandments, has failed? But I embrace those who are present with an unceasing embrace of the spirit for this reason: you have exhibited an unusual sight by being bonded together, each to the other. For each of us has become to the other like a grain of sand, not combined with each other but separated each from the other.[3] After all, it is impossible either to construct a building when what holds it together is missing, or to build up the church to the heights when it is not held together with the bonds of peace and love.   2   With patient ears attend to us for a moment, not because we seek to impress you with our discourse, but because we feel compelled to include you in the company of those who sorrow. For company with others who are sad brings consolation to the despondent. Perhaps when all our sorrows are united they will reach the Lord with greater intensity. Or will each of us be heard on his own because of our feeble efforts?

The present spectacle is but a remnant of the ancient love of the fathers. For its sake they inaugurated the practice of holding these

---

[3]The point of Basil's odd simile seems to be that even though grains of sand are closely compacted, they remain distinct from each other and are not blended together to the loss of individual identity.

festal assemblies, so that the estrangement that develops over time could be dissipated through personal interaction at set intervals, and those who live far away, by gathering in this one place, could use the event to initiate relationships of friendship and love. This is a spiritual assembly that renews old relationships and provides a starting point for those to come. For we have not come to make an exchange of salable goods, but to give each other a mutual exchange of love, to give love fully and to receive love fully. All this was established by our fathers.[4] Even though this is the tradition we have received, the present spectacle shows why it has come to an end. Most of those here are spies more interested in scrutinizing my statements than in being disciples of the doctrines I teach. Indeed, they attend my discourse not to be edified by being present but to ambush me with insults and abuse. If perhaps I say anything that harmonizes with what those who reject my point of view want to catch me saying, he who heard it departs as if he got from me what really belongs to him.[5] Let these considerations be inscribed on your hearts. Testify to the truth and to us against those who cause such disturbances, bearing witness that we have renewed the ancient gift.

3   For this is what those who do not fear the Lord say, opening their mouths against us on the grounds that we proclaim three gods: "What does this man who preaches three gods seek in the church of the Lord? Elsewhere polytheism can be found but here there is piety toward God. If he says three, why not dare to say even four? Why not extend the number to twelve?"[6] So then, see the madness of those who have sharpened their tongue against the truth! I am not fainthearted when it comes to refuting, but I await the judgment seat of Christ. There I will confront those who cook up such insults and abuse. *The Lord knows those who are his own* [2 Tim 2.19]. And: *Whoever abuses a poor man insults the one who made him* [Prov 14.31].

[4]Cf. the purpose of synods stated in *Lak* 5.
[5]See also *Sab* 4.
[6]Basil reports this accusation of polytheism elsewhere; see *Ep.* 131.2; *Sab* 4.

If I am handing on the faith of the fathers, why do you skip over the fathers and impugn me? If I believe in the Father, if I confess the Son, if I do not denigrate the Spirit; if anyone who confesses the Trinity names three gods, he denigrates baptism and impugns the faith. Why do you suppose that I am the source of this confession? Do you not realize that you impugn the Lord? Who bequeathed to us that we are to baptize *in the name of the Father, and of the Son, and of the Holy Spirit* [Mt 28.19]? Did I, or did the Master? Whose words are these? The one who proclaimed them or the one whom he commissioned? Why do you find me liable to these calumnies of yours when I repeat this confession? Do you not realize that by attacking me you impugn the truth? Do you not realize that by assaulting me you shake the stronghold of faith? While I may be easily snared by you, the faith remains unshaken. *One Lord* [Eph 4.5]. Learn from Paul. He did not say "two" or "three." Even if I name the Son "Lord," I do not dole out the lordship to two lords or to many gods. The Father is Lord; the Son is Lord. *One faith* [Eph 4.5], because one Lord. One follows one: one faith follows one Lord and *one baptism* [Eph 4.5] follows one faith. Thus there is confirmation of one from one through one.

If I do not denigrate the Spirit, nor place him in the category of those who serve, then for this reason I become the object of your calumnies. Do not say that I say something which I do not say. Let us look into how plausible your calumnies are. Why do you conceal your insults and abuse? O cursed one,[7] you lie when you say that we proclaim three gods, nor do you openly acknowledge that we are the ones who anathematize those who claim that the Holy Spirit is a creature. As for this accusation, I am guilty as charged. For this I am willing to submit myself to fire and a sharp sword. Even if the wheel of torture were to tear me to pieces, even if the instruments of torment were to be unleashed upon me, I would accept these instruments with the same confidence with which the martyrs who lie here did and thereby were deemed worthy of crowns. Therefore, make this accusation against me, since I do not number the Holy Spirit

[7] See Mt 25.41.

together with the creatures. But if you were to say anything more than this, you will have to give your reasons to the judge.

When the Paraclete comes [Jn 15.26] was just read. But you have taken even this passage as an opportunity for insulting and abusing me with your calumnies. "The Paraclete," one of you says, "is the one who intercedes for you." You show disrespect to the very means by which the Lord confers benefits! Have you not then received the benefits of the Paraclete? Has not the Lord decreed that this designation is suitable for himself? *I shall send to you another Paraclete* [Jn 14.16+16.7]. By saying *another*, does he not indicate that he too is called Paraclete if there is *another*? If I speak on my own authority, do not listen to me. If I read what has been written, bow down to the truth![8]

«The perfect is neither decreased nor increased. There is one unbegotten, God. There is one only-begotten of him, the Son and God. Just as there is not another co-unbegotten God with the one [unbegotten], so too there is not another co-begotten Son. Just as the Father is not the Father in name alone, so too the Son is not the Son in name alone. The Father is God; the Son is God. The Father is perfect God; the Son is also perfect God. The Father is incorporeal; the Son is incorporeal, the *representation* [Heb 1.3] of the incorporeal and the incorporeal *image* [Col 1.15].

Do you believe that he has been begotten? Do not inquire how. For if it is possible to inquire how the unbegotten is unbegotten, it is possible to inquire also how the one who has been begotten has been begotten. But if the unbegotten does not allow inquiry into how he is unbegotten, thus not even the one who has been begotten allows inquiry into how he has been begotten. Do not inquire about what cannot be discovered, since you will not find it. For if you inquire, from what can you learn it? From the earth? It did not exist. From the sea? There were no waters. From the sky? It was not raised up. From the sun and the moon and the stars? They were not fashioned.

---

[8]That the Son and Spirit are both called "Paraclete" is also mentioned by Didymus, *De spiritu sancto* 120.

Perhaps from the ages? The Only-Begotten is before the ages. Do not examine what has not always existed to learn about what always exists. But if you do not want [to desist from this line of inquiry], but rather contentiously pursue it, I deride your stupidity, or rather, I lament your audacity.

4 *In the beginning was the Word, and the Word was with God, and the Word was God* [Jn 1.1]. The *was* precludes "was not," and *God* precludes "not God." Believe in what has been written in Scripture. Do not inquire into what has not been written in Scripture. This Word, the Son of God, *became* [Jn 1.14] a human being for the sake of the fallen human being, Adam. For the sake of Adam the incorporeal one came into a body. For the sake of the body,[9] the Word assumed a body as a cloud, lest he incinerate visible beings. He descended to the flesh, so that the flesh might also be raised together with him. The invisible one came into a visible one, so that he might enter into visible beings. As a human being, he is subject to time. As God, he is before time. In both cases, the "as a human being" and "as God" should be understood not in terms of likeness but in terms of the true reality. He *was God* [Jn 1.1]; he *became* [Jn 1.14] a human being for the economy.»

The *became* did not come first and then the *was*; on the contrary, the *was* came first and then the *became*. So then, do not take away the divinity of the Only-Begotten because of the events of the economy. For a view such as this is nothing more than the distortions of the heretics and the madnesses of the Manichees. *For no one can lay another foundation besides that which is laid, which is Jesus Christ* [1 Cor 3.11]. He was begotten by a woman, so that he might bring all those begotten to rebirth.[10] He was willingly crucified, so that he might take down [from the cross] those unwillingly crucified. He died willingly, so that he might raise up [from the grave] those who died involuntarily. He accepted a death that he need not

---

[9]That is, Adam's body, namely, human beings.
[10]Cf. Jn 3.3.

have accepted, so that he might give life to those subjected to death. «*Death devoured* [Is 25.8] him in ignorance, but after it devoured him it came to know what it had devoured. It devoured Life; it was swallowed up by Life.[11] It devoured the One along with all the rest; it lost all the rest because of the One. *It seized him like a lion* [Ps 7.3]; its teeth were smashed.» And so for this reason it is scorned as weak. For we no longer fear it as we would a lion, but we tread upon it as we would a lion's hide.

Let the begetting of the Only-Begotten from the Father be revered in silence. For only the one who has begotten him and the one who has been begotten understand it. Indeed, we ought to know about what we can speak and about what we must keep silent. Not all words can be uttered by the tongue, for fear that our intellect, like an eye that wants to take in the whole of the sun, will lose even the light that it has. For knowledge is a question of knowing that you do not fully comprehend. So then, that begetting which is ineffable, let us revere it in silence. And indeed if we should find that this wears us out, let us not be sad. For that ineffable begetting is awesome because of its nature, but this nature is hard to explain because of its otherness. John was said to be *the voice of one crying in the wilderness* [Mt 3.3; Mk 1.3; Lk 3.4; Jn 1.23; Is 40.3], but he was a human being by nature. So then, do not take away the subsistence[12] of the Only-Begotten because of the name "Word."

But perhaps you may say: "Why is the one seated at the right hand more honored?" Now if he has honor through himself, he is more honored, but if he receives it from his begetter, it belongs to the one who freely gave the gift. There was not another Son who could be seated at the left hand. One unbegotten, God. One only-begotten of him, Son and God. So then, it was appropriate for the Son not to cede the place at the right hand to the Father, but for the Father to cede it to the Son.

[11]See 1 Cor 15.54.
[12]Gk. ὑπόστασιν.

It is clear that when the nature is far distant from us, under-standing it is also far distant from us. For among us a father is from another father, and involves time, nurturing, development, and other kinds of care, and a father does not beget whatever he wants. But God, whose power is concurrent with his will, begot one worthy of himself, begot as he himself knows, *to whom be glory and might for ever and ever. Amen* [1 Pet 4.11].

Homily against the Sabellians, Anomoians, and Pneumatomachians

INTRODUCTION

Basil's *Against the Sabellians, Anomoians, and Pneumatomachians* is a rhetorical and theological masterpiece.[1] Not only is it the fullest expression of his rhetorical depiction of his theological opponents, but it is also a detailed account of his Trinitarian theology from late in his career that reflects the mature development of several currents of his thought. In this homily Basil polemically presents his own doctrine of the Trinity as the middle way between the extreme viewpoints of the "Sabellians" and "Anomoians," who are depicted as attempting to reintroduce into Christianity, respectively, Jewish denial of the Son of God and Hellenic polytheism. On full display here is Basil's arsenal of rhetorical techniques, deployed with great effect as he attempts to demolish the heretical ideas of his major opponents: the modalist followers of Marcellus of Ancyra, the Heteroousian followers of Eunomius of Cyzicus, and

---

[1] The title of this homily varies in the mss. The Latin title, *Contra Sabellianos et Arium et Anomoeos*, is based on the most frequent Greek title, κατὰ Σαβελλιανῶν καὶ Ἀρείου καὶ τῶν Ἀνομοίων ("Against the Sabellians and Arius and the Anomoians"). See BBV ii.1120–1. But this title is inaccurate, as Basil never mentions or refutes Arius in the homily; see Joseph T. Lienhard, "Ps-Athanasius, *Contra Sabellianos*, and Basil of Caesarea, *Contra Sabellianos et Arium et Anomoeos*: Analysis and Comparison," *Vigiliae Christianae* 40 (1986): 365–89 at 370. Furthermore, a major portion of the homily refutes the Pneumatomachians, whom Basil mentions by name in the last sentence of §6. The Sabellians and Anomoians are also mentioned by name (§1–3). It seems best not to perpetuate this inaccurate title, which may not be original to Basil anyway. Therefore, I have revised the title of the homily to accurately reflect its contents and Basil's own labels for his opponents.

the Pneumatomachian followers of Eustathius of Sebasteia. In many ways this homily constitutes a synthesis and summation of Basil's Trinitarian thought.

In this homily the labels employed by Basil for his opponents reflect fourth-century polemics; they are not his own coinages. The "Sabellians" are Marcellus of Ancyra and his followers, who were seen as reviving the modalism of the third-century Sabellius.[2] The "Anomoians," who are today more commonly called Heteroousians, are Aetius, Eunomius, and their followers. The label "Anomoian" is based on the Greek word ἀνομοίος (*anomoios*), "unlike," and was used to reinforce the popular characterization of Heteroousian theology as teaching that the Son was unlike the Father.[3] Basil may also be using the same label as a deprecating play on the name "Eunomius;" if so, it could be translated "Anomoius." The label "Pneumatomachians" was first coined by Athanasius to refer to those who claimed that the Holy Spirit was a creature and one of the ministering spirits.[4] It means "Spirit-fighters" or "those who fight against the Spirit," and was adopted by Basil as a label for Eustathius of Sebasteia and his followers.[5]

The homily can be divided into two main parts. The first simultaneously refutes the errors of the Sabellians and Anomoians (§1–4) and focuses mainly on the relation between the Father and Son. The second part deals exclusively with errors of the Pneumatomachians (§4–7).[6] Nonetheless, in both parts of the homily one can detect a

[2]On "Sabellius" as a codename for "Marcellus," see Joseph T. Lienhard, *Contra Marcellum. Marcellus of Ancyra and Fourth-Century Theology* (Washington, DC: The Catholic University of America Press, 1999), 210–2, 229, and 231.

[3]This label is also found in Epiphanius, *Panarion* 76, which is roughly contemporary with *Sab*.

[4]Athanasius, *Letters to Serapion* 1.32.2 and 3.1.2. For a translation of these letters, see Mark DelCogliano, Andrew Radde-Gallwitz, and Lewis Ayres, *Works on the Spirit: Athanasius and Didymus*, PPS 43 (Yonkers, NY: St Vladimir's Seminary Press, 2011).

[5]*Ep.* 223.

[6]For another summary of this homily, see Hermann Dörries, *De Spiritu Sancto. Der Beitrag des Basilius zum Abschluss des trinitarischen Dogmas* (Göttingen: Vandenhoeck & Ruprecht, 1956), 94–7. Lienhard, "Ps-Athanasius and Basil of Caesarea,"

consistent, though not entirely systematic, account of the Trinity. Throughout Basil stresses the affinity of Father, Son, and Spirit. This communion is rooted in the fact that the Father is the source of the Son and Spirit, who are both "from" the Father, though in different ways. This "derivational" unity preserves their commonality and distinction. At the level of divinity, nature, substance, rank, dignity, honor, and glory they are eternally conjoined together, inseparable, and indivisible, yet at the same time they are three distinct, perfect individuals, or persons. According to Basil, Trinitarian orthodoxy is preserved only if one confesses that Father, Son, and Spirit are *both* three distinct persons *and* one nature.

Basil opens the homily by establishing the rhetorical framework that will govern its first half (§1). Just as the Egyptians and Assyrians were opposed to each other and to Israel, and just as cowardice and rashness are opposed to each other and to courage, so too are Judaism and the Hellenism opposed to each other and to Christianity. Why is Basil concerned with Jews and Hellenes here? Because according to him the Sabellians and Anomoians are nothing more than Jews and idolatrous Hellenes. The Sabellians are like Jews because they deny the existence of the Son of God just as the Jews did. And the Anomoians are tantamount to Hellenic polytheists (who are really atheists) because they idolatrously worship one whom they claim to be a creature (i.e., the Only-Begotten) and not the Creator. Hence Christianity is attacked on two sides at once by forces opposed both to each other and to orthodoxy. In what follows Basil presents his own Trinitarian theology as charting a middle course between the Sabellians and the Anomoians and avoiding both extremes.

Basil next lays out the basic ideas of the Sabellians and Anomoians and refutes them using scriptural argumentation. In other words, he demonstrates how their views are inconsistent with Scripture and in fact contradict it, and how his Trinitarian theology

370–2, gives a nice outline of the structure of the homily. Lienhard also provides a theological analysis of the homily which focuses on its technical terminology; see "Ps-Athanasius and Basil of Caesarea," 378–84, and *Contra Marcellum*, 228–32.

is rooted in a careful interpretation of the words of the Bible. Basil first attacks the Sabellian idea that the Father and Son are a single person because the Father's relation to the Word is analogous to a human being's relation to his own mental word (i.e., his internal thoughts). The Sabellians claim that, just as a human being is one person because he is not divided from the mental word in him, so too the Father is not divided from his Word, and thus the Father and the Word (i.e., the Son) are also one person. To refute this claim, Basil appeals to John 1.1, which shows the distinct existence of the Son since it speaks of the Father and Son as two different actors in the narrative.[7] Hence, far from being a mere mental word, which is "neither living nor subsistent" and quickly fades away, the Word of God is "life and truth" which endures forever (§1).

Basil next turns to the Anomoians (§2). In contrast to the Sabellians, they believe in the Son's distinct existence and the separate personhood of Father and Son, but they claim that the Father and Son are unlike in nature. Furthermore, while they use the name "Son," they consider the Son to be more like creatures than his divine Father. Once again, Basil cites a verse from the Gospel of John to refute these claims: John 14.9, *He who has seen me has seen the Father*. But this passage actually contradicts both the Sabellians and the Anomoians. Against the former, it affirms that the Father and Son are not the same person, but two distinct persons, for the same reasons as in John 1.1. Against the latter, it affirms that the Son has communion with the Father since he can make the Father known. Two further Johannine passages are cited to bolster Basil's point: John 10.30 against the Anomoians and John 16.28 against the Sabellians. The former teaches that the Father and Son are one because at the level of nature they are indistinguishable from each other, whereas the latter teaches that the Father and Son are distinct persons. Additional verses from John 8.14–18 are cited against the

[7]This verse was frequently employed by Basil to refute his opponents; see *Eun.* 2.14–15; 2.17; *Mam* 4; *Trin* 4; *Spir.* 6.14; and *Verb*. The exegesis found here is paralleled only in *Verb* 4.

Sabellians which make the same point about the distinctness of the persons. Against the Anomoians, Basil appeals to the Son's status as the image of God (Col 1.15) to affirm that the "living Image is indistinguishable from the archetypal Life" (§2). Because he is Son and not a creature, the Son is equal in nature and in honor to the Father (Jn 5.17; Phil 2.6).

Having presented and refuted his opponents' views, Basil now proceeds to an exposition of the true doctrine (§3). One must confess the persons because the Lord has clearly taught that Father, Son, and Paraclete are distinct persons (see John 16.7+14.16). There is thus no scriptural basis for conflating the three persons into a single reality as the Sabellians do. But this recognition of the distinctness of the persons does not imply that they are disjoined in nature, as the Anomoians think. The Father is God, and the Son is God, but they are not two gods because the same divinity, the same identical nature, is contemplated in each. (Note that Basil at this point neglects to affirm that the Spirit shares the same nature as Father and Son; he does this later in §4–7.) Therefore, in order to avoid the extremes of the Sabellians and the Anomoians, one must confess *both* the distinctness of the persons *and* one substance in both Father and Son. Both affirmations are necessary for an orthodox understanding the Trinity. Basil then clarifies for the Anomoians what he means by "one substance" (§4). The Father and Son are not siblings derived from a substance that transcends both; rather, the Father and Son share a single, identical substance because the Son is from the Father.

Then, somewhat surprisingly, Basil reports that some in his audience accuse him of polytheism.[8] Defending himself against this charge, he first says that only those who preach two fathers or two first principles, like the Marcionites, are polytheists. But he adds that Anomoian theology amounts to polytheism because its claim that the Unbegotten God is different in substance from the Only-Begotten implies two gods of unlike substance. Hence, it is the Anomoians who are the polytheists, says Basil, not he. In what

[8]For the historical context of this charge, see pp. 260–261 above.

follows Basil defends himself against the charge of polytheism along anti-Heteroousian lines.[9] Even though Father and Son are two distinct persons, they share the same nature because the Father is the principle and archetype from which the Son comes. As the image of the archetype, "by nature he expresses the Father in himself" and he is indistinguishable from the Father (§4). As something begotten of the Father, he is the same as the Father in substance (*homoousios*). Here Basil employs a frequently used metaphor of the emperor and his imperial image: just as the emperor and his image do not constitute two emperors but a single imperial rule, and just as a citizen treats the image of the emperor with the same respect as he would the emperor himself, so too are God the Father and his image the Son distinct but manifest the same power and are to be accorded the same respect. This analogy, however, only goes so far since the emperor and his image are perishable creatures. And so, the language of "image" must be understood in a way appropriate for God. Accordingly, as image, the Son is the perfect radiance of the Father's glory and the representation of his subsistence (Heb 1.3). The Son's status as image of God conveys that the Father and Son share one and the same divinity. While they are two in number (two persons), they have a nature that is indivisible. The same perfect divine form is contemplated in both Father and Son.

At this point Basil reports that his audience has grown restless since he has been discussing "points of agreement" and avoiding "the questions on everyone's mind" (§4). The hot topic of conversion which everyone wants to hear about is the Holy Spirit. Basil's trepidation over speaking about the Spirit is clear when he states that he will teach, without qualifications or refinements, only what the tradition has handed down to him. He reluctantly acknowledges that, as he hands on the tradition which he has received, he will have to answer probing questions about the Spirit posed by those who want to test

[9]On this tactic, see Mark DelCogliano, "Basil of Caesarea's Homily *On Not Three Gods* (CPG 2914): Problems and Solutions," *Sacris Erudiri* 50 (2011): 87–131 at 108–115.

him. Though Basil obviously finds this contentiousness distasteful, he exhorts his audience to listen to him without prejudice: "But we exhort you," he says, "not to seek to hear from us only what pleases you, but rather what is acceptable to the Lord, consonant with the Scriptures, and not in conflict with the fathers" (§4).

The remainder of the homily is refutation of Pneumatomachian views of the Holy Spirit. First, Basil affirms that what is true of the Father and the Son is also true of the Spirit: he is distinct person too. Scriptural verses such as John 4.24 and Romans 8.9–10 are misinterpreted if they are understood as conflating the Father and the Spirit or the Son and Spirit into a single person. Rather, these verses demonstrate the affinity of nature that exists between Father, Son, and Spirit. The Father is the source of both Son and Spirit. The Father, Son, and Spirit are eternally conjoined and co-existent, and nothing ever separates them. Yet at the same time, the Father, Son, and Spirit are not three "parts of single indivisible reality;" rather, there is an "inseparable consubstantiality (συνουσίαν) of three perfect incorporeals" (§5). This means that the presence of one implies the presence of the other two, as is especially shown in the baptismal command of Matthew 28.19. Since the Spirit is "numbered with" the Father and Son, the Spirit cannot be "foreign in nature" and therefore he is "ranked with the eternal nature" (§5).

In fact, those who separate the Spirit from the Father and Son and consider him a creature destroy the Trinity. For they insert a part of the created order into the Trinity. Basil points out the absurdity of this by suggesting that, if it is pious to add a created Spirit to the Trinity, why not add other creatures like the angels and the ministering spirits? Why not add the adversarial spirits too? Where does one draw the line? For Basil, nothing created can be ranked with the Trinity. Therefore, if Scripture demonstrates that the Holy Spirit is inseparable from the Father and Son, it implies that he is not created. In an aside Basil observes that whoever utters such blasphemies against the Spirit has surely been abandoned by the Spirit, the Enlightener. Accordingly, such people only utter blasphemies in the first place because their minds are dim and darkened, devoid of the light of the Spirit.

The tradition, continues Basil, teaches that the Holy Spirit should not be separated from the Father and the Son: "This is what the Lord taught, the Apostles preached, the Fathers preserved, the Martyrs confirmed" (§6). Basil then reports one of the sophistries used by the Pneumatomachians to "prove" that the Spirit is creature. They claim that there are three categories of existents: those unbegotten, those begotten, and those created. Since clearly, they say, the Spirit does not fall into the first two categories, he must fall into the third. Basil rejects this specious argumentation as it does not accord with the Scriptures. True, the Spirit is neither unbegotten nor begotten, but the Scriptures do affirm that he is with the Father and with the Son. This suggests that the Spirit has affinity with the Father and the Son (see Jn 15.26, Rom 8.9, Jn 14.17, and Rom 8.15). Therefore, Basil insists that this sophism of the Pneumatomachians has misled them. According to Basil, there are some things which cannot be grasped by the intellect. Not everything can be understood through logical argumentation. Since there are many things in this world about which we are ignorant, there is nothing wrong with professing ignorance about the way in which the Holy Spirit exists. It better to acknowledge one's ignorance about the Spirit than to utter blasphemies about the Spirit that are as impious as can be (§7). For the Pneumatomachians' claim that the Spirit is a creature implies a whole slew of heretical ideas about him: "estrangement from God according to nature itself, a humble state of servitude, servile ministries, deprivation of sanctity which is not present by nature, and the prospect of the Spirit participating in sanctity from the distribution of grace just as the rest of those sanctified do" (§7). Here Basil says as much about the doctrine of the Spirit as about theological epistemology.

Basil considers the faulty logic of the Pneumatomachians' sophism to be the result of an overconfidence in the power of the mind, a faulty epistemology which leads them to think that everything can be understood. He seeks to disabuse them of this assumption by using their brand of logical argumentation to "prove" that the sun does not exist and that we do not see with our eyes.[10] The conclusions of such specious arguments are obviously wrong, admits Basil, but they do proceed according to a logic which Basil claims is not unlike that which the Pneumatomachians employ in their syllogism. The fact is that Scripture affirms that the Spirit is from God. It is true that when Scripture says all things are from God (see Jn 1.3) it means they are created. But Christ is also said to be from God and yet he is not ranked with the creatures. Creatures are from God in one way, but the Son is from God in another way. We are from Christ as servants of the Master, but Christ is from God as the Son of the Father. Just as there are many sons, but one Son from God, so too there are many spirits, but one Spirit from God. The Son and Spirit alone are from God in the proper sense: the Son comes from the Father in a begotten way and the Spirit proceeds from the Father "in a way that cannot be explained" (§7). The Spirit glorifies and honors the Son in the same way that the Son glorifies and honors the Father, which indicates their communion. Basil concludes the homily with an affirmation of the Spirit's divinity against the Pneumatomachians: "If the Spirit is created, he is not divine" (§7). This conclusion is the result of the Spirit's inseparability from the Father and Son in terms of nature, rank, dignity, glory, and honor.

A noteworthy feature of *Sab* is its conspicuous preference for *prosōpon* ("person") over *hypostasis* ("subsistence") as the term for naming what is plural in God.[11] Some scholars have seen great significance in this. Jean Bernardi thought this indicated that the

---

[10]Similar arguments calling for epistemological humility are found throughout Basil's corpus; see *Eun.* 1.12–13; 3.6; *Trin* 3. The first passage is discussed in Mark DelCogliano, *Basil of Caesarea's Anti-Eunomian Theory of Names: Christian Theology and Late-Antique Philosophy in the Fourth-Century Trinitarian Controversy*, VCS 103 (Leiden: Brill, 2010), 137–8. Basil's argument about the eyes here parallels *Eun.* 3.6.

[11]Lienhard, "Ps-Athanasius and Basil of Caesarea," 382–3; idem, *Contra Marcellum*, 229; Volker Henning Drecoll, *Die Entwicklung der Trinitätslehre des Basilius von Cäsarea: Sein Weg vom Homöusianer zum Neonizäner* (Göttingen: Vandenhoeck & Ruprecht, 1996), 161 n. 69.

homily should be dated to the last years of Basil's career.[12] In contrast, Stephen Hildebrand considered Basil's preference for *prosōpon* in this homily as a third stage in the development of his Trinitarian theology, since *hypostasis* belongs to the fourth and final stage.[13] Yet, as Joseph Lienhard noted, "That Basil avoids *hypostasis* is clear, but its import is not."[14] And so, it remains to be seen whether Basil's preferred technical terms in *Sab* signify (or should even be used to evaluate) a development in his Trinitarian theology. The question of development is perhaps better assessed by comparing the overall intention and conclusions of Basil's arguments and interpretations of Scripture in this homily with earlier works.

Another remarkable feature of this homily is the numerous parallels which it exhibits with the pseudo-Athanasian *Contra Sabellianos*.[15] These parallels have been explained in various ways. The Maurist scholar Bernard de Montfaucon, whose 1698 Benedictine edition of the text remains the best, held that the pseudo-Athanasian homily is a later reworking of Basil's homily by a forger.[16] Theodor Zahn thought that the two homilies were merely different versions of the same work.[17] In a series of articles and a monograph Reinhard Hübner has argued for a line of influence running in the direction opposite of Montfaucon's, suggesting that in *Sab* Basil has borrowed from the homily of pseudo-Athanasius, which he ascribes to Apollinarius of Laodicea and dates to 350–360.[18] Joseph Lienhard

[12]On this, see below p. 289.

[13]Stephen M. Hildebrand, *The Trinitarian Theology of Basil of Caesarea: A Synthesis of Greek Thought and Biblical Truth* (Washington, DC: Catholic University of America Press, 2007), 82–92.

[14]Lienhard, "Ps-Athanasius and Basil of Caesarea," 388 n. 17.

[15]CPG 2243.

[16]PG 28.95–96. Montfaucon's 1698 edition was republished with additions in 1777 and then reprinted by J.-P. Migne in his *Patrologia graeca* in 1857 at PG 28.96–121.

[17]*Marcellus von Ancyra. Ein Beitrag zur Geschichte der Theologie* (Gotha: Friedrich Andreas, 1867), 208 n 4.

[18]Reinhard Hübner, "Die Hauptquelle des Epiphanius (*Panarion*, haer. 65) über Paulus von Samosata, Ps.-Athanasius, *Contra Sabellianos*," *Zeitschrift für Kirchengeschichte* 90 (1979): 201–20; idem, "Epiphanius, *Ancoratus* und Ps.-Athanasius, *Contra Sabellianos*," *Zeitschrift für Kirchengeschichte* 92 (1981): 323–33; idem, *Die Schrift des*

confirmed that Basil's *Sab* borrows from the pseudo-Athanasian homily, but denied that Apollinarius was its author.[19] Manlio Simonetti rejected the theses of both Hübner and Lienhard, reviving the view of Montfaucon that *Sab* was used by the author of the pseudo-Athanasian homily, which Simonetti ascribes to an Apollinarian between 380 and 400.[20] Finally, Volker Drecoll has suggested that the pseudo-Athanasian *Contra Sabellianos* is a conflation of another pseudo-Athanasian writing and fragments of *Sab*.[21] Clearly, scholarly consensus on the relationship between the homilies of Basil and pseudo-Athanasius remains elusive.

Authenticity. Nearly all noted Basilian scholars since the sixteenth century have affirmed the authenticity of this homily.[22] Only Volker Drecoll has dissented from this majority position based on

---

Apolinarius von Laodicea gegen Photin (Pseudo-Athanasius, Contra Sabellianos) und Basilius von Caesarea, Patristische Texte und Studien 30 (Berlin: Walter de Gruyter, 1989). The scope of Hübner's project is larger than assessing the relationship between the pseudo-Athanasian *Contra Sabellianos* and *Sab*. He detects the influence of the pseudo-Athanasian *Contra Sabellianos* in many texts from the 360s and 370s, thereby suggesting the pervasive influence of Apollinarius upon many Trinitarian theologians, particularly Basil of Caesarea. For a critique of Hübner's thesis, see Drecoll, *Die Entwicklung*, 34–7.

[19]Lienhard, "Ps-Athanasius and Basil of Caesarea," 365–89; idem, *Contra Marcellum*, 221 n. 48 and 229. In the article Lienhard suggested that a younger Basil was the author of the pseudo-Athanasius homily. This thesis was refuted by Reinhard Hübner, "Ps-Athanasius, *Contra Sabellianos*: Eine Schrift des Basilius von Caesarea oder des Apollinarius von Laodicea?," *Vigiliae Christianae* 41 (1987): 386–95. Lienhard has accepted Hübner's critique on this point, but remains unconvinced that the pseudo-Athanasian homily should be ascribed to Apollinarius; see Lienhard, *Contra Marcellum*, 221 n. 48.

[20]Manlio Simonetti, "Sulla recente fortuna del *Contra Sabellianos* Ps.-Atanasiano," *Rivista di storia e letteratura religiosa* 26 (1990): 117–32.

[21]Drecoll, *Die Entwicklung*, 36.

[22]It has been included as an authentic homily in all major editions of Basil's homiletic corpus, including Erasmus (1532), Ducaeus (1618), and Garnier (1721–1730); see BBV ii.1121. Its authenticity is also supported by Hermann Dörries, Jean Gribomont, Philip Rousseau, and Paul Jonathan Fedwick (see the notes below for precise references). It is also accepted as a genuine homily of Basil by in recent works on Basil's Trinitarian theology: see Bernard Sesboüé, *Saint Basile et la Trinité: Un acte théologique au IVe siècle* (Paris: Descleé, 1998), 215–6, and Hildebrand, *The Trinitarian Theology of Basil of Caesarea*, 83–4.

an attestation in the manuscript tradition that is not as strong as for other genuine homilies, even while admitting that there is "no definitive argument against authenticity."[23] At the same time, of those homilies whose authenticity Drecoll believes to be suspect, he holds *Sab* among those most likely to be Basil's.[24] It should be noted, however, that Drecoll was unable to avail himself of Paul Jonathan Fedwick's monumental study of the manuscript tradition of Basil's moral homilies, which confirmed the authenticity of *Sab* based on its wide attestation in the best manuscripts.[25] Therefore, on the basis of external and internal evidence, nothing precludes Basil's authorship of this homily and in fact everything points to its genuineness.

Context and Date. There is little in this homily to suggest a particular context or a firm date. Hermann Dörries demonstrated that it has several descriptions of the Spirit in common with *Spir.* 18, which may indicate that both works were composed around the same time, about 375.[26] But, as was the case with *Fide,*[27] here Basil may be articulating ideas about the Spirit that either would later find expression in *Spir.* or were repeated after this treatise was already written. So the parallels identified by Dörries cannot be used to estimate a precise date.

Scholars such as Jean Gribomont, Bernard Sesboüé, and Stephen Hildebrand dated *Sab* to around or after 372, presumably since it is mentioned in §4 that questions about the Holy Spirit were currently the hot topic of conversation.[28] Philip Rousseau narrowed the date to 372–375, noting the fact that "its treatment of the Holy Spirit looks

[23]Drecoll, *Die Entwicklung*, 161–2.

[24]Drecoll, *Die Entwicklung*, 161 n. 69. Drecoll notes that "lexicographically and stylistically *Hom.* XXIV (i.e., *Sab*) does not significantly diverge from Basil." In this same footnote, Drecoll lists a number questions about the structure and the contents of the homily that need to be considered when judging its authenticity. In particular he compares it to *Ep.* 52. But in my opinion none of the points raised here suggests that the homily should not be attributed to Basil.

[25]See BBV ii.1120–2.

[26]Dörries, *De Spiritu Sancto*, 94–97.

[27]See p. 232 above.

[28]Jean Gribomont, *In Tomum 31 Patrologiae Graeae Introductio*, 6 ("after 372"); Sesboüé, *Saint Basile et la Trinité*, 215 ("after 372"); Hildebrand, *The Trinitarian Theology of Basil of Caesarea*, 83 ("around 372").

more like a build-up toward the *De spiritu sancto* than something subsequent to so assured a formulation."[29]

Jean Bernardi dated *Sab* to late in Basil's career.[30] He was impressed by the homily's frank and developed account of the Spirit compared to the discretion used in his treatment of the Spirit in *Fide* (which Bernardi dated to 372). Such a shift in Basil's public stance on the Holy Spirit is attributed not only to a significant lapse of time but also to the death of Valens in 378 (or at least the relaxation of his pressure on Basil starting in 377). Also noted by Bernardi is the homily's use of technical terms associated with Basil late in his career, such as his preference for *prosōpon* over *hypostasis*. Thus according to Bernardi the homily is to be dated 377–378. Paul Jonathan Fedwick initially followed Bernardi and provisionally adopted 378 as a possible date for the homily, but subsequently he suggested that it could have been delivered at any time during his ecclesiastical career (362–378).[31] Yet Fedwick's extreme prudence here is unwarranted. In line with the opinions of Gribomont and others, a date from 372 onwards seems almost certain.

Perhaps a more precise date can be offered based on Basil's rhetorical depiction of his opponents in the homily. Sabellianism and Heteroousianism are depicted as diametrically opposed heresies which each fight against orthodox Christianity from opposite sides. Furthermore, Sabellians are construed as Jews and Heteroousians as Greek polytheists who have attempted to mix their own doctrine with Christianity. While seeds of this rhetoric can be found in earlier writings of Basil,[32] the full-blown version is found only in

[29]Philip Rousseau, *Basil of Caesarea* (Berkeley: University of California Press, 1994), 247 n. 60 ("around 372").

[30]Jean Bernardi, *La prédication des pères cappadociens* (Paris: Presses universitaires de France, 1968), 87–88.

[31]*The Church and the Charisma of Leadership in Basil of Caesarea* (Toronto: Pontifical Institute of Mediaeval Studies, 1979), 153; "A Chronology of the Life and Works of Basil of Caesarea," in idem, ed., *Basil of Caesarea: Christian, Humanist, Ascetic. A Sixteen-Hundredth Anniversary Symposium* (Toronto: The Pontifical Institute of Mediaeval Studies, 1981), 3–19 at 10.

[32]For example, see *Eun.* 2.22 and *Ep.* 69.2.

several texts from 375–376.[33] These texts suggest that in this period Basil was in the habit of employing a similar rhetoric to discredit his theological opponents. As with the parallels between *Spir.* and *Sab* mentioned above, the mere fact of parallels between two texts cannot be used to estimate a precise date. But since the same rhetoric appears in a number of texts from the same period, there is an increased likelihood that *Sab* belongs to the same period as the other texts. Therefore, almost certainly *Sab* is to be dated after 372 and quite possibly to the years 375–376.

Translation. The following translation is based on Julien Garnier's edition as reprinted in De Sinner ii.265–275 (=PG 31.599–617).[34] In crafting my translation, I benefited from Garnier's Latin translation and from an unpublished translation by Susan R. Holman, as well as from the excerpt translated in English by Blomfield Jackson.[35]

TRANSLATION

1 Judaism fights with Hellenism, and both of them fight with Christianity, just as the Egyptians and the Assyrians used to war against each other and against Israel. We find a similar thing in the case of vice: cowardice and rashness oppose each other and courage.[1] Such also is the battle joined by each side against orthodoxy,[2] which is attacked on the one side by Sabellius and on the other by those who preach the "unlike."[3] Now just as we have fled from the Hellenes, having rejected their evil idol-worship and condemned their polytheism as atheism, so too have we fled the blasphemy of the Jews who deny the Son of God, since we are fearful of that threat:

---

[33]*Spir.* 30.77 dated to 375; *Ep.* 210.4 dated to 376; *Ep.* 226.4 dated to 375.
[34]CPG 2869.
[35]"Prolegomena. Sketch of the Life and Works of Saint Basil," NPNF 2.8, lx–lxi.

[1]See Aristotle, *Nicomachean Ethics* 3.6–7 (1115a7–1116a14).
[2]Literally, "the correctness of confession."
[3]That is, the Anomoians, or Heteroousians.

Whoever denies me before men, I also will deny before my Father who is in heaven [Mt 10.33].

Therefore, it makes sense that we should also flee those who have concocted teachings against the word of truth that are akin to these. For the devil is crafty in his evildoing, and when he saw the estrangement of Christians from both Hellenes and Jews and realized that we are hostile to them simply on the basis of their names, he added our name to each of theirs and thereby tried to reintroduce Jewish denial and Hellenic polytheism. For those who claim that the Only-Begotten is a work of God and something made, then adore him and speak of him as divine, are clearly introducing Hellenic teaching because they worship a creature and not the Creator.[4] But those who deny God from God and confess the Son in name, but in deed and truth eliminate his existence, once again revive Judaism.[5]

For indeed when they confess the Word, they see him as analogous to the internal word that resides in the mind; when they call him Wisdom, they mean that he is like the state that arises in the soul of the learned. Thus they speak of the Father and Son as one person because a human being is also said to be one, not being divided from the word and wisdom that exist in him. And yet the Evangelist immediately cries out from the prologue: *And the Word was God* [Jn 1.1], granting the Son his distinct existence.[6] For if the Word was in the heart, how could he have been understood as God? How could he have been *with God* [Jn 1.1]? Indeed, the word that is in a man is not a man, and we do not say that such a word is "with" him but rather "in" him.[7] For such a word is neither living nor subsistent, but the Word of God is life and truth.[8] And as soon as our word has been spoken it no longer exists, but what does the Psalm say about the Word of God? *Your Word, O Lord, endures in the heavens forever* [Ps 118.89].

[4]See Rom 1.25. These are the Heteroousians.
[5]These are the Sabellians.
[6]Gk. ἰδίαν ὕπαρξιν.
[7]See *Verb* 4.
[8]See Jn 14.6.

2 This, then, is the war on the one side. But what is the battle against the truth on the other side? What sort of battle is it? While they concede the Son's existence[9] and agree that the Son and the Father each has a distinct person,[10] they introduce unlikeness of nature.[11] Furthermore, they concede the name "Son" as far as the term is concerned, but in actuality bring it down to the level of creation,[12] feeling no shame at that saying of the Lord where he points to himself in reply to the one who was eager to contemplate the Father: *He who has seen me has seen the Father* [Jn 14.9].

Now this saying, if any think about it correctly, puts an end to the blasphemies of both sides. For he does not claim that he is the Father since he clearly distinguishes the persons by saying: *He who has seen me*. This statement shows his distinct person.[13] *Has seen the Father* refers to the Father's person[14] and clearly distinguishes it from his own, as when he said. *If you had known me, you would have also known my Father* [Jn 14.7]. For these passages do not disclose a conflation of the persons, but communicate the indistinguishability of the divinity.[15] Let their adversaries also listen to the same verse, that whoever is deemed worthy of communion with the Son is not deprived of the Father.[16] For the begetter has not begotten one who is foreign to him but one who is such as he is.[17] Listen to this, Anomoian:[18] *I and the*

[9]Gk. ὕπαρξιν.

[10]Gk. ἴδιον εἶναι πρόσωπον Υἱοῦ καὶ Πατρός.

[11]Gk. ἀνομοιότηνα τῆς φύσεως. Unlike Sabellians, the Heteroousians teach that the Son really exists as a distinct person alongside the Father who is also a distinct person, but claim that Father and Son are unlike each other at the level of their basic nature.

[12]While the Heteroousians agree that the name "Son" can be used for the Son, they do not understand this term to imply the natural affinity that exists between the Son and the Father (as Basil would), but interpret the name as signifying that the Son is a creature who is substantially different from the Father.

[13]Gk. τὸ ἴδιον αὐτοῦ πρόσωπον.

[14]Gk. τὸ πατρικὸν πρόσωπον.

[15]Gk. τὸ ἀπαράλλακτον τῆς θεότητος.

[16]This is Basil's interpretation of Jn 14.7 and 14.9.

[17]Gk. οὐ γὰρ ἀλλοῖον ὁ γεννήτωρ ἐγέννα, ἀλλὰ τοιοῦτον οἷος αὐτός ἐστιν.

[18]Literally, "unlike." It could also be translated "Anomoius," an insulting pun on the name of Basil's chief Heteroousian opponent, Eunomius.

Father are one [Jn 10.30]. And you, Sabellius, listen to this: *I have come from the Father and I go to him* [Jn 16.28+16.10]. Let each of you be healed of his particular wound from the teaching of the gospel. One of you should understand that their unity is a question of indistinguishability of nature; the other, that *I have come from him and I go to him* is a question of the distinction of the persons. So then, let us agree on these matters, and make peace, and bring this long war against piety to an end, throwing down these sharpened weapons of impiety and refashioning our spears into plowshares and our swords into pruning hooks.[54]

Nor should you, [Sabellius], say "one alone," but follow him who says: I am not alone because *the one who sent me, the Father, is with me* [Jn 8.16+24]. So then, one is the Father who sent and another is the Son who was sent. And again, he says: *I testify to myself and the Father who sent me testifies to me* [Jn 8.14+18]. He also says: *In your law it is written that the testimony of two people is true* [Jn 8.17]. If you like, count the persons. He says: *I myself testify* [Jn 8.18]. That's one. *And the Father who sent me testifies to me* [Jn 8.18]. That's two. And it is not I who count so audaciously, but the Lord himself taught this, saying: *In your law it is written that the testimony of two people is true* [Jn 8.17].

And as for you, [Anomoian], you fight against God with another form of impiety, claiming that the Son is unlike God in nature, not granting their equality, introducing an interval of life.[55] Honor Paul who says: *He is the image of the invisible God* [Col 1.15], and grant that the living Image is indistinguishable from the archetypal Life. Confess that the Father has produced a Son, not a creature. And in this true confession of the Father, grant that the one begotten to him is of the same honor, mindful of the testimony of the gospel: *he called God his Father, making himself equal to God* [Jn 5.18]. Now his equality with the begetter is understood in terms of nature, not in terms

[19]See Is 2.4: *and they shall beat their swords into plowshares and their spears into pruning hooks.*

[20]That is, an interval of life between the Father and Son. According to the Heteroousians, the life of the Son is not coterminous with the life of the Father because the Father pre-existed the Son.

of physical size. How *did he not consider equality with God a thing to be grasped* [Phil 2.6], if, as you blaspheme, he was never equal to him? How *was he in the form of God* [Phil 2.6], when, according to your account, he was never like him?

3   Such is the war against us on both sides. But what is the truth? Do not fear to confess the persons, but say "Father" and say "Son" too. In this confession you do not attribute two names to one reality, but learn from each designation a distinct notion.[21] For it is the utmost foolishness not to accept the teachings of the Lord, who clearly distinguishes for us one person from the other.[22] For he says: *if I go away, I will ask the Father and he will send you another Paraclete* [Jn 16.7+14.16]. Therefore, the Son asks, the Father is asked, and the Paraclete is sent. So then, isn't your shamelessness clear when, hearing *I* about the Son, *he* about the Father, and *another* about the Holy Spirit, you mix all of them together, conflate them all, and attribute all the names to one reality?

Nevertheless, you should not usurp the distinction of the persons for impiety. For even if they are two in number, they are not disjoined in nature. Nor does anyone who says "two" introduce estrangement [between them]. There is one God because there is one Father.[23] But the Son is also God, and there are not two gods because the Son has identity with the Father. For I do not behold one divinity in the Father and another in the Son. Nor is one nature this and the other that. So then, in order to make clear for you the distinctness of the persons,[24] count the Father by himself and the Son by himself, but in order to avoid secession into polytheism, confess one substance in both. In this way both Sabellius falls and the Anomoian[25] will be shattered.

[21]Gk. ἰδίαν ἔννοιαν. The names "Father" and "Son" have specific meanings that the theologian needs to take into account.

[22]Gk. τῶν προσώπων τὴν ἑτερότητα, literally, "the difference of the persons."

[23]Here I adopt the repunctuation suggested by Lienhard, "Ps-Athanasius and Basil of Caesarea," 388 n. 14.

[24]Gk. τῶν προσώπων ἡ ἰδιότης.

[25]See n. 18 above.

4   But when I say "one substance," do not think that two are separated off from one, but that the Son has come to subsist from the Father, his principle.[26] The Father and Son do not come from one substance that transcends them both. For we do not call them brothers, but confess Father and Son. There is an identity of substance because the Son is from the Father, not made by a command but rather begotten from his nature, not separated from him but the perfect radiance of the Father, who himself remains perfect.

And those of you who have not come around to my position, as much as you have either imperfectly followed what we have said or stood around only hoping to insult us, not seeking to receive any benefit from us but looking to seize on something that we have said, still you say: "He preaches two gods! He proclaims polytheism!"[27] There are not two gods because there are not two fathers. Whoever introduces two first principles preaches two gods. Such is Marcion and anyone similar to him in impiety. Once again, whoever says that the one begotten is different in substance from the one who has begotten him implies that there are two gods, introducing polytheism by maintaining the unlikeness of substance. For if there is one divinity that is unbegotten and one that is begotten, you are preaching polytheism, implying that the unbegotten is contrary to the begotten and clearly positing too that their substances are contrary—that is, if indeed unbegottenness is the substance of the Father and begottenness is the substance of the Son. Thus you imply not only that there are two gods but also that they are opposed to each other. And the worst of it is that you do not locate their conflict in the will[28] but in a natural dissension which can never be peacefully resolved.

But the word of truth flees these contradictory teachings from each side. For wherever there is one principle and one thing from it,

---

[26]Gk. ἐκ τῆς ἀρχῆς τοῦ Πατρὸς.

[27]Elsewhere Basil reports that he was charged with polytheism; see *Ep.* 130; *Trin* 2–3.

[28]Gk. προαιρέσει.

wherever there is one archetype and one image, the formula of unity is not destroyed. Therefore, the Son exists from the Father in a begotten way and by nature he expresses the Father in himself: as image he has indistinguishability,[29] as something begotten[30] he preserves sameness in substance.[31] After all, whoever gazes at the imperial image in the forum and calls the one on the panel "emperor" does not confess two emperors, namely, the image and the one whose image it is. Nor when he points to the depiction on the panel and says, "This is the emperor," does he deprive the exemplar of the designation "emperor." Rather, he affirmed the emperor's dignity by acknowledging his depiction. For if the image is equivalent to the emperor, even more so is it true that the emperor has provided the image with the reason for its existence. But here below wood and wax and the skill of a painter produce a perishable image that is an imitation of someone perishable and an artificial likeness of someone who has been made. But there above whenever you hear "image," take this to mean *the radiance of glory* [Heb 1.3]. What is this radiance? And what is this glory? The Apostle himself wastes no time explaining this, adding: *And the representation of the subsistence* [Heb 1.3]. So then, the subsistence is the same as the glory and the representation the same as the radiance. Thus while the glory remains perfect and never diminishes, perfect radiance proceeds. And so, the formula of the image, if taken in a way appropriate to God, communicates to us the unity of the divinity. For the one is in the other and the other in him because the one is such as the other and the other is such as he. Thus the two are united by not being different in kind, nor is the Son understood according to another form and an alien representation. So then, once again I say: "One and one,

[29] Gk. τὸ ἀπαράλλακτον. That is, as image the Son is indistinguishable from the Father.

[30] Gk. γέννημα. On Basil's use of this term here, see Mark DelCogliano, "Basil of Caesarea on the Primacy of the Name 'Son,'" *Revue des Études Augustiniennes et Patristiques* 57 (2011): 46–69 at 64.

[31] Gk. τὸ ὁμοούσιον. That is, as one begotten from the Father, the Son's substance is the same as the Father's. This is the only use of the term *homoousios* in this homily.

but their nature is indivisible and their perfection unwavering." So then, God is one because through both we contemplate one form which is shown in its entirety in both.

But for quite some time now I have realized that what I am saying bores you. And it seems to me that you have all but stopped listening to me because I dwell upon points of agreement and do not touch upon the questions on everyone's mind. For all ears these days are eager to hear debates about the Holy Spirit. Now I especially wish that, just as I received the tradition without qualification, just as I agreed to it without refinements, so too may I hand it on thus to my audience, without being constantly challenged on these issues, but having disciples persuaded on the basis of one confession. But since you stand around us more like judges than disciples, wanting to test us and not seeking to learn anything, we are obligated, as if in a court of law, to respond to objections, to submit over and over again to questioning, and to state over and over again what we have received. But we exhort you not to seek to hear from us only what pleases you, but rather what is acceptable to the Lord, consonant with the Scriptures, and not in conflict with the fathers.

Therefore, what we said about the Son, namely, that it is necessary to confess his distinct person, this we must also say about the Holy Spirit. For it does not mean that the Spirit is the same as the Father when it is written that *God is Spirit* [Jn 4.24]. Nor again does it mean that the Son and Spirit constitute a single person[32] when it is said: *If anyone does not have the Spirit of Christ, he does not belong to him. But Christ is in you* [Rom 8.9–10]. For on the basis of these passages some are deceived into thinking that the Spirit and Christ are the same. But what do we say? That these passages demonstrate their affinity of nature, not a conflation of persons. There exists the Father with perfect being, self-sufficient, and the root and source of the Son and of the Holy Spirit. There exists the Son, living Word in full divinity and the self-sufficient offspring begotten of the Father.

---

[32]Gk. υἱοῦ καὶ πνεύματος ἓν πρόσωπόν ἐστιν, literally, "there is a single person of Son and Spirit."

Full too is the Spirit, not part of another, but considered perfect and complete in himself. In addition, the Son is inseparably conjoined to the Father and the Spirit to the Son. For nothing separates them, nor does anything sever their eternal conjunction. No age intrudes between them, nor indeed does our soul admit the concept[33] of separation, as if either the Only-Begotten were not always together with the Father or the Holy Spirit were not co-existent with the Son.

5   So then, whenever we conjoin the Trinity, do not imagine the three as parts of a single indivisible reality—such a thought is impious! Instead, admit the inseparable consubstantiality[34] of three perfect incorporeals. For wherever there is the presence of Holy Spirit, there also is the dwelling of Christ, and wherever Christ is, there clearly the Father is also present. *Do you not know that your bodies are a temple of the Holy Spirit within you?* [1 Cor 6.19]. And: *If anyone destroys the temple of God, God will destroy him* [1 Cor 3.17]. So then, when sanctified by the Holy Spirit, we receive Christ who dwells *in our inner man* [Eph 3.16], and along with Christ we also receive the Father who makes a home with him in those who are worthy.[35] This conjunction is declared in both the teaching handed down to us about baptism and the confession of faith.[36] For if the Spirit were foreign in nature, how could he be numbered with them? And if he were added to the Father and Son later in time, how could he be ranked with the eternal nature? Those who separate the Spirit from the Father and Son and number him with the created order render baptism incomplete and the confession of faith defective. For the Trinity does not remain the Trinity when the Spirit is subtracted. Then again, if one of the creatures were added, all creation will enter into the connumeration of the Father and Son. For what would hinder anyone from saying: "We believe in the Father and Son and in the entire creation"? After all, if it were pious to believe

[33]Gk. ἐπίνοια.
[34]Gk. συνουσίαν.
[35]See Jn 14.23.
[36]See Mt 28.19.

in a part of creation, then perhaps it would be even more devout to include all creation in the confession! By believing in all creation, you believe not only in the angels and the ministering spirits, but also in whatever adversarial powers there may be. Since these too are part of creation, you also assent to these being in the faith. Thus the blasphemy against the Spirit leads you into impious and wicked teachings. For as soon as you make inappropriate statements about the Spirit, you have a sign that the Spirit has abandoned you. After all, just as anyone who has closed his eyes sits in a darkness of his own making, so too anyone who has withdrawn from the Spirit, now that he is outside the Enlightener, is confounded by the blindness in his soul.

6 Let the tradition shame you into not separating the Holy Spirit from the Father and Son. This is what the Lord taught, the Apostles preached, the Fathers preserved, the Martyrs confirmed. Be satisfied with speaking as you have been taught, and do not bother me with these sophistries: "The Spirit is either unbegotten or begotten. If unbegotten, he is a father; if begotten, he is a son; if neither of these, he is a creature." As for me, I have come to know that the Spirit is with the Father, not that he is the Father, and I have received that he is with the Son, not that he is named Son. But I understand his affinity with the Father, since he proceeds from the Father.[37] I understand too his affinity with the Son, since I hear: *If anyone does not have the Spirit of Christ, he does not belong to him* [Rom 8.9]. For if the Spirit does not have affinity with Christ, how can he bring us into affinity with Christ? But I also hear that he is called the *Spirit of Truth* [Jn 14.17]. And the Lord is Truth.[38] Whenever I hear the *Spirit of adopted sonship* [Rom 8.15],[39] I come to understand his unity with the Son and Father

[37]See Jn 15.26.

[38]See Jn 14.6.

[39]The Greek word for "adopted sonship" is υἱοθεσία, which literally means "adopting as a son (υἱός). Therefore, for Basil and many other Greek fathers, the title "Spirit of adopted sonship" shows Spirit's intimate connection with the Father's adoption of sons in Christ. See, for example, Athanasius, *Letters to Serapion* 1.19; Basil, *Eun.* 3.4; Didymus, *On the Holy Spirit* 195–196.

by nature. For how can what is foreign to them adopt us as sons? How can what is alien to them bring us into affinity with them?

So then, here I am neither generating innovative formulations nor denying his dignity, but rather I bewail those who dare to designate him a creature and I mourn the fact that through their petty sophisms and spurious reasoning they cast themselves into the pit of perdition. For they say: "Our intellect has comprehended these three, and among existents there is nothing that does not fall under the category of existents. For the Spirit," they continue, "is either unbegotten or begotten or created. But indeed he is neither the first nor the second. Therefore, he must be the third." This "therefore" of yours will make you liable to that everlasting curse![40] Have you investigated everything? In your thoughts have you placed everything in a category? Have you left nothing unexamined? With your intellect have you grasped everything? With your mind have you comprehended everything? Do you know what's under the earth? Do you know what's in the deep? That's what the demons brag about: "I know the number of the sands and the measure of the sea."[41] Now if you are ignorant about many things, and if what you don't know infinitely surpasses what you do know, why not put your shame aside and along with everybody else admit your ignorance about the way in which the Holy Spirit exists, seeing that such ignorance is not fraught with danger?

As for me, I do not have the leisure to refute your stupid ideas, nor to point out how many existents there are which have escaped the comprehension of your thoughts. But I would be happy to ask you questions, and I do declare with confidence that someday you

[40] In Mt 12.32 (cf. Mk 3.29; Lk 12.10) speaking against the Holy Spirit will not be forgiven, "either in this age or the age to come." In this sentence Basil plays on "therefore" (ἄρα) and "curse" (ἀρᾷ). The rhetorical figure used here is known as parechesis.

[41] Here Basil cites the Pythian oracle, recorded by Herodotus 1.47. It is also cited, for example, by Origen, *Contra Celsum* 2.9; Porphyry, *Vita Plotini* 22; Philostratus, *Vita sophistarum* 1; and Julian, *Commentary on Job* (Dieter Hagedorn, ed., *Der Hiobkommentar des Arianers Julian*, Patristische Texte und Studien 14 [Berlin: De Gruyter, 1973], 233, 15). On Julian, see p. 154 n. 15 above.

will repent of this godless wisdom, claiming the Holy Spirit is a creature. Don't you fear the forbidden sin?[42] Or do you think that you can utter a blasphemy more impious than this? For this one statement alone raises the most terrible possibilities [for the Holy Spirit]: estrangement from God according to nature itself, a humble state of servitude, servile ministries, deprivation of sanctity which is not present by nature, and the prospect of the Spirit's participating in sanctity from the distribution of grace just as the rest of those sanctified do. And just as *the manifestation of the Spirit is given to us for the common good* [1 Cor 12.7], and just as he is measured out to each *in proportion to faith* [Rom 12.6], so too the Spirit will participate in sanctity, if he is really created as the Pneumatomachians[43] suppose.

7 But let us not allow this foolishness to go unrefuted, I mean the foolishness of those who think that everything can be comprehended with their mind. Therefore, let them now answer our questions. So, what in the world is the substance of the perceptible sun? Is it one of the four elements, or it is a compound of the four? But indeed neither is it earth, nor air, nor is it water, nor fire. For these move vertically: some go up, others go down. Earth and water go down because of their heaviness, whereas air and fire move with upward motion because of their lightness. But the motion of the sun is circular. Therefore, it is not one of the four elements. But indeed neither is it a compound of these. For compounds are held together only with great effort, being assembled from contraries which pull each other in opposite directions by their motion. But the motion of the sun is effortless, and for this reason also unceasing. Hence it is not a compound. But indeed each corporeal entity is either simple or compounded. But the sun is neither a simple corporeal entity since it does not move vertically, nor a compound since it moves effortlessly. Therefore, the sun does not exist. Such is what results from your clever categorizations, which are ridiculed by anyone with eyes

[42]See Mt 12.32.
[43]Or, "fighters against the Spirit."

to see! Then again, how do we human beings see? Do we receive the forms of visible objects, or do we emit some power from ourselves? But indeed it is neither. We do not receive the images of visible objects. For how could the hemisphere of the heaven be seen by the tiny opening of the pupil? Nor do we emit something from ourselves. For again how could what is emitted suffice to spread across the heaven? But if we neither receive the images of visible objects, nor emit some power from ourselves, therefore we do not see.[44]

What then? Shall I refute your syllogisms or pray for you, that your conclusions be true? What difference is there between such arguments and your logic-chopping about the Spirit, which you flaunt before wretched, silly women[45] and eunuchs who are nearly women? Listen to me without spitefully twisting my words. If the Spirit is from God, how can you categorize him with creatures? For indeed would you not say that all things are from God? Christ is said to be of God, but he is not a creature like us, for *we are of Christ, but Christ is of God* [1 Cor 3.23]. We say instead that we are of Christ in one way, as servants of the Master, but Christ is said to be of God in another way, as the Son of the Father. So too it is with the Spirit: not because all things are from God and he is like all things, nor because there are ministering spirits[46] and the Holy Spirit is just like them on account of their [shared] designation. For only one is the true Spirit. Indeed, just as many are sons but only one is the true Son, so too, even though all are said to be from God, nonetheless the Son is from God and the Spirit from God in the proper sense.[47] For the Son comes forth from the Father and the Spirit proceeds from the Father. But while the Son is from the Father in a begotten way, the Spirit is from God in a way that cannot be explained.[48]

[44]*Eun.* 3.6 employs the same argument about the eyes. The two theories Basil mentions appear to be those of Epicurus and Plato. See Mark DelCogliano and Andrew Radde-Gallwitz, *St. Basil of Caesarea: Against Eunomius*, FOTC 122 (Washington, DC: Catholic University of America Press, 2011), 193 n. 20, for further discussion.

[45]See 2 Tim 3.6.
[46]See Heb 1.14.
[47]Gk. κυρίως.
[48]Gk. ἀρρήτως.

So then, be on guard against the great danger of disparaging the glory of the Paraclete. The Son does not receive the honor given to him when the Spirit is denigrated. For the Son says: *That one will glorify me* [Jn 16.14]. It is not as a servant together with the creatures [that the Spirit glorifies the Son]. For if the Spirit had glorified the Son together with all things, the Son would not have said *that one*. In this verse the reference to the single entity[49] communicates that the glory is accorded [to the Son by the Spirit] in a way far superior to others, not like those who say: *Glory to God in the highest* [Lk 2.14], but like the one who said: *Father, I glorified you; I accomplished the work that you gave me* [Jn 17.4], and also like the Father, who glorifies the Son, as when he says: *And I glorified you, and I will glorify you again* [Jn 12.28]. Thus does the Son receive the Spirit into the communion of the Father and himself. If anyone can show me greater glory than this, I will concede that my adversaries speak the truth in everything. *Whoever rejects you rejects me* [Lk 10.16]. Why? Clearly because the Spirit dwells in them. Hence whoever does not honor the Spirit does not honor the Son, *and whoever does not honor the Son does not honor the Father* [Jn 5.23].

Therefore, a willful misunderstanding of any one of those in whom we believe[50] is a denial of the whole divinity. If the Spirit is created, he is not divine. But indeed it says: *the divine Spirit is the one who made me* [Job 33.4]. And it says: *God filled Bezalel with the divine Spirit of wisdom and understanding* [Ex 35.31]. So, in which do you find access to the divine? In creation? Or in the divinity? If in creation, you will say that even the Father of our Lord Jesus Christ is a creature! For it is written about him: *His eternal power and deity* [Rom 1.20]. But if in divinity, stop your blasphemy and recognize the dignity of the Spirit. You are so stupid that not even by the term itself can you be brought to worthy notions about the Spirit.

---

[49] Gk. ἕν, namely, *that one*.

[50] Gk. ἡ περὶ ἕν τι τῶν πιστευομένων ἀγνωσύνη. These words could also be interpreted: "a willful misunderstanding of any single point of our beliefs . . ."

The Traditional Numbering of the Moral Homilies

The following tables correlate the abbreviations for Basil's Moral Homilies (apart from the homilies on the Psalms) with the traditional numbers assigned to them. These are used in De Sinner and PG, and most scholarship refers to Basil's homilies by these numbers. Numbers omitted from the series refer to homilies once attributed to Basil but now considered spurious.

Att	3		1	*Iei1*
Bapt	13		2	*Iei2*
Chr	27		3	*Att*
Dest	6		4	*Grat*
Div	7		5	*Iul*
Ebr	14		6	*Dest*
Fam	8		7	*Div*
Fide	15		8	*Fam*
Gord	18		9	*Malo*
Grat	4		10	*Ira*
Hum	20		11	*Inv*
Iei1	1		12	*Prov*
Iei2	2		13	*Bapt*
Inv	11		14	*Ebr*
Ira	10		15	*Fide*
Iul	5		16	*Verb*
Lak	26		18	*Gord*

Malo	9	19	*Mart*
Mam	23	20	*Hum*
Mart	19	21	*Mund*
Mund	21	23	*Mam*
Prov	12	24	*Sab*
Sab	24	26	*Lak*
Trin	29	27	*Chr*
Verb	16	29	*Trin*

Note that Garnier did not assign numbers to those homilies which he considered inauthentic (*Lak, Chr, Trin*). The numbers assigned to them above are found in neither De Sinner nor PG (as far as I can tell); they are derived, apparently, from the order in which they were printed among the spurious works of Basil.[1]

---

[1]See Paul Jonathan Fedwick, ed., *Basil of Caesarea: Christian, Humanist, Ascetic. A Sixteen-Hundredth Anniversary Symposium* (Toronto: The Pontifical Institute of Mediaeval Studies, 1981), xix-xxxi; and Philip Rousseau, *Basil of Caesarea* (Berkeley: University of California Press, 1994), 388–9.

English Translations of the Moral Homilies

The following lists all known English translations of Basil's Moral Homilies. Full references can be found in the Bibliography. Translations are listed in reverse chronological order.

Att PPS 30, 93–105 (Harrison); FOTC 9, 431–446 (Way).

Bapt PPS [forthcoming] (Holman); Hamman, *Baptism*, 75–87 (Halton); Kenrick, *A Treatise on Baptism*, 225–241.

Chr PPS [forthcoming] (DelCogliano).

Dest PPS 38, 59–71 (Schroeder); Toal, *The Sunday Sermons*, vol. 3, 325–32.

Div PPS 38, 41–58 (Schroeder); Silvas, "The Emergence of Basil's Social Doctrine," 161–176.

Ebr PPS [forthcoming] (DelCogliano).

Fam PPS 38, 73–88 (Schroeder); Holman, *The Hungry Are Dying*, 183–192.

Fide PPS 47, 234–239 (DelCogliano); Toal, *The Sunday Sermons*, vol. 4, 75–78; Boyd, *The Fathers not Papists*, 86–99.

Gord Leemans, Mayer, Allen, and Dehandschutter, *Let Us Die That We May Live*, 56–67 (Allen); Boyd, *The Fathers not Papists*, 44–69.

Grat PPS [forthcoming] (Holman).

Hum PPS 47, 108–119 (DelCogliano); Toal, *The Sunday Sermons*, vol. 3, 360–366; FOTC 9, 475–486 (Wagner).

Iei1 PPS [forthcoming] (DelCogliano); Berghuis, *Christian Fasting*, 185–194; Pole, *A Treatise of Iustification*, vol. 2, 48–57.

Iei2 PPS [forthcoming] (DelCogliano); Berghuis, *Christian Fasting*, 195–201.

Inv	PPS 47, 132–144 (DelCogliano); Toal, *The Sunday Sermons*, vol. 4, 142–148; FOTC 9, 463–474 (Wagner).
Ira	PPS 30, 81–92 (Harrison); Toal, *The Sunday Sermons*, vol. 4, 270–278; FOTC 9, 447–461 (Wagner).
Iul	PPS [forthcoming] (Holman).
Lak	PPS 47, 195–210 (DelCogliano).
Malo	Silvas, "The Emergence of Basil's Social Doctrine," 145–160; PPS 30, 65–80 (Harrison).
Mam	PPS [forthcoming] (Holman).
Mart	Leemans, Mayer, Allen, and Dehandschutter, *Let Us Die That We May Live*, 67–77 (Allen); Boyd, *The Fathers not Papists*, 44–69.
Mund	PPS 47, 164–181 (DelCogliano); FOTC 9, 487–505 (Wagner).
Prov	PPS 47, 53–78 (DelCogliano).
Ps1	FOTC 46, 151–164 (Way).
Ps7	FOTC 46, 165–180 (Way).
Ps14a	PPS 47, 92–101 (DelCogliano).
Ps14b	PPS 38, 89–99 (Schroeder); FOTC 46, 181–191 (Way).
Ps28	FOTC 46, 193–211 (Way).
Ps29	FOTC 46, 213–225 (Way).
Ps32	FOTC 46, 227–246 (Way).
Ps33	FOTC 46, 247–274 (Way).
Ps44	FOTC 46, 275–295 (Way).
Ps45	FOTC 46, 297–309 (Way).
Ps48	FOTC 46, 311–331 (Way).
Ps59	FOTC 46, 333–340 (Way).
Ps61	FOTC 46, 341–350 (Way).
Ps114	FOTC 46, 351–359 (Way).
Ps115	PPS 47, 218–226 (DelCogliano).
Sab	PPS 47, 290–303 (DelCogliano).
Trin	PPS 47, 269–276 (DelCogliano).
Verb	PPS 47, 250–257 (DelCogliano).

Select Bibliography

Texts

Courtonne, Yves. *Saint Basile. Homélies sur la richesse: Éditions critique et exégetique.* Paris: Typographie Firmin-Didot et Cie, 1935.

———. *Saint Basile: Lettres.* 3 vols. Paris: Société d'édition 'Les Belles Lettres', 1957–1966.

Deferrari, Roy Joseph, and Martin R.P. McGuire. *Basil: Letters.* Loeb Classical Library 190, 215, 243, and 270. Cambridge, MA: Harvard University Press, 1926–1934.

DelCogliano, Mark, and Andrew Radde-Gallwitz. *St. Basil of Caesarea: Against Eunomius.* FOTC 122. Washington, DC: Catholic University of America Press, 2011.

De Sinner, Gabriel Rudolf Ludwig. *Sancti Patris nostri Basilii, Caesareae Cappadociae archiepiscopi, opera omnia quae exstant, vel quae sub eius nomine circumferuntur, ad manuscriptos Codices Gallicanos, Vaticanos, Florentinos et Anglicos, necnon ad antiquiores editiones castigata, multis aucta: Nova Interpretatione, criticis Praefationibus, Notis, variis Lectionibus illustrata, nova sancti Doctoris Vita et copioissimis Indicibus locupletata. Tomus Primus et Secundus: Opera et studio Domni Iuliani Garnier, Presbyteri et Monachi Benedictini, e Congregatione Sancti Mauri. Tomus Tertius: Opera et studio Monachorum Ordinis Sancti Benedicti, et Congregatione Sancti Mauri.* Editio Parisina altera, emendata et aucta. Paris: Gaume Fratres, 1839.

Garnier, Julien, and Prudentius Maran. *Sancti Patris nostri Basilii, Caesareae Cappadociae archiepiscopi, opera omnia quae exstant, vel quae sub eius nomine circumferuntur, ad manuscriptos Codices Gallicanos, Vaticanos, Florentinos et Anglicos, necnon ad antiquiores editiones castigata, multis aucta: Nova Interpretatione, criticis Praefationibus, Notis, variis Lectionibus illustrata, nova sancti Doctoris Vita et copioissimis Indicibus locupletata. Tomus Primus et Secundus: Opera et studio Domni Iuliani Garnier, Presbyteri et Monachi Benedictini, e Congregatione Sancti Mauri. Tomus*

Tertius: Opera et studio Monachorum Ordinis Sancti Benedicti, et Congregatione Sancti Mauri. Paris: Coigard, 1721–1730.

Giet, Stanislas. *Basile de Césarée: Homélies sur l'hexaéméron.* 2nd ed. SChr 26. Paris: Cerf, 1968.

Harrison, Nonna Verna. *St Basil the Great: On the Human Condition.* PPS 30. Crestwood: St Vladimir's Seminary Press, 2005.

Hildebrand, Stephen. *St Basil the Great: On the Holy Spirit.* PPS 42. Yonkers: St Vladimir's Seminary Press, 2011.

Holman, Susan R., and Mark DelCogliano. *St Basil the Great: On Fasting and Feasts.* PPS. Yonkers: St Vladimir's Seminary Press, forthcoming.

Mendieta, Emmanuel Amand de, and Stig Y. Rudberg. *Basilius von Caesarea: Homilien zum Hexaemeron.* GCS n.f. 2. Berlin: Akademie-Verlag, 1997.

Migne, Jacques-Paul. *Sancti Patris nostri Basilii, Caesareae Cappadociae archiepiscopi, opera omnia quae exstant, vel quae sub eius nomine circumferuntur, ad manuscriptos Codices Gallicanos, Vaticanos, Florentinos et Anglicos, necnon ad antiquiores editiones castigata, multis aucta: Nova Interpretatione, criticis Praefationibus, Notis, variis Lectionibus illustrata, nova sancti Doctoris Vita et copioissimis Indicibus locupletata. Tomus Primus et Secundus: Opera et studio Domni Iuliani Garnier, Presbyteri et Monachi Benedictini, e Congregatione Sancti Mauri. Tomus Tertius: Opera et studio Monachorum Ordinis Sancti Benedicti, et Congregatione Sancti Mauri.* PG 29–32. Paris: J.-P. Migne, 1857; repr. Paris: Garnier, 1886; Turnhout: Brepols, 1959–1961.

Pruche, Benoît. *Basile de Césarée: Sur le Saint-Esprit.* Reímp. de la deuxiéme éd. rev. et aug. SChr 17 bis. Paris: Cerf, 2002.

Rudberg, Stig Y. *L'homélie de Basile de Césarée sur le mot 'Observe-toi-même.' Édition critique du texte grec et étude sur la tradition manuscrite.* Uppsala: Almquist & Wiksell, 1962.

Schroeder, C. Paul. *St Basil the Great: On Social Justice.* PPS 38. Crestwood: St Vladimir's Seminary Press, 2009.

Sesboüé, Bernard, Georges-Matthieu de Durand, and Louis Doutreleau. *Basile de Césarée, Contre Eunome suivi de Eunome Apologie.* SChr 299 and 305. Paris: Cerf, 1982–1983.

Wagner, M. Monica. *Saint Basil: Ascetical Works.* FOTC 9. New York: The Fathers of the Church, Inc., 1950.

Way, Agnes Clare. *Saint Basil: Letters. Volume 1 (1–185).* FOTC 13. New York: The Fathers of the Church, Inc., 1951.

————. *Saint Basil: Letters. Volume 2 (186–368).* FOTC 28. New York: The Fathers of the Church, Inc., 1955.

————. *Saint Basil: Exegetic Homilies.* FOTC 46. Washington, DC: The Catholic University of America Press, 1963.

Studies

Altaner, Berthold. *Patrology.* Translated by Hilda C. Graef from the fifth German edition. Freiburg: Herder, 1960.

Amand, David. "Essai d'une histoire critique des éditions générales grecques et gréco-latines de S. Basile de Césarée." *Revue Bénédictine* 52 (1940): 141–161; 53 (1941): 119–151; 54 (1942): 124–144; and 56 (1944/1945): 126–173.

Arnim, Hans Friedrich August von. *Stoicorum veterum fragmenta.* 4 vols. Leipzig: Teubner, 1903–1905.

Ayres, Lewis. *Nicaea and its Legacy: An Approach to Fourth-Century Trinitarian Theology.* Oxford: Oxford University Press, 2004.

Bardenhewer, Otto. *Patrology: The Lives and Works of the Fathers of the Church.* Translated from the second edition by Thomas J. Shahan. St. Louis: Herder, 1908.

Bardy, Gustave. "L'homélie de saint Basile *Adversus eos qui calumniantur nos.*" *Recherches de science religieuse* 16 (1926): 21–28.

Behr, John. *The Nicene Faith.* Crestwood: St Vladimir's Seminary Press, 2004.

Berghuis, Kent D. *Christian Fasting: A Theological Approach.* S. l.: Biblical Studies Press, 2007.

Bernardi, Jean. *La prédication des pères cappadociens.* Paris: Presses universitaires de France, 1968.

Blowers, Paul M. "Envy's Narrative Scripts. Cyprian, Basil, and the Monastic Sages on the Anatomy and Cure of the Invidious Emotions." *Modern Theology* 25 (2009): 21–43.

Boyd, Hugh Stuart. *The Fathers not Papists; or Six Discourses by the Most Eloquent Fathers of the Church. With Numerous Extracts from Their Writings. Translated from the Greek. A New Edition Considerably Enlarged.* London: Samuel Bagster, 1834.

Campbell, James Marshall. *The Influence of the Second Sophistic on the Style of the Sermons of St. Basil the Great*. Washington, DC: Catholic University of America Press, 1922.

Cavalcanti, Elena. "Dall'etica classica all'etica cristiana: il commento al prologo del libro dei Proverbi, di Basilio di Cesarea." *Studi e materiali di storia delle religioni* 56 (1990): 353–378.

DelCogliano, Mark. *Basil of Caesarea's Anti-Eunomian Theory of Names: Christian Theology and Late-Antique Philosophy in the Fourth-Century Trinitarian Controversy*. VCS 103. Leiden: Brill, 2010.

————. "Basil of Caesarea's Homily *On Not Three Gods* (CPG 2914): Problems and Solutions." *Sacris Erudiri* 50 (2011): 87–131.

————. "Basil of Caesarea on the Primacy of the Name 'Son.'" *Revue des Études Augustiniennes et Patristiques* 57 (2011): 45–69.

————. "Origen and Basil of Caesarea on the Liar Paradox." *Augustinianum* 51 (2011): 349–66.

————. "Basil of Caesarea on John 1.1 as an Affirmation of Pro-Nicene Trinitarian Doctrine." [forthcoming].

————. "Basil of Caesarea on Psalm 115 (LXX): Origen and Anti-Eunomian Rhetoric." [forthcoming].

Dickie, Matthew. "The Fathers of the Church on the Evil Eye." Pages 9–34 in Henry Maguire, ed. *Byzantine Magic*. Washington, DC: Dumbarton Oaks, 1995.

Dörries, Hermann. *De Spiritu Sancto. Der Beitrag des Basilius zum Abschluss des trinitarischen Dogmas*. Abhandlungen der Akademie der Wissenschaften in Göttingen, Philologisch-Historische Klasse, Folge 3, Nr. 39. Göttingen: Vandenhoeck & Ruprecht, 1956.

Drecoll, Volker Henning. *Die Entwicklung der Trinitätslehre des Basilius von Cäsarea: Sein Weg vom Homöusianer zum Neonizäner*. Forschungen zur Kirchen- und Dogmengeschichte 66. Göttingen: Vandenhoeck & Ruprecht, 1996.

Du Pin, L. Ellies. *Nouvelle bibliothèque des auteurs ecclésiastiques*. 19 vols. Utrecht: Jean Broedelet, 1731.

Fedwick, Paul Jonathan. *The Church and the Charisma of Leadership in Basil of Caesarea*. Toronto: Pontifical Institute of Mediaeval Studies, 1979.

————, ed. *Basil of Caesarea: Christian, Humanist, Ascetic. A Sixteen-Hundredth Anniversary Symposium*. 2 vols. Toronto: The Pontifical Institute of Mediaeval Studies, 1981.

————. "A Chronology of the Life and Works of Basil of Caesarea." Pages 3–19 in idem, ed. *Basil of Caesarea: Christian, Humanist, Ascetic. A Sixteen-Hundredth Anniversary Symposium.* 2 vols. Toronto: The Pontifical Institute of Mediaeval Studies, 1981.

————. *Bibliotheca Basiliana Vniversalis.* 5 vols. Turnhout: Brepols, 1993–2005.

Garnier, Julien. "Praefatio" (to Vol. 1). De Sinner i.i–lxxxi; PG 29.clxxvii–ccxli.

————. "Praefatio" (to Vol. 2). De Sinner ii.i–xci; PG 31.9–158.

Geerard, Maurice. *Clavis Patrum Graecorum.* 5 vols. Turnhout: Brepols, 1974–1983.

Girardi, Mario. "Basilio di Cesarea esegeta dei *Proverbi.*" *Vetera Christianorum* 28 (1991): 25–60.

————. *Basilio di Cesarea interprete della Scrittura. Lessico, principi ermeneutici, prassi.* Quaderni di «Vetera Christianorum» 26. Bari: Epipuglia, 1998.

Gribomont, Jean. *In Tomum 29 Patrologiae Graecae ad editionem operum Sancti Basilii Magni Adnotationes.* Turnhout: Brepols, 1959.

————. *In Tomum 30 Patrologiae graecae ad opera Sancti Basilii Magni Adnotationes.* Turnhout: Brepols, 1960.

————. *In Tomum 31 Patrologiae graecae ad editionem operum rhetoricorum, asceticorum, liturgicorum Sancti Basili Magni Introductio.* Turnhout: Brepols, 1961.

————. "Notes biographiques sur s. Basile le Grand." Pages 21–48 in Paul Jonathan Fedwick, ed. *Basil of Caesarea: Christian, Humanist, Ascetic. A Sixteen-Hundredth Anniversary Symposium.* 2 vols. Toronto: The Pontifical Institute of Mediaeval Studies, 1981.

Hamman, André. *Baptism: Ancient Liturgies and Patristic Texts.* Translated by Thomas Halton. Staten Island: Alba House, 1967.

Hanson, R.P.C. *The Search for the Christian Doctrine of God: The Arian Controversy 31–381 AD.* Edinburgh: T & T Clark, 1988.

Hildebrand, Stephen M. *The Trinitarian Theology of Basil of Caesarea: A Synthesis of Greek Thought and Biblical Truth.* Washington, DC: Catholic University of America Press, 2007.

Holl, Karl. *Amphilochius von Ikonium in seinem Verhältnis zu den grossen Kappadoziern.* Tübingen / Leipzig: J.C. Mohr, 1904.

Holman, Susan R. *The Hungry are Dying: Beggars and Bishops in Roman Cappadocia.* Oxford: Oxford University Press, 2001.

————. "Rich City Burning: Social Welfare and Ecclesial Insecurity in Basil's Mission to Armenia." *Journal of Early Christian Studies* 12 (2004): 195–215.

Jackson, Blomfield. "Prolegomena. Sketch of the Life and Works of Saint Basil." NPNF 2.8, xiii-lxxvii.

Kenrick, Francis Patrick. *A Treatise on Baptism; with an exhortation to receive it, translated from the works of St. Basil the Great. To which is added a treatise on confirmation.* Philadelphia: M. Fithian, 1843.

Kopecek, Thomas A. *A History of Neo-Arianism.* 2 vols. Patristic Monograph Series, No. 8. Cambridge: The Philadelphia Patristic Foundation, Ltd., 1979.

Leemans, Johan, Wendy Mayer, Pauline Allen, and Boudewijn Dehandschutter. *Let Us Die That We May Live: Greek Homilies on Christian Martyrs from Asia Minor, Palestine and Syria (c. AD 350-AD 450).* London and New York: Routledge, 2003.

Lienhard, Joseph T. "Ps-Athanasius, *Contra Sabellianos*, and Basil of Caesarea, *Contra Sabellianos et Arium et Anomoeos*: Analysis and Comparison." *Vigiliae Christianae* 40 (1986): 365–89.

————. "Basil of Caesarea, Marcellus of Ancyra, and 'Sabellius'." *Church History* 58 (1989): 157–67.

————. *Contra Marcellum. Marcellus of Ancyra and Fourth-Century Theology.* Washington, DC: The Catholic University of America Press, 1999.

Limberis, Vasiliki. "The Eyes Infected by Evil: Basil of Caesarea's Homily, *On Envy*," *Harvard Theological Review* 84 (1991): 163–84.

Long, A.A., and D.N. Sedley. *The Hellenistic Philosophers.* 2 vols. Cambridge: Cambridge University Press, 1987.

Maran, Prudentius. *Vita Sancti Basilii Magni Archiepiscopi Caesariensis.* De Sinner iii. xxxviii–ccliv; PG 29.v–clxxvii.

Pole, Reginald. *A Treatise of Iustification. Founde among the writings of Cardinal Pole of blessed memory, remaining in the custodie of M. Henire Pyning, Chamberlaine and General Receiuer to the said Cardinal, late deceased in Louaine. Item certaine translations touching the said matter of Iustification, the Title whereof. see in the page following. Namely, A Treatise of St Augustine, which he entitled: Of Faith and Workes. Item, a Sermon of Chrysostome, of Praying unto God. Item, a Sermon of St.*

Basil, of Fasting. Item, certaine Sermons of St Leo the Great, of the same matter. Last of al, a notable Sermon of St Cyprian, of Almes dedes. Al newly translated into English, 2 vols. Louanii apud Ioannem Foulerum. anno 1569. cum priuilegio; facsimile repr. Farnborough, Hants.: Gregg Press, 1967.

Quasten, Johannes. *Patrology, Vol. 3.* Westminster, MD, Newman Press, 1960.

Radde-Gallwitz, Andrew. *Basil of Caesarea, Gregory of Nyssa, and the Transformation of Divine Simplicity.* Oxford: Oxford University Press, 2009.

———. "Ad Eustathium de sancta trinitate." Pages 89–109 in Volker Henning Drecoll and Margitta Berghaus, eds. *Gregory of Nyssa: The Minor Treatises on Trinitarian Theology and Apollinarianism. Proceedings from the 11th International Colloquium on Gregory of Nyssa (Tübingen, 17–20 September 2008).* VCS 106. Leiden: Brill, 2011.

———. *Basil of Caesarea: A Guide to His Life and Doctrine.* Eugene: Cascade Books, 2012.

Rouillard, Édouard. "Recherches sur la tradition manuscrite des *Homélies diverses* de Saint Basile." *Revue Mabillon* 48 (1958): 81–98; 57 (1967): 1–16 and 45–55.

———. "La tradition manuscrite des *Homélies diverses* de Saint Basile." *Studia Patristica* 3 (1961): 116–121.

———. "Peut-on retrouver le texts authentique de la prédication de Saint Basile?" *Studia Patristica* 7 (1966): 90–101.

———. "Basile de Césarée a-t-il corrigé lui-même un premier état de texte de ses homélies?" *Studia Patristica* 22 (1989): 65–68.

———. "L'édition des *Homélies morales* de Basile de Césarée." *Studia Patristica* 22 (1989): 75–78.

——— and Marie-Louise Guillaumin. "Recherches à la Bibliothèque Nationale de Paris sur quelques manuscrits grec du Xe siècle: leur intérêst pour l'édition des *Homélies morales* de Basile de Césarée." *Revue d'histoire des textes* xiv-xv (1984–1985): 23–53.

Rousseau, Philip. *Basil of Caesarea.* Berkeley / Los Angeles / London: University of California Press, 1994.

Rudberg, Stig Y. *Études sur la tradition manuscrite de saint Basile.* Lund: Hakan Ohlssons Boktryckeri, 1953.

———. "Manuscripts and Editions of the Works of Basil of Caesarea." Pages 49–65 in Jonathan Paul Fedwick, ed. *Basil of Caesarea: Christian,*

Humanist, Ascetic. A Sixteen-Hundredth Anniversary Symposium. 2 vols. Toronto: The Pontifical Institute of Mediaeval Studies, 1981.

Sesboüé, Bernard. *Saint Basile et la Trinité: Un acte théologique au IVe siècle.* Paris: Descleé, 1998.

Silvas, Anna M. "The Emergence of Basil's Social Doctrine." Pages 133–176 in Geoffrey D. Dunn, David Luckensmeyer, and Lawrence Cross. *Prayer and Spirituality in the Early Church. Volume 5. Poverty and Riches.* Strathfield, Australia: St Pauls Publications, 2009.

Tillemont, Louis-Sébastien Le Nain de. *Mémoires pour servir à l'histoire ecclésiastique des six premiers siècles.* 16 vols. Venice: Pitteri, 1732.

Tixeront, J. *A Handbook of Patrology.* Translated from the fourth French edition. St Louis / London: Herder, 1920.

Toal, M.F. *The Sunday Sermons of the Great Fathers.* 4 vols. Chicago: Henry Regnery; London: Longmans, Green, 1957–1963.

Vaggione, Richard Paul. *Eunomius of Cyzicus and the Nicene Revolution.* Oxford: Oxford University Press, 2000.

Van Dam, Raymond. *Kingdom of Snow: Roman Rule and Greek Culture in Cappadocia.* Philadelphia: University of Pennsylvania Press, 2002.

_____. *Becoming Christian: The Conversion of Roman Cappadocia.* Philadelphia: University of Pennsylvania Press, 2003.

_____. *Families and Friends in Late Roman Cappadocia.* Philadelphia: University of Pennsylvania Press, 2003.

Zachhuber, Johannes. *Human Nature in Gregory of Nyssa: Philosophical Background and Theological Significance.* VCS 46. Leiden: Brill, 2000.

Index of Scripture

OLD TESTAMENT

New Testament

POPULAR PATRISTICS SERIES

ST VLADIMIR'S SEMINARY PRESS
1-800-204-2665 • www.svspress.com